I0147639

GHOSTS, TROLLS AND THE HIDDEN PEOPLE

GHOSTS, TROLLS
AND THE
HIDDEN PEOPLE
AN ANTHOLOGY OF
ICELANDIC FOLK LEGENDS

Edited by
DAGRÚN ÓSK JÓNSDÓTTIR

REAKTION BOOKS

*This book is dedicated to my parents, Ester Sigfúsdóttir
and Jón Jónsson. Thank you both for all your support and
encouragement, for the stories you have told me and for not
getting me that portable DVD player.*

Published by
Reaktion Books Ltd
Unit 32, Waterside
44–48 Wharf Road
London NI 7UX, UK

www.reaktionbooks.co.uk

First published 2025
Copyright © Dagrún Ósk Jónsdóttir 2025

All rights reserved

EU GPSR Authorised Representative
Logos Europe, 9 rue Nicolas Poussin, 17000, La Rochelle, France
email: contact@logoseurope.eu

No part of this publication may be reproduced, stored in a retrieval
system, or transmitted, in any form or by any means, electronic,
mechanical, photocopying, recording or otherwise, without the
prior permission of the publishers. No part of this publication
may be used or reproduced in any manner for the purpose of
training artificial intelligence technologies or systems.

Printed and bound in Great Britain by Bell & Bain, Glasgow

A catalogue record for this book is available from the British Library

ISBN 978 1 83639 025 1

CONTENTS

EDITOR'S NOTE

THE TRANSLATIONS of the stories found in this book come from three main sources. First, the book *Icelandic Legends*, which was published in two volumes in the years 1864 and 1866 and included translations by George E. J. Powell (1842–1882) and Eiríkur Magnússon (1833–1913) of selected legends from the collection of Jón Árnason.[1] It is important to note that in the introduction to Powell's and Eiríkur's translations they state that they have made some changes to the stories. These include making additions, inserting phrases and removing repetitions and content they deemed irrelevant. Furthermore, between Jón Árnason's first publication of his legend collection (translated by Powell and Eiríkur) and the second edition of his collection, minor changes were made to some of the legends. Nevertheless, in the references for the stories (cited in the Bibliography), I use the second edition as it is more accessible and more often used. For this book, minor changes were made to the old translations to make the text more accessible.

Other legends in this book are translated by a dear friend of mine and colleague in the folklore department at the University of Iceland, Alice Bower, and Sigurður Líndal, a colleague in Strandir who studied arts and policy management at the University of London. The rest are translated by me. Naturally, each translator has their own style, and a clear difference can be seen between the antique and modern transla-tions, as the older ones use a more formal language, something that offers an interesting comparison. In the modern translations we remain true to the source material; however, complicated genealogy, which is sometimes included in the legends, has been removed to make them more understandable and enjoyable. Throughout the book I use the Icelandic naming system when referring to Icelanders, using their per-sonal name rather than the patronymic, as few Icelanders have surnames.

The book has been illustrated with images created by various art-ists who, throughout the years, have drawn inspiration from Icelandic folk legends and beliefs. Through their art they make the invisible become visible, allowing us to see how these supernatural beings, told of in the stories, might have been imagined by the artists. It is inter-esting to note here that the first Icelander to make art their primary profession was Ásgrímur Jónsson (1876–1958), who drew great inspi-ration from the Icelandic folk tale collection of Jón Árnason. However, it is worth acknowledging that there is a certain gender bias in the illus-trative material, as artistry was for a long time more accessible to men than women.[2] The illustrations in the book span from the sixteenth century to the present day.

Foreword:
Enthralling Icelandic Legends

Though it has often been assumed that fantastic legends about ghosts, trolls, elves, witches, sorcerers, devils, outlaws and other supernatural creatures emanated primarily from major European countries and North America, nothing could be further from the truth. Indeed, it is important to know that Iceland also played a significant role in spreading fantastic stories about these creatures and perhaps created more unusual ones than readers have ever encountered. Thanks to Dagrún Ósk Jónsdóttir's extraordinary *Ghosts, Trolls and the Hidden People*, an enthralling collection of tense Icelandic legends, we may now understand why we tend to be attracted to supernatural creatures, if not believe in them.

Dagrún has divided her anthology into six categories: the farm, the wilderness, the dark, the church, the ocean and the shore, for it is in these places that the supernatural creatures lurked – and still lurk – in Iceland. They have not sprung solely from the imagination. Throughout her book, Dagrún provides social-historical commentaries that reveal how the legends have embedded themselves in Icelandic culture. She is a most insightful guide, not hesitant to reveal how closely the stories deal with real and traumatic events in the lives of Icelanders.

Up to the present, Iceland has been a beautiful but rugged country, first ruled by farming elites, priests and bureaucrats, and did not become an independent nation until 1944. From its very beginning in the ninth century, life was difficult for most of the inhabitants of the island, which came under the rule of the Norwegian and then the Danish kingdoms. By the medieval period the Lutheran Church had played a major role in the education of the people. They were mainly farm labourers or fishermen and had to deal with poverty and plagues up to the twentieth century. Moreover, it is important to remember there was no electricity or radio on the island until the twentieth century. So, in the evenings after work, storytelling was a way to deal with the living conditions people experienced. Wonder legends were among the tales told about people's relations to supernatural creatures. These stories were based on the struggles of the people to survive incomprehensible forces that threatened to overwhelm them.

Many of their experiences were unusual, if not incredible, and they shared them in stories told to one another. The supernatural creatures were not particularly friendly to the people, but they could at times help them if they showed respect, and this is why most of the legends raise the question of ethics and justice. One of my favourite legends is "Nineteen Outlaws", about a young woman who guards her home on the family farm during Christmas Eve. Bravely, she cuts off the heads of eighteen outlaws to protect the farm. She is an enterprising, smart woman. Later she weds the captain of a ship, who is actually the disguised nineteenth outlaw, and she disposes of him as well and then marries a good man. There is something comic and bloody about this tale, but it also has its virtue, as do all the legends in this collection. The majority of the tales feature male protagonists, but there are also many tales that depict strong women and the difficulties faced by women, as is the case in "Nineteen Outlaws".

This tale was told by an old woman to Jón Árnason, the first librarian of the national library in Reykjavík. He and his friend Magnús Grímsson, a student at the Latin school in Reykjavík, were inspired by the Brothers Grimm, whose works on legends were well known in Iceland. Together, Jón and Magnús began collecting folk tales and legends in the late 1840s and published their first book in 1852. Magnús died in 1860, and Jón, who went on to become the most famous folk tale collector in Iceland, continued to publish several volumes until his death in 1888. Dagrún's anthology is based largely on Jón's works, and the additional translations of the legends were done by her colleagues at the University of Iceland and in Strandir, whom she cites in her Editor's Note. To Dagrún's credit, she has done a superb job of organizing and honouring the rich history of Icelandic folklore.

Very little research into Icelandic folk and fairy tales has been undertaken in the United Kingdom and North America. This is indeed a pity because the Icelandic stories, before and after Jón Árnason, have woven motifs and themes with those of European countries in intricate and original ways. The contexts of the tales are, to be sure, Icelandic, but their meanings have international value. Dagrún has made a great contribution to folklore by reviving the spirits of Icelandic legends.

Jack Zipes

Introduction

My family is haunted by a ghost. I remember when I first heard the story of it: I was probably around seven years old, it was late in the evening, and my family was driving home to the Westfjords of Iceland after a visit to Reykjavík. This was at a time when portable DVD players were all the rage, but my parents refused to buy me one, feeling it was entertaining enough to look out of the window. Outside, however, there was complete darkness, as should be expected on a winter evening in Iceland. "Here lives our family ghost," my father said out of nowhere. We had just driven past the farm Skriðinsenni, and the family ghost is called Ennis-Móri owing to its connection to the farm. My father then proceeded to tell me the chilling story of how the ghost came to be.

The tale recounts the tragic fate of a man deeply in love with a girl who did not return his affections, rejecting his advances. Consumed by bitter heartbreak, the man sought revenge by conjuring a ghost from the lifeless body of a young man who had washed ashore. Using sorcery, he transformed the body into the vengeful spirit known as Ennis-Móri. The scorned man then sent the ghost to the farm of the girl. When the ghost arrived at the farm it observed the family dining on porridge through the keyhole. Seizing the opportunity, Ennis-Móri transformed into a tiny fly, landing on the girl's spoon and ending up in her mouth. The ghost then changed back into its true form, causing the girl's head to explode (making this one of the few splatter stories in the Icelandic folk legend corpus). The ghost then went back to kill the sorcerer who had brought it back from the dead and finally returned to haunt the family of the girl he killed, my ancestors and the farm Skriðinsenni.

Despite the eerie nature of Ennis-Móri's story, I found it more curious and captivating than terrifying when my father narrated it to me. The ghost Ennis-Móri is first mentioned in a written account in Jón Árnason's Icelandic legend collection from the nineteenth century,[1] but is also still very much a part of living oral tradition. Because the ghost is connected to a specific family – the one that lived in Skriðinsenni – as well as the place where the old farm stood, and where a new one now stands, new stories continue to emerge.

In 1943 my great-grandmother Guðbjörg Jónsdóttir (1871–1952) published her memoirs. Her book is quite extraordinary, as it was unusual at the time for women to write their stories. In her book she writes about life in the late nineteenth century. Her brother Þorsteinn lived on the farm Skriðinsenni, but in December 1877 he, along with three others, drowned when collecting driftwood and moving it by boat to the farm. As she writes, some people blamed the ghost:

> This is the worst accident that people in this area can remember. Fortunately, it was not often that people drowned in good weather, just off the land, as was the case here. In those years, superstition was so prevalent among the public that some believed that an evil spirit had been at work there, in other words that the ghost of Ennis-Móri had overturned the boat.[2]

Even today, stories are still told about the ghost Ennis-Móri. It is sometimes seen by local truckers passing by the farm. One told of seeing a young man appear right in front of his truck, just as he crashed into him. Terrified, the trucker left his vehicle to search for a body, but he never found it. It had been the ghost. Others see the ghost standing by the road when they drive by. The ghost is also known to choose specific family members and follow them more than others. It is sometimes seen with those family members, and when they visit people, the ghost usually arrives before them, knocking on the door a few minutes prior to the arrival of the guest.

The stories of Ennis-Móri are still part of oral tradition in the area, as well as among the families it is connected to. A couple of years ago, I told two of my younger cousins the same story that my father had told me all those years ago. I told them that as they are descendants of the girl's family, the ghost also follows them. The next day I got a phone call from their grandmother, who was not happy. To my surprise, the girls had not been as excited by the ghost as I was when I heard the story; rather, they had been terrified.

Iceland is rich with legends and tales that tell of encounters with the supernatural. Many of the legends are still present today, passed down from one generation to the next, and some of them are taught in primary school. We are reminded of these stories when we travel around Iceland since so many of them are embedded in the landscape. When travelling, one can see trolls that have been turned into stone by the sun, the rocks and hills that are the homes of the hidden people and deserted and abandoned houses that immediately make one think of ghosts. When I first heard these stories, they amazed me and filled both my mind and the landscape around me with magic and mystery. Later, when I studied folklore and ethnology at the University of Iceland, I gained further insight into the importance of these stories, which are indeed so much more, and how they can work as windows into the past.

In this book selected legends from the nineteenth and early twentieth centuries are presented in English translation. The legends reflect the ideas of the people who told them; those that are still told today hold relevance either to specific places or people, or through the issues or messages they convey. To better understand the legends and the messages they carry, it is therefore important to put them in context with Icelandic society at the time in which the legends were collected.

In the following introductory sections I will briefly introduce Icelandic society in the nineteenth and twentieth centuries, discuss the collection of Icelandic folk tales, explore how legends can be used as sources on society and, finally, explain how this book is organized.

Icelandic Society

The settlement of Iceland started in the late ninth century. The settlers mostly came from Scandinavia and the Celtic countries. When coming to Iceland they naturally brought with them various things: tools, building materials, clothes and farm animals. The settlers also brought with them their traditions, beliefs, place names, folk stories and legends. In 930 Icelanders established their parliament (Alþingi) at Þingvellir, and in the year 1000 it was decided at parliament that Icelanders should become Christian. In the mid-thirteenth century, Iceland became part of the Norwegian kingdom and remained so until the late fourteenth century, when the Kalmar union was created, joining Denmark, Sweden and Norway under a single monarch. Later Iceland, along with Norway, moved under the Danish crown.

Iceland has never been a big nation. In terms of population records, the first people's census in Iceland took place in 1703. At that time there were 50,358 people living in the country. More than 170 years later, in 1880, there were only 72,445 people, meaning that while population growth was taking place, it was not fast. Indeed, the eighteenth century had been extremely difficult for Icelanders; during 1707–9 plague had ravaged the country, and in the late eighteenth century a large volcanic eruption known as *Skaftáreldar* shook the land, followed by famine, resulting in the deaths of thousands and so reducing the population. At the time medical knowledge was also limited, and the death rate among infants was extremely high, all of which affected the slow population growth in Iceland.[3]

The nineteenth and twentieth centuries in Iceland were a time of rapid change. During that period, Iceland was mostly a rural society with relatively few people, many of whom had to face rough conditions and close cohabitation with nature. From the time of settlement until the twentieth century, Icelanders lived in so-called turf houses, built from stone, turf and wood. The Icelandic society of the nineteenth century was essentially a farming and fishing society. Poverty was prevalent, and the rough weather conditions could make the lives of the people difficult. There were no big villages or towns; the farm was the cornerstone of society. As the Icelandic historian Sigurður Gylfi Magnússon puts it:

> The country was almost entirely rural, with farmsteads scattered usually with long distances between them throughout the lower lying areas. Isolation was the norm rather than the exception. Communication was extremely difficult due to the complete absence of roads and the frequent obstacles presented by glaciers and fast-flowing rivers. Each farm was in this sense an island of its own, often with minimal contact with the outside world, especially during the long, cold, dark months of winter.[4]

Most of the farmers rented the farms and land they utilized, but a few owned property and land. The Church and the Danish king owned a great deal of land and were sometimes also entitled to part of the benefits of the farm. Owing to how rural Iceland was at the time, the farm was both the home and workplace of most people, and the efficiency of these farms was largely dependent on the land the farmers had access to and the number of working hands available.[5]

The Icelandic nation was greatly affected by social restrictions and laws, not least those relating to class and gender. At the top of the Icelandic class system were government officials and priests, followed by those who owned land and property. Next came tenant farmers, then workers and finally the paupers. This system made it extremely hard for people to move out of poverty once they fell into it. This was, among other factors, due to a set of laws called *Vistarbandið* (labour bondage), which remained in effect until the late nineteenth century.[6] The laws stated that every man and woman who did not own a farm had to take up employment on a farm for a year at a time. This was meant to guarantee that everyone had a place to live, while ensuring that farmers had a cheap workforce as well. The law attempted to reduce population growth by placing difficult marriage restraints on workers. Iceland was also a patriarchal society. While the support of the family rested on the shoulders of both men and women, the man was the head of the family and the only one who could take part in public affairs. Women first got the right to vote in parliament in 1915 and equal voting rights in 1920.[7]

Education was also part of home life in the nineteenth century. Until 1880 all education in Iceland (outside the two schools for boys in Skálholt (which later moved to Reykjavík) and Hólar) took place at home on the farms. In 1746 an order from the Danish king Christian VI called *Húsagatilskipun* (in Danish: Anordning om Hustugt paa Island) was passed regarding the upbringing, education and religion of Icelandic children, where it was stated that all Icelandic children should learn to read. Priests were responsible for ensuring that education was carried out, although all the teaching rested on the shoulders of the farmers.[8] One of the main sources of education was the evening wakes often held on farms in winter, during which various homilies and sermons were often read out loud. The purpose of the readings was to entertain and educate people while they worked to turn wool into clothing. Storytelling was also an important part of the evening wakes, as people would read out loud from books, manuscripts and papers. However, the folklorist Júlíana Þóra Magnúsdóttir concludes that the main time for oral storytelling was during *rökkrin* (twilight gatherings), which refers to the period in the evening before the evening wake took place. *Rökkrin* was the time when men came in from working outside, and adults used the opportunity to take a nap; at the same time, low-key storytelling would often take place in a corner of the

This illustration, created in 1862 by artist August Schiøtt (1823–1895), depicts a traditional evening wake. It shows people in a wooden farm living room, some of whom appear to be working with wool, and a young boy reading from a book, probably out loud for the others.

living room for children, teenagers and other household members who did not need sleep. The storytelling at *rökkrin* was usually aimed at the younger generation and was often in the hands of the women at the farm.[9]

From 1907 attending school from the ages of ten to fourteen became mandatory in Iceland, and in 1936 this was expanded to children of seven to fourteen. However, this was not strictly enforced, and some children were still taught at home. While schools were built in every town, the most common approach in rural areas was for teachers to travel between areas, staying at farms for three to six weeks at a time, where they would educate children from neighbouring farms.[10] Nevertheless, it seems that literacy in Iceland was relatively high from an early point, in both rural and the growing urban areas. Somewhere between 10 and 30 per cent of women and 20 to 50 per cent of men are estimated to have been capable of writing in 1839, something that was particularly important for the collecting of folk tales that took place in the nineteenth century.[11]

In Iceland the process of industrialization and urbanization took place much later than in most other European countries, but by 1870 big changes were evidently starting to occur in both the living and working environments of the people.[12] In the late nineteenth century, the population was growing fast, farms were overflowing with people and fishing villages started to form, mostly around former commercial fishing stations.[13] Many people had also moved to Canada and the United States in search of new opportunities.

After urbanization finally began, it happened quickly. In 1890 only 14 per cent of Icelanders had lived in settlements of fifty residents or more, a figure that included the 8,886 people living in the capital, Reykjavík. However, by 1930 more than half of the population lived in urban areas.[14] The old turf houses grew fewer in number, and wood, concrete and different forms of housing became more common.[15] More rapid changes occurred during the twentieth century as Iceland gradually became an independent nation. Iceland got home rule in 1904, became a sovereign state in 1918 and became fully independent in 1944.[16]

Folk Tale Collection in Iceland

The late eighteenth and early nineteenth centuries saw the rise of the Romantic nationalist movement in Europe, which played a big role in the growing interest in folkloric material. Much was also changing in Western societies at the time: people were moving from the countryside to the cities, the two being posed as opposites. Life in the countryside was now presented as an incarnation of the old, original, calm, natural and uncorrupted elements of society. Many in the cities feared that the old knowledge, folklore and legends that preserved the ancient spirit of the nation were disappearing. The aim of the collectors was to gather this material from the countryside to create a new sense of common identity that could be shared by both groups. Iceland was no exception, and the early collections of the nation's folk tales have been closely linked to Iceland's struggle for independence.[17]

In Europe the beginning of the collection of folk tales is usually traced back to the work of the brothers Jacob and Wilhelm Grimm, who collected folk tales in Germany, publishing wonder tales in *Kinder- und Hausmärchen* (Children's and Household Tales) in 1812–15, and legends in *Deutsche Sagen* (German Legends) in 1816–18. Even though some folk tales had been published before that, the key to the Grimms' originality was their stance as collectors, and their claim that these narratives were the creation of the folk and the heritage of the nation.[18] The Scandinavian countries followed one by one, collecting legends and publishing their own national collections of tales, with Iceland following relatively late, in the middle of the nineteenth century.

In Iceland the beginning of the collection of folk legends is usually connected to Jón Árnason (1819–1888) and Magnús Grímsson (1825–1860). Jón was one of the pioneer folk tale collectors in Iceland. He was born in the north of Iceland but later moved to Reykjavík, where he became a teacher and a librarian (and later the bishops' secretary). Magnús Grímsson was an associate of Jón Árnason's who was born in the south of Iceland. He was a farmer's son but went to Reykjavík to study, after which he stayed there for a while before becoming a priest in Mosfell, a rural area in the southwest of the country. Jón and Magnús started collecting stories together and published their first small folk tale collection, *Íslenzk ævintýri* (Icelandic Wonder Tales), in 1852. This was the first published collection in Iceland to contain stories from oral tradition, and it was not well received.[19] Magnús Grímsson died in 1860, but Jón Árnason continued to collect material following the encouragement of Konrad Maurer (1823–1902), a German professor of law and legal history who was very interested in Icelandic literature and culture and who even published a book of Icelandic folk tales of his own, *Isländische Volkssagen* (Icelandic Folk Legends), in 1860.[20] For Jón's later collection, he received stories from all over Iceland, sent by various individuals (often priests), and collected some legends himself in

Reykjavík. All the same, as folklorist Terry Gunnell states, some people seem to have been hesitant about telling the clerics their stories. Many letters written to Jón suggest that it was difficult to obtain stories from the people, and it is also possible that people feared appearing ignorant or superstitious.[21]

The legends were collected from oral tradition. In the introduction to Jón Árnason's collection, he emphasizes this, noting that these stories "are the poetry of the nation and its spiritual offspring century after century and therefore better than most describe its ways of thinking and habits".[22] Jón also states that he has tried to stay true to the material, as was suggested by the Brothers Grimm in their guide to collecting folk legends. However, as in other legend collections, Jón admits to having made changes to the stories. It is also important to note that due to the oral nature of the storytelling tradition, it is likely that each of these legends had existed in many different versions and variations and gone through changes as new ideas emerged and the general world view changed. Good storytellers would also have made their own changes when telling them, for example to make them more entertaining, or based on their own world view or even their audience.[23] When the legends were collected and written down, however, they became frozen in time. Today, the written version has become the "correct" one, and in some cases other variations have disappeared.

Jón Árnason's collection, *Íslenzkar þjóðsögur og æfintýri* (Icelandic Folk Tales and Wonder Tales), was first published in two volumes in 1862 and 1864 with selected legends and wonder tales. It was not until nearly a hundred years later, in 1954–61, that the full collection was first published, in six volumes. Most of the legends found in this book are from this collection.

Jón Árnason's collection is often said to mark the beginning of legend collecting in Iceland, but it was certainly not the end. More folk tale collections followed in the years after. As in other countries, these legends were mostly collected and published by men. In the collections, more of the legends attributed to specific storytellers are ascribed to male storytellers than female ones. However, in many cases the story-teller is not known. This gender bias must be kept in mind when considering the legends. As the folklorist Rósa Þorsteinsdóttir notes, stories bear witness to the attitudes and environments of those who told them, and the background of the storytellers seems to affect which tales they tell and how they tell them.[24] Various scholars have pointed out that women's storytelling tended to be classed as a secondary matter in the estimation of many rural communities, often dismissed by collectors as minor genres, old wives' tales or gossip. The power relations that existed between those who collected the legends and those who told them must also be kept in mind, since in Iceland the collectors were educated men or clerics, and people often censor themselves when talking to authorities or someone of a higher class.[25]

For each legend in this book, I note both the name of the story-teller (when it is known) and who collected it. This book also includes tales from other collections: *Íslenzkar þjóðsögur* (Icelandic Folk Tales), collected by Ólafur Davíðsson (1862–1903) in the nineteenth century and first published in 1895; *Þjóðsögur og sagnir* (Folk Tales and Legends), collected by Torfhildur Þ. Hólm (1845–1918) in the late nineteenth century and first published after her death in 1962; *Íslenskar þjóðsögur og sagnir* (Icelandic Folk Tales and Legends), collected by Sigfús Sigfússon (1855–1935) in the early twentieth century and first published in 1922–54, mainly collected in the east of Iceland; and *Rauðskinna* (lit. Redskin – the name references a legendary book of magic), published by Jón Thorarensen (1902–1986) in 1929–62.

Most of the Icelandic legend collections are divided into categories and chapters based on what supernatural phenomenon can be found in the stories; chapters on ghosts, trolls and elves are therefore found in most of them. This classification, first established by the Brothers Grimm, also shines through in this book, as certain settings have become closely connected to specific supernatural beings.

In 2014 the online database Sagnagrunnur.com was launched. The database makes the Icelandic legend material more accessible: there, one can find legends from published Icelandic legend collections, and today over ten thousand legends have been registered within the database.[26] It is thus safe to say that the legend archive in Iceland is quite extensive.

Legends as a Window to the Past

Folk tales are usually defined as stories told by the people and are most often divided into two main categories: legends and wonder tales (also known as fairy tales). When defining legends, they are often placed in opposition to wonder tales, making their differences define them. One of the first definitions was put forth by the Brothers Grimm in their introduction to the first volume of their *Deutsche Sagen* in 1816, where they note that the wonder tale is more poetic, while the legend is more historical.[27] The legends are often set in a specific time and place within the realm of those who listen, while wonder tales are more often set to happen "once upon a time, in a kingdom far away". As the folklorist Max Lüthi asserts, wonder tales are one-dimensional, while legends have more layers and depth. In legends everything takes time, seasons pass, and they tend to include more detailed descriptions of people and changes, while wonder tales are more abstract.[28] In this book the emphasis will be on Icelandic folk legends; however, these are sometimes longer than similar stories in the neighbouring countries, meaning that the border between legend and wonder tale can sometimes seem blurred. Nevertheless, as in other countries, Icelandic legends purport to take place in the real world of the people who told them and are often connected to specific times, places and people. As with all categories, they often overlap with other types of narrative, meaning that similar motifs and ideas can be found across various genres.

Both legends and wonder tales include narrative characters who often encounter something supernatural or otherworldly, but they differ when it comes to that encounter being a common part of the character's world or an unusual experience. In wonder tales such encounters are a natural part of the hero's world, while in legends the encounter is always unusual and something that is hard to explain: it is not a part of their everyday world. This is important in relation to another distinguishing feature of legends, which is that they are told in such a way that they are meant to be believed. As the folklorist Elliott Oring points out, legends employ an extensive rhetoric in establishing truth. They make a claim about the truth of an event, as can be seen in various legends included in this book.[29] Sometimes legends can also challenge the beliefs of whoever is listening. This element of the legend is something that is often mentioned by scholars, and the American Hungarian folklorist Linda Dégh even makes belief a central factor in her main definition of legends:

> The legend is a legend once it entertains debate about belief. Short or long, complete or rudimentary, local or global, supernatural, horrible, mysterious, or grotesque, about one's own or someone else's experience, the sounding of contrary opinions is what makes a legend a legend.[30]

Legends can thereby bring to the forefront questions about what one believes, both for the storyteller and for those who listen. However, as Oring has noted on many occasions, they cannot go too far in challenging the beliefs of people, as a legend is more likely to be persuasive if it reflects the morality of the listener. While the question of belief is important in regards to the legends, to a folklorist it is not important to know whether there really is an elf in the rock or whether the family is really terrorized by a ghost: the stories themselves are what is of interest, to understand what they are telling us about society.

Legends cannot be considered accurate historical sources about events of the past. Nevertheless, they contain a different kind of truth. Legends reflect the ideas of the people who told them, and in that way, they can work as windows to the past. Repeated themes can be said to reflect the dominant world views and beliefs of the societies in which they were told, collected and recorded.[31] In legends we can see a reflection of people's ideas about the world around them, their beliefs and their fears, their prides and prejudices, criticism of authority, sympathy with the underdog and so on.

As the Swedish folklorist Ulf Palmenfelt notes, legends of conflicts between people and supernatural beings often reflect the conflicts people faced in real life, making it easier for them to process those problems mentally.[32] Thus, legends also have a degree of healing power and can also help spark conversations about sensitive matters, such as religion, trauma and authority, as well as being an effective way for people to make their opinions known indirectly.

Indeed, legends had to be relevant and in touch with the daily lives of people to continue to be told.[33] As the Finnish folklorist Anna-Leena Siikala states, legends tend to have an ideological dimension that reflects the culture from which they emerge and to which they belong. While they belong to an oral tradition that considers events of the past, they are always affected by the present.[34]

Legends also include messages on how people should or should not behave. As the folklorist Terry Gunnell puts it:

> They served as a map of behaviour, underlining moral and social values and offering examples to follow or avoid . . . If the map was followed you had a good chance of living in safety. If you broke it, you stood an equally good chance of ending up in a folk legend yourself.[35]

This is made clear in legends: if you break the official or even unofficial rules of the society reflected in a legend, you are brutally punished.[36] Legends therefore are both shaped by the society to which they belong and have the possibility to affect it by confirming or rejecting the ruling ideology.

Even though we have some knowledge of the wider context of the legends, such as the laws of the time and various official details concerning the rights of certain groups, in many cases the closer context of the stories is difficult to establish. While we do have some information about the settings in which stories were told, when they were told and who the audience was, it is important to keep in mind that the meanings that modern readers of legends see in the text might not always be the same as those intended by the original storytellers or how they were understood by listeners at the time. Indeed, there is always a possibility that the legend telling was originally framed within another discourse, one that might, for example, have made fun of the legend and the messages contained within it. It is thus important to remember that the same legend could have numerous different meanings that varied according to the circumstances, with variations of a single legend offering a range of interpretations. Unfortunately, when narratives are published in legend collections, this context is often lost.[37]

Icelandic legends and folk beliefs are in many cases similar to those found elsewhere in Europe, especially in Scandinavia and the Celtic countries. Legends that have been passed on to different places and countries are said to be migratory. When a migratory legend travels to different places, it must be able to adapt to the new society, often becoming connected to new people or places.[38] When this occurs, it is particularly interesting to note the differences that exist between the Icelandic variations and those stories found elsewhere, considering what might have made them different. To get a better overview of these diverse variants found in different countries, scholars have compiled extensive bibliographies of various tale types, known as the Aarne–Thompson–Uther classification system (ATU).[39] Later, the same approach was taken with migratory legends (ML), with bibliographies of legend types found in specific countries being made in a number of countries in northern Europe, such as Norway and Sweden.[40] In this book, these are sometimes referenced in the text, however more often in endnotes.

Some of the supernatural beings, beliefs and motifs found in the Icelandic legend collections can also be found in older sources, such as the Icelandic sagas and medieval literature (which was in many cases highly influenced by other European literature) from the thirteenth to fifteenth centuries.[41] For this book's context it is important to note that these sagas were often read at evening wakes, and many people knew some of these stories in the nineteenth century. It is nevertheless also important to remember that while the legends often build on themes that can be seen in these older stories, it is impossible to know how long the legends themselves had circulated in oral tradition before they were written down, and they therefore should only be considered to reflect the time in which they were collected.

Legends and stories are often connected to a particular landscape or a specific place. For those who know the stories, the places to which they are attached gain a new dimension. The stories can thus be said to work to create places, in the sense that they have the power to transform seemingly ordinary places into meaningful and magical settings by infusing them with emotional, cultural and narrative significance.

This strange rock formation might remind those familiar with Icelandic folk legends of a troll woman turned to stone. However, no such legend is linked to this rock, at least not one that has been preserved. This shows how the landscape can also create stories.

The stories enrich and deepen people's appreciation and understanding of those locations. This can also work the other way around, a place being the inspiration for a story. An unusual rock in the sea might remind people of the stories they have heard about supernatural beings and the ocean, thereby immediately awakening the imagination and creating new stories.

The legends can offer important insights into the lives and world views of the people who told them, as will be seen in the following chapters of this book.

The Book

This book is divided into six chapters, each centred around a specific setting in which the legends take place: the farm, the wilderness, the dark, the church, the ocean and the shore. It is an anthology of Icelandic legends, stories of the hidden people, trolls, ghosts, sea monsters, polar bears and seals, to name but a few. Many of these stories are about love and revenge. They show conflict between Christianity and paganism, past and present, nature and humans, men and women, different classes, and the supernatural and non-supernatural. These are stories that were told for entertainment, legends that include warnings to those who heard them, and narratives that convey empathy, prejudice, dreams and the ideas of those who told them.

In each chapter I have chosen a selection of Icelandic legends from the nineteenth and twentieth centuries. I have tried to include a wide range of legends and supernatural beings to give the reader a good, hopefully representative, impression of the legend corpus in Iceland. Most of them, as mentioned earlier, are from the collection of Jón Árnason, since his collection is both the largest and the oldest. Some of the legends included here are among the best-known legends in Iceland, while others are stories that hold a special place in my own heart, ones that I heard when growing up or have researched in my career as a folklorist. The stories I have chosen are usually found in several different variants in the Icelandic legend corpus, something that indicates that they were widespread and therefore offer a better insight into the past.

In the first chapter, we will examine the role of the farm in the lives of Icelanders and get to know the hidden people (or elves), beings that are similar to humans in both appearance and demeanour. They live in hills and rocks often close to farms and can therefore be said to have been the supernatural neighbours of Icelanders in the past. The second chapter focuses on the Icelandic wilderness. Icelanders often found themselves in the wilderness when travelling, herding sheep or collecting herbs. Legends that take place there often include encounters with trolls, outlaws or even polar bears. In the third chapter we take a closer look at the darkness, a quality that is predominant in Iceland and naturally the perfect setting for eerie ghost stories. The fourth chapter includes legends that take place in a church, since churches were one of the cornerstones of Icelandic society in the nineteenth century and in the context of legends were often considered to be a space that offered safety, where one could escape the threatening supernatural. The fifth and sixth chapters examine stories that take place at the shore and out at sea. Many Icelanders lived near the ocean and utilized it for fishing, something that was not without risk, and the shore – the border between Iceland and the rest of the world – can be seen as a liminal space where anything can happen. Many Icelandic legends tell of the horrible sea monsters found in these places.

I hope this book offers a different understanding of Icelandic society in the nineteenth and early twentieth centuries and an interesting glimpse into the Icelandic legend tradition. Ultimately, I hope that those who read it will never see an unusual rock the same way again but will from now on be reminded of the hidden people who might live in it, or the trolls that might once have been turned to stone when touched by the first rays of sunlight.

1

The Farm

In the nineteenth century, farms were the very heart of Icelandic society. They were the home, the workplace and the main focus of people's social lives. There could be great distances between farms. Frequently, many people lived on one farm. This meant it was quite crowded and people had limited privacy. Life on the farm followed a well-worn routine. There were various jobs that had to be done depending on the season, as the farming unit had to be self-sufficient. Tending to sheep, horses and cattle were year-round tasks. In the summer, the focus was on the harvest and collecting hay. Life on the farm was not always easy. The children on the farm would play, but as soon as they were old enough they would join the workforce. People would often eat together, and during the winter they would gather for the evening wake, telling stories and reading aloud.

Until the end of the nineteenth century, turf houses were the most common form of housing in Iceland, as they had been since the settlement. The walls of the houses were made of turf and stones, with a wooden frame to hold up a turf roof. The timber was often driftwood that had washed ashore from Siberia or Canada. The houses varied in size and build, but most farms from the eighteenth century until the middle of the nineteenth consisted of a few rooms or small buildings that stood in a cluster and were connected by tunnels. The most important area was the *baðstofa*, which will be translated hereafter as the living room, in which most of the people on the farm slept and ate.

During the winter this was also where they worked. This living room is a common setting in folk legends, as it was the heart of the farm. Other rooms were the kitchen and a pantry for food. On some larger farms there were specific sleeping rooms for workers, and if the owner was wealthy one might find a fancier living room that was specially designed to greet guests. As the houses were made of natural materials, they required a lot of maintenance. It was then handy for each room to be an individual unit, which made it easier to make changes or fix them one at a time.[1] While few legends tell of the maintenance of the houses, at least one legend type mentions something about their up-keep. The story tells of a young housemaid who is returning dishes to the pantry when she disappears. It then turns out that her fiancé has drowned on the night of her disappearance. Decades later, when the farmer is fixing the house, he finds the skeleton of the woman inside one of the walls, still carrying the dishes and looking over her shoulder in horror. The people on the farm conclude that the ghost of her fiancé must have lured her inside the wall with a trap door, which closed when she had entered.[2]

Animals and people lived close to each other on the farms, and in the eighteenth and early nineteenth centuries the living room was some-times placed on top of the cowshed, so the people could benefit from the warmth of the animals. In the late nineteenth century, it became more common for the rooms to be lined up side by side, with a wooden facade. This was the result of the Danish trading monopoly being lifted completely in 1855, which made wood and glass more accessible to Icelanders than before.[3] These natural turf houses were neverthe-less often described as both dark and dirty and sometimes made for an unpleasant living area. As described by the writer and poet Ólöf Sigurðardóttir (1857–1933) in an article written in a local paper in 1906 about her childhood home:

> The house was like the worst of our mud huts. The *baðstofa* was small with a low ceiling, all unpanelled, except for those loose

This illustration by Karel Sedivý (from *Illustreret Tidende*, 10 December 1882) depicts a late 19th-century turf house. By that time, it was more common for rooms to be lined up side by side with a wooden facade. The house shown is notably large, likely owned by someone of good standing and considerable wealth, as most Icelandic turf houses were typically smaller.

planks placed above the beds. The beds were made of turf blocks with a bed frame and a footboard made of wood. No tables, no seating other than the beds.[4]

Others have mentioned that the houses were often dark and wet, as when it rained the roofs would leak, as described by parliamentarian and priest Þorkell Bjarnason (1839–1902) in 1892:

As one might guess, many of these living rooms were far from pleasant or comfortable abodes. When it rained heavily, they leaked a lot. During the daytime, there were tubs and other containers in the rooms to collect the rainwater, but at night people hung animal skins over the beds or spread them on top of themselves. However, the bedding did not escape getting wet.[5]

These negative descriptions become even more striking in the writings of various scholars who travelled from abroad and visited Iceland in the nineteenth century. Many of them noted how they felt that the turf houses would be more fit for animals than people. One of these travellers was J. Ross Browne, an Irish-born American who visited Iceland in 1862 and was not impressed: "It is to the astonishment of the traveller who peers into these ugly, joyless lairs in which these poor people live, that they are not eaten by snails or die from rheumatism."[6] These travelling scholars also noted how dirty the farms were and described an awful smell inside the houses, as well as a strong odour from the inhabitants. In 1810, Henry Holland, a traveller from England, celebrated not having to stay at a farm where he noted that "the dirt and the smell inside was unbearable." Holland considered the smell to be characteristic of Icelandic people and their houses: "It could be said that all the most disgusting things imaginable come together there; dirt, darkness and a stench of fish in all possible degrees of curing . . ."[7] Here, it is important to note that the travellers were not used to these living conditions, unlike the Icelandic people.[8] Usually the legends themselves make little mention of the state of the farmhouse, nor the leakage or smell, something that might suggest it was too ordinary to be specified. When it came to housing, living and working conditions, most Icelanders knew nothing else but the turf houses. All the same, not everyone had such negative experiences with these houses; some remember them more fondly. These differing experiences must have varied based on the condition of the house in question, something that would have depended greatly on people's resources and their status in society. Interestingly enough, in some later writings there is a more nostalgic view of the turf houses, which after all were often warmer than the timber and concrete houses that followed.[9]

Each turf house was home to an average of seven people (based on the census of 1860). This number was usually made up of the nuclear family (mother, father and their children) along with a number of other people. These people could be divided into three categories: other relatives, hired workers and people who had been "placed" on the farm. These "placed" people included children who were being fostered, paupers and so on.[10] From the late eighteenth century until the early nineteenth, it was not uncommon for farmers in Iceland to have ten to fifteen children, a figure that was somewhat higher than in other neighbouring countries.[11] However, often only half of those children made it to adulthood as medical knowledge was still limited, and the death rate among infants was extremely high.[12]

On many farms, guests were a welcome change. How common this was depended greatly on where the farm was located. In the farming society, there was a great emphasis on hospitality, something that is also reflected in the legends, in which those who are inhospitable are usually punished. There was a social agreement that guests could stay at each farm for three nights before moving on.[13]

As mentioned earlier, the farm was the main field of work for most people in the nineteenth century. Most people might have dreamed of becoming a farmer or housewife on their own farm, but such dreams only came true for a few. Most people served as farmworkers or housemaids.[14] While both men and women worked side by side on the farms, their work tended to be different. Women often took care of housework as they oversaw the home. They turned milk into food, cooked, sewed, knitted, spun, washed, raised the children, milked the cows and were in charge of the housemaids.[15] The farmers were in charge of the work that took place outside the house and were the head of the family and in charge of its affairs.

It is therefore not surprising that many of the Icelandic legends take place on farms: they were the centre of people's worlds. As the home, the farm offered a certain protection, but it also needed to be protected. According to folk belief, while a number of dangerous supernatural beings such as trolls and outlaws lived some distance away from the farm, they were known sometimes to threaten the peace of the home, as can be seen in the story "Nineteen Outlaws" and in the wilderness chapter, in which we find stories about female trolls who kidnap farmers.

The Icelandic *huldufólk* or *álfar* (hidden people, or elves, terms that Icelanders use interchangeably) were somewhat different. They were the invisible neighbours of Icelanders of the past, and were said to live in rocks or hills, often in close proximity to the farm. They have counterparts in the folklore of other countries, the stories of the hidden people having many similarities to stories told in the other Nordic and Celtic countries.[16]

In the Icelandic legends, the hidden people are often described as being similar to humans in size and appearance, although they are usually invisible to the naked eye. The hidden people, like the Icelandic people of the nineteenth century, were farmers and fishermen. They were also considered to be Christian. Large and extravagant rocks were often said to be the churches of the hidden people, and some people claim to have heard singing when walking past such rocks.

The hidden people are described as being wealthier than humans, their homes being beautifully decorated and their belongings made of silver and gold. Some legends tell of the hidden people throwing big parties in which there is plenty of food. The world of the hidden people therefore appears as a slightly better world than that known by most people in Iceland, who were often poor and knew food had to be carefully distributed. The hidden people are good farmers, intuitive about the weather, and in some legends they are also capable of using magic and putting curses on those they do not like. People are often shown to respect them out of fear. Indeed, the legends underline that the hidden people are kind to those who help them, but if a person does them harm they are vengeful and harmful.

Jónas Jónasson (1856–1918), who in the nineteenth century published a book about folkways and folk beliefs, notes that people at the time still very much believed in the hidden people:

This photograph shows a rock near the farm Brúará in Strandir, believed to be home to a hidden woman who owns the grass field below, using it to feed her sheep. In the mid-20th century, a farmer at Brúará used stones from the rock and turf from the hill to build an outhouse. The people on the farm worked the whole day to build it. During the night they heard loud noises; the outhouse had collapsed by morning. Convinced it was the hidden people's doing, they returned all the materials. Today, stories persist about the hidden people in the rock, with some claiming to hear beautiful singing or see lights as if a window were inside the rock.

The belief in elves is by no means extinct – not more so than just a few years ago a young woman got engaged to a hidden person out in Fljót (not long after 1900). And the same thing can be seen in various stories of people today: individuals still see hidden people and often interact with them.[17]

The collector Jón Árnason was less convinced. He writes in his introduction, "The belief in elves has had proponents everywhere in Iceland. Although it is now considered dead, along with most of those who believed in the existence of elves, there are still a few remnants of it left."[18] In this regard it is interesting to note that even today, new stories are still emerging in Iceland about the hidden people. Indeed, foreigners are often captivated by Icelanders' belief in these supernatural beings, something that is often painted by the media and visitors as being somewhat bizarre. It is often reported that up to two-thirds of the population in Iceland believe in elves, which is an oversimplification. The following figures come from surveys sent out in 1974, 2006–7 and 2023, the first by the psychologist Erlendur Haraldsson and the others by Terry Gunnell, a professor in folkloristics, in consultation with Erlendur in 2006–7.[19] The surveys asked Icelanders about their belief in various supernatural beings, among others the hidden people and their homes. The results show that most people were not willing to deny the possibility of hidden people, without stating direct belief in them. When people were asked about their opinions on the existence of the hidden people or elves, the answers were as follows:

	1974	2006	2007	2023
Impossible	4%	15%	14%	27%
Unlikely	8%	24%	20%	28%
Possible	40%	35%	39%	25%
Likely	24%	18%	18%	12%
Certain	24%	9%	9%	8%

It is interesting to note how relatively little change there was between those who believed the existence of hidden people to be possible between 1974 and 2007. However, it does appear that the belief in these supernatural beings is decreasing today. It is also clear that the stories of the hidden people one hears today have changed quite a bit from those that were told in the nineteenth century.

The stories found in the legend collections from the nineteenth century show various communications between the hidden people and humans. They tell of collaboration, romantic relationships and conflicts between the two worlds. Since many of the legends take place on farms, the main protagonists are often women, something that underlines the women's place within the farm and household. These legends also often focus on communication between two women, one from the hidden world and one from the human world. Such communication takes place usually in the context of childbirth or is related to the upbringing of children, something that could be either good or bad.

Many of these legends signify the importance of helping those in need, something that was valued in Iceland's farming society, as people never knew when they themselves might be in need of assistance. Since Iceland was a very rural area, help was often hard to come by and far away. It is therefore not hard to imagine that people found consolation in the idea that they had a friendly neighbour in a nearby rock.

Young Woman Helps a Hidden Woman
to Give Birth

When elf women cannot give birth, they need nothing other than the touch of humans, and elves are well aware of this solution. One evening a woman was taking in her laundry. A man then approached her and asked her to come with him, as he was in great need. The young woman went and they came to a mound in the field. The mound opened up and the man led the young woman in. She came into a living room that was built on two raised platforms, with one at each end. The man led the young woman up on one platform, and there she saw a woman lying on the floor and nobody else. She helped the woman give birth and then bathed the child. The man then took a glass and asked her to apply the contents to the child's eyes, but to avoid letting it come into contact with her own eyes. She took the glass and applied it to the child's eyes. The young woman wanted to know what effect this would have. She then put her fingertip to her right eye, and it so happened that she saw a number of people around her at the other end of the living room. It seemed to her that this event had caused her to see elves, and in that moment the man came in. The young woman gave him the child and the glass, and he thanked her. She then said goodbye to the woman and walked away. The man accompanied her and said that she would be a woman of good fortune. He gave her something as they parted ways, and she then went home.

This woman later became the wife of a priest. She generally benefited from seeing elves, as she could observe their agricultural customs and conduct herself accordingly, for example with hay production during summertime. Once, the priest's wife visited the town and the elf man was there, as it is well known that elves go into town as we do and trade with elf merchants, although we don't see them. She greeted the man, but he was startled and put his finger in his mouth and then in the woman's eye. From that point, she never saw another elf and no longer had second sight.

Told by an unknown storyteller to Magnús Grímsson,
translated by Alice Bower

⋙ ⋘

Becoming a midwife was the first official education offered to women in Iceland. Even though women had been working as midwives long before that, it was not considered an official profession by the state. Giving birth in the farming society of the past was not easy, and these legends might be said to reflect society's understanding of women's fear of childbirth. Those women who were believed to have aided hidden women during childbirth were often considered blessed with the gift of becoming successful midwives, something that was likely to provide a sense of comfort to those seeking assistance from them.[20]

The Grateful Elf Woman

A peasant's wife once dreamed that a woman came to her bedside, who she knew to be a hidden woman, and who begged her to give her milk for her child, two quarts a day, for the space of a month, placing it always in a part of the house which she pointed out. The goodwife promised to do so and remembered her promise when she awoke. So she put a milk bowl every morning in the place which the other had chosen, and left it there, always on her return finding it empty. This went on for a month; and at the end of the month she dreamed that the same woman came to her, thanked her for her kindness, and begged her to accept the belt which she should find in the bed when she awoke, and then vanished. In the morning the goodwife found beneath her pillow a silver belt, beautifully and rarely wrought, the promised gift of the grateful elf woman.

Told by Svanhildur Helgadóttir to Guðmundur Gísli Sigurðsson,
translated by Eiríkur Magnússon and George E. J. Powell

The importance of helping out those in need is a common theme in Icelandic folk legends. In the case of the hidden people this is even more important, as those who do so usually receive a great reward.[21]

The Magic Scythe

A certain day-labourer once started from his home in the south, to earn wages for hay-cutting, in the north country. Once, when travelling over the mountains, he was suddenly overtaken by a thick mist and sleet-storm, and lost his way. Fearing to go on further, he pitched his tent in a convenient spot, and taking out his provisions, began to eat.

While he was engaged upon his meal, a brown dog came into the tent, so ill-favoured, dirty, wet, and fierce-eyed, that the poor man felt quite afraid of it, and gave it as much bread and meat as it could devour. This the dog swallowed greedily, and ran off again into the mist. At first the man wondered much to see a dog in such a wild place, where he never expected to meet a living creature, but after a while he thought no more about the matter, and having finished his supper, fell asleep, with his saddle for a pillow.

At midnight he dreamed that he saw a tall and aged woman enter his tent, who spoke thus to him, "I am beholden to you, good man, for your kindness to my daughter, but am unable to reward you as you deserve. Here is a scythe which I place beneath your pillow: it is the only gift I can make you, but despise it not. It will surely prove useful to you, as it can cut down all that lies before it. Only beware of putting it into the fire to temper it. Sharpen it, however you will, but in that way never." So saying, she was seen no more.

When the man awoke and looked forth, he found the mist all gone and the sun high in heaven; so getting all his things together and striking his tent, he laid them upon the pack-horses, saddling, last of all, his own horse. But on lifting his saddle from the ground, he found beneath it a small scythe-blade, which seemed well worn and was rusty. On seeing this he, at once, recalled to mind his dream, and taking the scythe with him, set out once more on his way. He soon found again the road which he had lost, and made all speed to reach the well-people district to which he was bound.

When he arrived at the north country, he went from house to house, but did not find any employment, for every farmer had labourers enough, and one week of hay-harvest was already past. He heard it said, however, that one old woman in the district, generally thought by her neighbours to be skilled in magic and very rich, always began her hay-cutting a week later than anybody else, and though she seldom employed a labourer, always contrived to finish it by the end of the season. When, by any chance – and it was a rare one – she did engage a workman, she was never known to pay him for his work.

Now the peasant from the south was already advised to ask this old woman for employment, having been warned of her strange habits.

He accordingly went to her house, and offered himself to her as a day-labourer. She accepted his offer, and told him that he might, if he chose, work a week for her, but must expect no payment.

"Except," she said, "you can cut more grass in the whole week than I can rake in on the last day of it."

To these terms he gladly agreed, and began mowing. And a very good scythe he found that to be which the woman had given him in his dream; for it cut well, and never wanted sharpening, though he worked with it for five days unceasingly. He was well content, too, with his place, for the old woman was kind enough to him.

One day, entering the forge next to her house, he saw a vast number of scythe-handles and rakes, and a big heap of blades, and wondered beyond measure what the old lady could want with all these. It was the fifth day – the Friday – and when he was asleep that night, the same elfwoman whom he had seen upon the mountains, came again to him, and said:

"Large as are the meadows you have mown, your employer will easily be able to rake in all that hay tomorrow, and if she does so, will – as you know – drive you away without paying you. When, therefore, you see yourself worsted, go into the forge, take as many scythe-handles as you think proper, fit their blades to them and carry them out into that part of the land where the hay is yet uncut. There you must lay them on the ground, and you shall see how things go."

This said, she disappeared, and in the morning the labourer getting up, set to work, as usual, at his mowing.

At six o'clock the old witch came out, bringing five rakes with her, and said to the man:

"A goodly piece of ground you have moved, indeed!"

And so saying she spread the rakes upon the hay. Then the man saw, to his astonishment, that though the one she held in her hand raked in great quantities of hay, the other four raked in no less, each, all of their own accord and with no hand to wield them.

At noon, seeing that the old woman would soon get the best of him, he went into the forge and took out several scythe-handles, to which he fixed their blades, and bringing them out into the field laid them down upon the grass which was yet standing. Then all the scythes set to work on their own accord, and cut down the grass so quickly that the rakes could not keep pace with them. And so they went on all the rest of the day, and the old woman was unable to rake in all the hay which lay in the fields. After dark, she told him to gather up his scythes and take them into the house again, while she collected her rakes, saying to him:

"You are wiser than I took you to be, and you know more than myself: so much the better for you, for you may stay as long with me as you like."

He spent the whole summer in her employment, and they got along very well together, mowing with mighty little trouble a vast amount of hay. In the autumn she sent him away, well laden with money, to his own home in the south. Next summer, and more than one summer following he spent in her employ, always being paid as his heart could desire, at the end of the season.

After some years, he took a farm of his own in the south country, and was always looked upon by all his neighbours as an honest man, a good fisherman, and an able workman in whatever work he might put his hand to. He always cut his own hay, never using any scythe but that which the elfwoman had given him upon the mountains; nor did any of his neighbours ever finish their mowing before him.

One summer it chanced that, while he was out fishing, one of his neighbours came to his house and asked his wife to lend him her husband's scythe, as he had lost his own. The farmer's wife looked for one, but could only find the one upon which her husband set such store. This, however, a little reluctant, she lent the man, begging him at the same time never to temper it in the fire, for that, she said, her good man never did. So the neighbour promised, and taking it with him, bound it to a handle and began to work with it. But, sweep as he would, and strain as he would (and sweep and strain he did right lustily), not a single blade of grass fell. Angry at this, the man tried to sharpen it, but with no avail. Then he took it into his forge, intending to temper it, for, thought he, what harm could that possibly do; but as soon as the flames touched it, the steel melted like wax, and nothing of it was left but a little heap of ashes. Seeing this, he went in haste to the farmer's house, where he had borrowed it, and told the woman what had happened: she was at her wits' end with fright and shame when she heard it, for she knew well enough how her husband set store by this scythe, and how angry he would be at its loss.

And angry indeed he was, when he came home, and he beat his wife well for her folly in lending what was not hers to lend. But this wrath was soon over, and never again, as he never had before, laid the stick about his wife's shoulders.

Told by an unknown storyteller to Magnús Grímsson,
translated by Eiríkur Magnússon and George E. J. Powell

The legend highlights farmwork and takes place during haymaking season, which was one of the most important times as the livelihood of the livestock, and thereby the people, depended on it. Here it is also interesting to note that in the first publication of Jón's collection, the man punishes his wife at the end of the legend (although not as severely as in the translation by Eiríkur and Powell shown here); however, in later editions that has been completely removed from the story.

The Elfin-Lover

A certain rich farmer and his wife had two daughters, who were named Margrét and Ólöf.

Margrét was the darling of her parents' hearts and used in the summer to take care of a dairy and pasture in the mountains, for her father and mother always put more trust in her than in anybody else.

One summer it happened that, while she was sitting milking the ewes, a little boy came to her several evenings in succession, and brought with him a small wooden jug, which he asked her to fill for him with milk. This Margrét always refused to do, and as he still came day after day with the same request, she at last became angry, and one evening threatened him with a good whipping if he troubled her again.

"For," she said, "I should think I had plenty to do without giving milk to all the little boys who choose to come with jugs for it. Begone!"

At this the child ran back crying to his mother, who was an elfwoman, and who lived near the mountain-farm, and told her how harshly Margrét had spoken to him. The elfwoman was mighty wroth at this, and said:

"Harsh words shall meet with a harsh lot. This shall be Margrét's fate. She shall spend and fritter away everything that comes into her hands just as lavishly as she has stingily refused to give you milk. She shall try how she likes poverty and loss of trust." And true enough she certainly did become such a spendthrift, that her father and mother soon noticed it, and not caring that she should waste all they had, withdrew her from the mountain pasture and sent Ólöf there in her stead.

When the latter had been there some little time, the same child came to her as she sat out in the evening milking the ewes, and, holding out his little porringer, said:

"Ólöf, my mother sends her love to you, and begs you to give her a little milk for her child. When your sister Margrét was here I often asked her for some, but she was harsh and said nay, and drove me out of her sight."

Ólöf was tender-hearted, and willingly gave the boy some milk to drink himself and filled his jug for him, at the same time telling him to come whenever he liked. The boy ran off to his mother and told her how different things were now, and how kindly the girl had spoken to him and treated him. Whereupon the elfwoman said:

"Good words shall have a good reward. This shall be Ólöf's fate. All that comes into her hands shall turn to fair luck, and all she has shall increase as many-fold as her kindness to you has been greater than her sister's cruelty."

So, for some summers the boy came often to Ólöf for milk. Now one autumn her companions in the mountain-farm noticed that she was soon to give birth to a child, but being discreet, and moreover loving her well, they kept their discovery from all else, though they could not help whispering among themselves that the boy who used to beg for milk was just as fond of Ólöf herself as her milk-pails, if not more so.

One night Ólöf was delivered of a child. As soon as it was born, an old man and old woman, together with the boy who had so often visited Ólöf on the mountains, came into the cottage, and taking the child in their arms went out with it, after bidding her an affectionate farewell. All this her companions saw, and that the youth often came and spoke with her, though Ólöf fully believed that not only the birth of her child, but also the visits of the elves were unknown to all but herself.

Time passed without any new occurrence, until Ólöf's mother fell into a sickness which was her last. After her mother's death, Ólöf took her place in keeping the house, but never seemed quite happy after what had happened at the mountain-hut. Many fine young fellows wooed and wished to win her, but she said nay to them all, and sent them all off without so much as turning her head to look after them.

At last one came, to whom Ólöf's father, wearied with her eternal refusals, bade her give herself. For some while she would not listen to him, but at length consented to marry him only on the condition that he would never allow anyone to pass the winter with them, until he had first spoken to her and asked her leave to do so. He made her this promise, and they were speedily married and went to live at the husband's farm (for he was a farmer, well to do), which was in the mountains, far from her old home.

She had not been there long, when her mother-in-law saw that some weight lay upon Ólöf's heart, and that her eyes were often filled with tears, and begged her to tell her the cause of her grief. But for a long time, Ólöf would not be persuaded and always put the other off with shirking answers. At last, however, her mother-in-law promised never, as long as she lived, to repeat to anyone the truth, if Ólöf would only tell it her. So Ólöf told her, and when she found how the good woman pitied her, and how kind and leal was that hearth into which she poured her sorrow, she wondered why she had not trusted her at first.

For there is no balm like pity to a wounded soul, however deep the wound and however long it may have ached in secret.

In the third year after Ólöf's marriage, but the twelfth from the birth of her child in the mountain-hut, it happened at autumn tide, towards the end of the hay harvest, that a man and a young boy came to their farmer's house and gave him greeting. He had never seen them before, but he noticed that they kept their hats slouched down over their brows, as if they were unwilling to be known. When the farmer had returned kindly their salutation, they begged him to allow them to pass the winter in his house. The farmer answered:

"It is not my custom to receive strangers thus. It is long since I have done so."

But on their becoming more urgent, he said:

"I cannot bid you welcome, nor will I send you away, until I have first seen my wife and spoken to her about it."

The man answered, "Truly you do well, and it becomes you to let your wife have the upper hand of you. If you send us away, be sure that all your neighbours shall know which of you two is master."

This taunt was more than the farmer could bear, so he promised to let them stay with him. Then going into the house he met Ólöf, who said to him:

"What men are these?"

"I know not," he replied: "they have come to me to ask lodging for the winter, and they urged me so, that I promised it them, and bade them welcome to stay with us."

Then Ólöf said, "In so doing you have broken your promise to me, but some voice in this matter I will have. These men shall not sleep in the house with the rest of the workers, but shall spend the winter in one of the outbuildings."

And she left him, and went to her own room weeping.

So the farmer made ready one of the outlying buildings, furnished it with every necessary from the farm, and gave it up as a winter dwelling for the two strangers; but his wife never set foot inside its door, nor went near it. The man and boy took up their abode there, joining the farmer's family every evening in the living room, as was the custom, but always sitting apart in a dark corner, and never speaking unless the farmer first addressed them. Ólöf always seemed as if she did not see them, never even once looking at or speaking to them. Thus the winter passed and spring came.

Now it happened one Sunday, that the farmer and his wife were going to church in order to take the Holy Communion, having bidden farewell to all their household. When they were a little way from home, the farmer asked Ólöf:

"Have you bidden farewell to all at home?"

She said, "To all."

Then he asked again, "Have you bidden farewell to the strangers also?"

"No," she said, "I have not, nor need I, for the whole winter through I have neither spoken to nor looked at them. How then can I have trespassed against them?"

But the farmer was not well-pleased at this, and urged her to return and bid the strangers farewell, and the more she refused, the more he waxed wroth, till at length she seeing that he would be obeyed, said:

"Well! I will return, as you have bidden, but for what comes of it, blame yourself, not me."

She went, and the farmer waited for her, but she stayed so long away that he turned back after her, to see what had delayed her. When he came to the outhouse in which the two strangers lived, he found the door unlatched, and stopping by it to listen if his wife were there, he heard her say these words:

"This is the sweetest draught that ever passed my lips from thine."

He waited a while to hear if more would be said, but no other sound came from the house. So he went in, and there on the couch lay his wife and the stranger dead (for their hearts had broken from sorrow); and over them the young boy stood weeping. When he asked the lad what this meant, and how death had befallen them, he only said, "These are my parents."

But the farmer's mother told him Ólöf's story, for she held herself free from her promise now that Ólöf was dead. And the farmer, full of grief, bade the lad welcome to stay with him, and as he had been Ólöf's child, so to be his. But from the moment when Ólöf and her elfin lover were hidden by the earth, the boy was no more seen.

Told by an unknown storyteller to Magnús Jónsson,
translated by Eiríkur Magnússon and George E. J. Powell

⟶≫ ≪⟵

Several legends tell of romantic relationships between humans and hidden people, something that usually ends tragically in Icelandic legends. Stories similar to this one make one wonder about the position of women who became pregnant out of wedlock, something that was frowned upon during the time in question. Supernatural beings in legends are commonly used to portray everyday human conflicts, making it easier to discuss them and process them mentally.[22] This legend also gives an interesting insight into the gender hierarchy that existed on the farms, something that becomes very obvious when the husband betrays the promise he made to his wife. In the translation of Powell and Eiríkur they have added the direct quotes of the hidden woman.

The Father of Eighteen Elves

At a certain farm, long ago, it happened that all the household were out one day, making hay, except the goodwoman and her only child, a boy of four years old. He was a strong, smart little fellow, who could already speak almost as well as his elders, and was looked upon by his parents with great pride and hope. But as his mother had plenty of other work to do besides watching him, she was obliged to leave him alone for a short time, while she went down to the brook to wash the milk-pails. So she left him playing in the door of the cottage, and came back again as soon as she had placed the milk-pails to dry.

Directly when she spoke to the child, it began to cry in a strange and unnatural way, which amazed her not a little, as it had always been so quiet and sweet-tempered. When she tried to make the child speak to her, as it was wont to do, it only yelled the more, and so it went on for a long time, always crying and never would be soothed, till the mother was in despair at this change in her boy, who now seemed to have lost his senses.

Filled with grief, she went to ask the advice of a learned and skilful woman in the neighbourhood, and confided to her all her trouble.

Her neighbour asked her all sorts of questions – How long ago this change in the child's manner had happened? What his mother thought to be the cause of it? And so forth. To all of which the wretched woman gave the best answers she could. At last the wise woman said: "Do you not think, my friend, that the child you now have is a changeling? Without doubt it was put at your cottage door in the place of your son, while you were washing the milk-pails." "I know not," replied the other, "but advise me how to find it out." So the wise woman said, "I will tell you. Place the child where he may see something he has never seen before, and let him fancy himself alone. As soon as he believes no one to be near him, he will speak. But you must listen attentively, and if the child says something that declares him to be a changeling, then beat him without mercy."

That was the wise woman's advice, and her neighbour, with many thanks for it, went home. When she got to her house, she set a cauldron in the middle of the hearth, and taking a number of rods, bound them end to end, and at the bottom of them fastened a porridge-spoon. This she stuck into the cauldron in such a way that the new handle she had made for it reached right up the chimney: as soon as she had prepared everything, she fetched the child, and placing him on the floor of the kitchen left him and went out, taking care, however, to leave the door ajar, so that she could hear and see all that went on.

This 1971 illustration by Þórdís Tryggvadóttir (1927–2012) depicts the story of "The Father of Eighteen Elves". Þórdís often drew inspiration from Icelandic folk legends, and many of her works portray these tales. Here, the women are dressed in versions of the Icelandic national costume, complete with the traditional headpiece.

When she had left the room, the child began to walk round and round the cauldron, and eye it carefully, and after a while he said:

"Well! I am old enough, as anybody may guess from my beard, and the father of eighteen elves, but never in all my life, have I seen so long a spoon to so small a pot."

On hearing this the goodwoman waited not a moment, but rushed into the room and snatching up a bundle of fire-wood flogged the changeling with it, till he kicked and screamed again. In the midst of all this, the door opened, and a strange woman, bearing in her arms a beautiful boy, entered and said, "See how we differ! I cherish and love your son, while you beat and ill-use my husband"; with these words, she gave back to the farmer's wife her own son, and taking the changeling by the hand, disappeared with him.

But the little boy grew up to manhood, and fulfilled all the hope and promise of his youth.

Told, among others, by Sigurður Guðmundsson to Jón Árnason and Magnús Grímsson, translated by Eiríkur Magnússon and George E. J. Powell

→→》 《←←

This legend tells of an *umskiptingur* or changeling, a phenomenon known all around the world (see, for example, K141-70 and ML5080, 'The Changeling'). Several Icelandic stories tell of hidden women who steal human children and exchange them for their old, wrinkly elven husbands, whom they have disguised as children. When this happens, the previously well-behaved child becomes difficult and impossible to soothe. As Jón Árnason notes, it was considered risky to leave children unsupervised, as they could be taken and replaced by the elves. In most legends of this kind, the mother is working outside and momentarily looks away from her child. When she returns, the child is unpleasant and crying, and in some versions its appearance has even changed. According to many of these legends, the best way to get rid of the changeling is to inflict violence on it, until the hidden woman returns the original child.[23] In these stories, as with most tales that have to do with childbirth or raising children, the responsibility lies entirely with the mother; the father is not mentioned. The setting of these stories is also often in or around the kitchen, which was the housewife's territory, as she would be in charge of cooking for the home.

In recent years, various scholars have written about the phenomenon of the changeling, focusing on its potential connection to children with disabilities. In short, the sudden change in the child's behaviour and sometimes appearance might represent a disability that was not visible at birth. The Icelandic folklorist Eva Þórdís Ebenezersdóttir has researched this in the case of the Icelandic legends, asking the question of what messages these stories convey with regard to society's response to disabled people, something that makes the violence, for example, in these legends that much more horrible.[24]

The Hidden Woman in Múli

West of Barðaströnd in the parish of Flatey, in Látrar, there lived a man named Ingimundur, well-off in wealth, whose great-grandchildren are still alive today. This Ingimundur was diligent and of strong character. On the farm where he lived there was a small grassy islet, which has been said to be called Múli; it had never been mowed, as it was forbidden, but the grass grew thick on the islet. This sight troubled Ingimundur greatly, seeing the islet with so much grass that he could not use for anything, and at last he could no longer bear it and ordered his men to mow the islet. His wife begged him not to do so, but he paid her no heed and had the islet mowed against his wife's wishes. Thus, the islet was mowed, and the grass proved to be excellent. There was plenty of hay from it, and Ingimundur was pleased with his decision.

However, one autumn night, Ingimundur's wife had a dream in which she felt that another woman was approaching her with a troubled countenance. She said, "Your husband acted poorly, he had my islet mowed, therefore I have to slaughter my cow, which has been my saving grace. Your husband shall benefit from your warning; but nevertheless he shall bear the consequences of my loss of the cow." Thus she went away to Ingimundur, who was sleeping in a different bed, and said to him in his sleep: "You owe it to your wife that I do not pay you a worthy remuneration for what you have done, as you did not obey your wife and had the islet mowed, and because you had the grass cut there I have to slaughter my cow; and yet you shall remember this." She then took his hand and said, "You will never feel anything as hard as this." Then she left, and when he woke up, he felt a pain in his hand. Thus it withered, and after that he was never able to do any work with it again. This is true, and serves as proof that the hidden people work the land the same way we do.

Told by an unknown storyteller to Ólafur Sveinsson,
translated by Dagrún Ósk Jónsdóttir

⟶≫ ≪⟵

Beliefs and stories about hidden people are still very present in Icelandic society, something that applies especially when it comes to nature preservation.[25] Many of the old legends tell of the close connection the hidden people have to nature, as their homes are often said to be located in big stones and hills. According to these stories, it is forbidden to damage the houses of the hidden people or any land that belongs to them. The stories also carry messages about not being greedy; one should never take more than is needed, and when taking something one must also leave something behind, in this case for the hidden people. These stories also reflect conflicts between the past and the ever-changing present, between the old and the new, as in the older stories where one often encounters an older woman who warns a young and irresponsible farmer about not taking from the elves; when the young one does not heed these warnings, he ends up being punished.

Una the Elf Woman

A certain man named Geir lived at a farm called Rauðafell, and was
rich, young and active, and a widower at the time to which this story
refers. Once, in the haymaking season, a large quantity of hay being
left for the women to rake up – almost more than they could do, for
he kept but a few maids – Geir saw a young and fair woman enter
the field, and begin raking up the hay with the others. She uttered
not a word to anybody, but worked quietly, and so quickly, that very
soon after she arrived, the hay was all got in, till the farmer fancied
there must be some magic power in the rake she used. Every evening,
when the work was over, she went away, but came on the morrow,
and every day through the season, always doing more work than
all the rest, and always departing at nightfall without exchanging a
syllable with anybody. On the last night of the hay-cutting, however,
the farmer went up to her and thanked her for having worked so
diligently all the summer. She received his thanks kindly, and they
talked a long time together, the farmer concluding by asking her
to come to his house and act thenceforth as his housekeeper. She
consented, and went away.

Next morning she came to Rauðafell, bringing with her a large
chest, and at once entered upon her duties in the house. The chest
was put into one of the outhouses, as she was unwilling, for some
reasons of her own, to keep it in the farm itself. She stayed there
through the winter, and Geir had every cause to be pleased with
her management of the house, for she was clean and thrifty, and
an active manager. She never would tell the farmer where she came
from, but went so far as to allow that her name was Una: nor would
she ever enter the church, though urged to do so over and over again
by the farmer; and this was the only cause of offence which he could
find in her.

It was the custom on Christmas Eve for every person on the
farm to go to church except one, who was left behind to take care

of the house. On this occasion Una always refused to go with the rest, which much displeased the farmer; she remained at home, and when the family returned from church, she had finished all the household work.

Three years passed, during which time Una remained with the farmer, who became so fond of her that were it not for her one fault – her dislike of going to church – he would have married her.

On Christmas Eve in the third winter Una was, as usual, while others went to service, left alone in the house. When the family had gone some little distance from home on their way to church, one of the male workers declared himself unwell, and, sitting on a stone, said that he would remain there till the illness passed over, and that he did not wish anyone to remain behind with him. The farmer, therefore, and the rest of the family left him there, and went on to the church.

When they were out of sight, the man got up and went back to the farm – for his illness was only feigned in order to enable him to play the spy upon Una. On arriving there he saw that Una was sweeping and washing the whole house, and seemed in great haste to finish her work. He hid himself so that Una should not know of his return, and, when she had finished her work, saw her leave the house. He followed her, and saw her go to the outhouse and unlock her chest, from which she took out handsome and cunningly embroidered clothes, and, having dressed herself in them, she looked so lovely, that the worker thought he had never seen anybody so beautiful before. Then she took out of the chest a red cloth, which she put under her arm, and, locking the box, left the outhouse, and closed the door behind her. She ran across the meadow near the farm till she came to a soft slough, upon the surface of which she spread the scarlet cloth, and stepped into the centre of it, just leaving room by chance at one of the corners for the worker, who (having with sorcery, in which he was well skilled, made himself quite invisible) stepped on to the cloth after her.

No sooner was he there than the cloth sank with them through the earth, which seemed like smoke round them, until they came to some wide and fair green fields, where Una stepped off the cloth and put it again under her arm. Some little way off stood a vast and stately palace, into which Una went, and the man after her. Here he found a great number of people assembled, who rose at her entrance, and received her with every show of love and respect. The whole hall in which they stood was adorned as if for a feast. When they had greeted Una they all sat down again, Una amongst them, and the most costly dainties, and rarest wines in gold and silver vessels, were set before them.

But as for our invisible friend, the worker, all he could get hold of was a rib-bone of smoked mutton, wonderfully fat and good, which he, without tasting, thrust into his pocket.

When the supper was over, the guests amused themselves with drinking and various games, and kept up the revel all night with a great show of joy. About daybreak Una rose and declared that she must now depart, as the farmer, her master, and his family would by this time be leaving church. Then bidding a courteous farewell to all, she went out again into the fair green fields, where she spread the cloth out once more, and stepped upon it, and the worker on to the corner, as before. The cloth rose with them through the earth, till they arrived at the slough, where they had started. And now, gathering up the cloth under her arm, Una ran into the outhouse, where she locked it, together with her beautiful clothes in the chest, and again donning her everyday apparel, went back into the farmer's house. Pretty well content with having seen all this, the worker took his visible form, and hastened back to the stone, where he had feigned illness the evening before. On their way homewards from the church, the farmer and his family found him; and inquiring how he was, received for answer that he had passed a wretched night, but was much better, and was now able to return home with them, which he did.

When they were all assembled at breakfast, and were eating, the farmer (suspecting nothing) took up a rib-bone of mutton from his plate, and holding it up, said:

"Did any of you ever see so fat a rib-bone as this?"

"Possibly, my master," replied the worker; and taking from his pocket the rib-bone of mutton he had stolen from the elfin-feast, held it up.

Directly as she saw it, Una changed colour, and without a word vanished from their sight: nor was she ever seen afterwards. So the man told the farmer all that he had seen in the night, and Geir no longer wondered why Una should avoid going to church.

Told by an old woman from Rangárþing to Magnús Grímsson,
translated by Eiríkur Magnússon and George E. J. Powell

⟶⟶ ⟵⟵

This legend, like a few others, tells of royalty among the hidden people. It shows their riches well, with regard to clothing, food and drink. While the hidden people are often noted to be Christian, some legends suggest that they do not do well in a human church.

The Worker and the Water Elves

In a large house, where all the chief rooms were panelled, there lived, once upon a time, a farmer, whose ill fate it was that every worker of his that was left alone to guard the house on the night of Christmas Eve, while the rest of the family went to church, was found dead when the family returned home. As soon as the report of this was spread abroad, the farmer had the greatest difficulty in procuring workers who would consent to watch alone in the house on that night; until at last one day a man, a strong fellow, offered him his services to sit up alone and guard the house. The farmer told him what fate awaited him for his rashness, but the man despised such a fear, and persisted in his determination.

On Christmas Eve, when the farmer and all his family, except the new worker, were preparing for church, the farmer said to him:

"Come with us to church; I cannot leave you here to die."

But the other replied, "I intend to stay here, for it would be unwise for you to leave your house unprotected; and, besides, the cattle and sheep must have their food at the proper time."

"Never mind the beasts," answered the farmer. "Do not be so rash as to remain in the house this night, for whenever we have returned from church on this night, we have always found every living thing in the house dead, with all its bones broken."

But the man was not to be persuaded, as he considered all these fears beneath his notice; so the farmer and the rest of the workers went away and left him behind, alone in the house.

As soon as he was by himself, he began to consider how to guard against anything that might occur, for a dread had stolen over him, in spite of his courage, that something strange was about to take place. At last he thought that the best thing to do was, first of all, to light up the living room, and then to find some place in which to hide himself. As soon as he had lighted all the candles, he moved two planks out of the wainscot at the end of the room, and, creeping into the space between it and the wall, restored the planks to their places, so that he could see plainly into the room, and yet avoid being himself discovered.

He had scarcely finished concealing himself, when two fierce and strange-looking men entered the room and began looking about.

One of them said, "I smell a human being."

"No," replied the other, "there is no human being here."

Then they took a candle and continued their search, until they found the man's dog asleep under one of the beds. They took it up, and, having dashed it on the ground till every bone in its body was broken, hurled it from them. When the worker saw this, he congratulated himself on not having fallen into their hands.

Suddenly the room was filled with people, who were laden with tables and all kinds of table furniture, silver, cloths, and all, which they spread out, and having done so, sat down to a rich supper, which they had also brought with them. They feasted noisily, and spent the remainder of the night drinking and dancing. Two of them were appointed to keep guard, in order to give the company due warning of the approach either of anybody, or of the day. Three times they went out, always returning with the news that they saw neither the approach of any human being, nor yet the break of day.

But when the worker suspected the night to be pretty far spent, he jumped from his place of concealment into the room, and clashing the two planks together with as much noise as he could make, shouted like a madman:

"The day! The day! The day!"

On these words the whole company rose scared from their seats, and rushed headlong out, leaving behind them not only their tables and all the silver dishes, but even the very clothes they had taken off for ease in dancing. In the hurry of flight many were wounded and trodden under foot, while the rest ran into the darkness, the worker after them, clapping the planks together and shrieking, "The day!

The day! The day!" until they came to a large lake, into which the whole party plunged headlong and disappeared.

From this, the man knew them to be water-elves.

Then he returned home, gathered the corpses of the elves who had been killed in the flight, killed the wounded ones, and making a great heap of them all, burned them. When he had finished this task, he cleaned up the house and took possession of all the treasures the elves had left behind them.

On the farmer's return, his worker told him all that had occurred, and showed him the spoils. The farmer praised him for a brave fellow, and congratulated him on having escaped with his life. The man gave him half the treasures of the elves, and ever afterwards prospered exceedingly.

This was the last visit the water-elves ever paid to *that* house.

Told by a farmer from Biskupstungur to Jón Árnason,
translated by Eiríkur Magnússon and George E. J. Powell

⸻ ⸺⸻

Many Icelandic legends tell of supernatural beings that burst into the home, disturbing the peace. The idea of the sacredness of the home and the danger of threats from outside is a universal idea in folklore. In Iceland the intruder is an elf, a troll, some kind of Christmas creature or an outlaw. In a number of Icelandic legends, the intruders show up – often around Christmas time – and pose a threat to those individuals who have stayed behind while the other family members have gone to church.[26]

Nineteen Outlaws

In the Westfjords, as in other regions, it was the tradition that
all the people on each farm attended church on Christmas Eve.
However, someone always had to be home to watch over the farm.
At one farm there, it had become customary that on Christmas
Eve, while the people were at church, the one who was at home
was killed and the farm was robbed of many things, both food
and other valuables. This had gone on for several Christmas
nights one after another, and no one knew how this came to be.
As a result, no one wanted to stay home on Christmas Eve, and
those who did not need to thought themselves lucky.

As Christmas approached once more, no one at the farm
wanted to stay home, until the farmer's daughter volunteered.
The farmer did not want his daughter to do it because he thought
she might meet the same fate as those who had stayed home before,
and the household did not want to lose her, but all the same, in
the end she stayed behind alone.

When the people had left, the farmer's daughter carefully made
all the doors, closed them, and locked them, so now no creature
could enter unless it crawled in through a chute that ran out of
the kitchen. At this chute, the farmer's daughter sat and waited.
Soon after, she heard a clamour outside, a cacophony, and human
speech. Someone walked to the door, and, finding it locked,
attempted to move the chute at which the farmer's daughter
sat with a big axe by her side. She heard someone crawling on his
stomach through the chute, and when he had his head so far along
that it was in the kitchen completely, the farmer's daughter cut his
head off with the axe and pulled the torso all the way through onto
the kitchen floor. Then she heard that another was coming, and
he got the same treatment as the first, until eighteen had been
dealt with. But as the eighteenth poked his head in, he called out,
"We are betrayed!" But he could not return, both because the

chute was narrow and because the farmer's daughter was swift in beheading him.

Time passed, until the people came home; when they arrived, they were greeted by the farmer's daughter, who was healthy and calm as if nothing had happened. People marvelled at this, and she told them everything, but added that she was afraid that one of these robbers or outlaws might have escaped because of the eighteenth's warning. After that, nothing further was heard of this. Many came to ask for the farmer's daughter's hand in marriage, as she was a good prospect, but she refused everyone, and always said that one outlaw must have been left behind by the chute.

Later, a foreign ship dropped anchor near the farm, captained by a great man, powerful and rich. He often came to see the farmer, who took pride in these visits, and before long he proposed to the farmer's daughter. The farmer was delighted with the proposal, as was expected, but the farmer's daughter did not want to accept him. After her father's persuasion, she finally accepted the suitor, and they, she and this ship's captain, were wed, and a great feast was celebrated by the farmer because he was wealthy and had a good house.

On their wedding night, the couple were supposed to sleep in the loft where there were no people, and the captain of the ship had a large ironbound chest moved up to their bedroom. When all had left the room, he told his wife, the farmer's daughter, that he must now repay her for his old companions in the chute. He opened the chest and took out of it iron bars, and went downstairs to heat them in the fire, in the meantime locking the door so that the farmer's daughter could not get out. The farmer's daughter saw what was going to happen, and grabbed a duvet from the bed, broke the window, covered herself with the duvet, and jumped out of the window. She fell to the ground, breaking her arm because the fall was high. She ran to her father's window and told him to grab the ruffian, and the farmer reacted quickly, calling his workers to him, and they met the man holding the hot iron bars on the stairs. The farmer took hold of him there and tied him up. Then he was tortured into confessing all, after which he was killed. But the farmer's daughter did not grieve him and soon remarried a good man and lived long and well with him.

Told by an old woman in Reykjavík to Jón Árnason,
translated by Sigurður Líndal

⟶≫ ≪⟵

In this story, the focus is not on the hidden people but the outlaws, who will be more fully explained in the next chapter. They are described as liminal beings at the margins of human society, living in the wilderness like trolls in Icelandic folklore. However, just like the trolls, outlaws sometimes intrude into farms, especially around Christmas. A few legends of this kind can be found in Icelandic folk collections, horror stories that tell of women who are forced to marry outlaws who later turn out to want to torture and kill them. In other versions, legends of this kind often note that the women in question have refused every man who has asked for their hand in marriage, thereby explaining why, when a well-educated, wealthy and powerful man arrives, their fathers feel compelled to take action and force them to marry.[27]

The Raven at Skíðastaðir

At a farm, called Skíðastaðir, in the north of Iceland, which stood
under a steep and very high mountain, there lived, long ago, a
very rich farmer. He had many household workers, and kept them
sharply at work, summer and winter. In summer, he was wont to
keep his people so hard at work, that no maid was ever allowed to
be at home at the farm for cooking; this he made them do on the
Sabbath, and then get over the cooking for the whole week, thus
hindering them from going to church or hearing the Word of
God read at home.

Amongst other of his workers there was a girl who, although
dissatisfied with her place, and with the household ways and
ungodliness of the farmer, had for a long while served at Skíðastaðir.
She was of a peaceful temper, and ready to do all she was bidden,
wherefore she was beloved by her masters and fellow workers.
It had most often fallen to her lot to do the cookery on Sundays,
but no other reward did she get for it than to have the scourings
of the pans for her share.

One winter was a particularly hard one, in so much that both
men and beasts died from starvation. The farmer at Skíðastaðir
refused all help and aid to his fellow parishioners who asked him
for help for themselves and their beasts, and drove many a needy
man from him, with harsh refusals instead of kind assistance.
Neither were the workers at Skíðastaðir so well fed (although
enough provisions were always at hand) that they could afford
any aid to hungry visitors.

This girl, however, always tried to leave somewhat of her
meals, and sometimes not a little to her pain, for those who
came needy and hungry to Skíðastaðir.

This winter, all creatures were so worn out with hunger
that they were found, in heaps, dead on the ground. For a long
time not even a hungry sparrow could find as much food as he

could pick up in his little bill. The ravens, therefore, as is their wont
in such times, flocked to the different farms, in order to get hold
of whatever eatable was cast out in the sweepings of the house.
This was their only support this winter. The kindly girl tried to
throw out, in the sweepings of the kitchen, as much as she could
of small scraps of food, to help the poor, starving ravens. This
she continued to do, and one of the ravens became so attached to
her, that he followed her nearly everywhere, outside the house,
and, the following spring and summer, he used to come home to
Skíðastaðir, early in the morning, to get his breakfast from the girl's
hand, for she always had something in store for him, and amused
herself much with him.

Now, one Sunday morning, the girl had risen very early, to boil
the stirabout for the household, and tried to have done scraping the
pot before her raven friend came, that she might please him with
the scrapings. Just as she had done scraping the pot, she heard the
voice of her friend, outside. She went out with the scrapings in a
large ladle, and put them outside where she had been wont to put
them before.

But the raven first began hopping round the ladle, and then fled
away, a short distance into the field.

The girl ran after him with the ladle, but he would not yet take
the scrapings, and flew a short distance from her and waited there
for his kind friend, who followed him, not knowing what could
possibly be the matter with her poor raven that had until now
always devoured the scrapings with a raven's appetite.

This game went on between them till the raven had made the
girl follow him to a good distance from the home-field, and she was
beginning to think of returning home and letting her raven alone.

But while this was going on between the raven and the girl,
the people at different farms which stood in the valley, opposite
Skíðastaðir, saw a man in white garments, walking along the ridge
of the high mountains which stood over Skíðastaðir, with a staff in

his hand, till he came to a spot on the mountain, just above the farm. Here he stopped at the very minute the girl was about to leave the raven, and struck with his staff on the mountain, and there at once slid down a large piece of it, ever increasing in its fall, and rolled over the farm, destroying every house and every life in the place, except that of the girl. Then she broke out into loud praises to God for having thus saved her from a terrible death by the aid of a raven.

Told by unknown storytellers from Vatnsdalur to Jón Árnason,
translated by Eiríkur Magnússon and George E. J. Powell

⟶⟩⟩⟩ ⟨⟨⟨⟵

While this legend does not revolve around hidden people, it shares many of the same themes, particularly emphasizing the importance of aiding those in need. In this tale the one in need of help is a raven. While ravens are often seen as omens of death and danger in Icelandic legends, a number of stories depict their benevolent deeds. In Icelandic there is a saying, *Guð launar fyrir hrafninn* (God rewards the raven), which conveys the idea that God rewards those who assist those in need, as is also illustrated in this legend. While in this case, the threat to the farm is not supernatural, the legend underlines the very real danger posed by Iceland's natural forces. It is interesting to note that the man dressed in white is nowhere to be found in Jón Árnason's version of the story, and is an addition made by Powell and Eiríkur. In the Icelandic version, the avalanche falls without any explanation, while the young girl still thanks God for having saved her.

2

The Wilderness

In the wilderness, away from civilization, few things are easier than
letting the surroundings, storms, and darkness seize you, when you
are travelling alone or in trouble. At such times, the mind is filled
with tales of getting lost in the wilderness, desolate shelters, and
grim fates, not to mention worries about the family back home.[1]

Iceland was very rural in the nineteenth century, and there were sometimes great distances between farms. Although the farm was people's
home and workplace, they would still have to travel for various reasons. Well into the twentieth century, the most common means of
travel was by boat, on foot or on horseback. In Iceland the horse was
often called *þarfasti þjónninn*, or the most necessary servant, making
it clear that the importance of having a good riding horse could not
be underestimated. As a man born in 1896 recalls:

Preparation for longer journeys around 1900 and some way
into the next century had to take into account a terrain without
roads and unbridged rivers. During that time, it was the horse
that had to be relied upon for travel, transporting people and
other goods across steep moors and mighty rivers.[2]

As noted above, there were often no proper roads connecting
places but rather paths that were often used to travel to and from

Ásgrímur Jónsson (1876–1958), born in southern Iceland, was the first Icelandic
painter to make art his primary occupation after studying at the Royal Danish
Academy of Art from 1900 to 1903. His extensive body of work includes numerous
drawings and paintings inspired by Icelandic folk legends, earning him recognition
as a pioneer in this genre. This 1955 illustration by Ásgrímur depicts a group of
people travelling over mountains, surrounded by the dangerous supernatural beings
that inhabit the wilderness.

specific places, called *þjóðleiðir* (national paths). These paths could be
short or long: some journeys might take a few hours of walking, others
a couple of days. These paths were often marked with *vörður* (cairns),
piles of rocks that stood out in the landscape and led the way for those
who travelled. Some of them are still visible today.[3]

The length of a trip and the weather conditions were factors that
people always had to keep in mind. People travelled for a variety of
reasons: they might go to church or visit a neighbouring farm.
Additionally, they often needed to travel to fetch a doctor or midwife.
Different seasons called for specific tasks that required them to venture
even further from the farm. For example, in the autumn people went

up to the mountains to herd sheep, which had roamed free on the mountains during the summer. They would also pick berries and collect herbs.

When travelling or herding sheep, people sometimes had to enter the highlands of Iceland, an area that in the past was largely unexplored. The highlands have been defined as covering all those parts of Iceland that are more than 500 metres (1,640 ft) above sea level. This includes most of Iceland's centre, and up to 40 per cent of the country as a whole.[4] The highlands are unsuitable for human habitation. It is colder than in the rest of the country, it snows more heavily and there is very little land for farming. The landscape is nonetheless breathtaking and at times otherworldly, filled with geological phenomena such as active volcanoes, lava fields, sands, glaciers, rivers, waters and flora. In the past, a number of key walking paths across Iceland passed through the highlands. Travelling along these paths could be dangerous. The weather could be harsh, with heavy snow and storms being common over the wintertime.

The means of travel did not change until the early twentieth century. The first car arrived in Iceland in 1904, when a man called Ditlev Thomsen got a grant from the Icelandic parliament to buy it. However, the car did not work as well as people had hoped; a news article from the time stated, "The vehicle is running poorly, often breaks down, and the engine is too underpowered for the car to make it up hills, that are often quite steep."[5] There were also few roads in Iceland at the time, which did not make things easy.[6] A more elaborate road system was established in the years 1920–30, and shortly after that, cars became more common. Despite this, there are still places in Iceland where there are no roads and which can only be accessed by sea or on foot, such as the Hornstrandir area in the Westfjords which is now uninhabited.

In Iceland there is little risk of running into dangerous wild animals when travelling. The main wild mammals are the arctic fox, who has been in Iceland since before human settlement, and reindeer in the east which were first imported to Iceland in the late eighteenth century. Both animals are harmless to humans. Alongside these, the occasional polar bear wanders to Iceland, either on drift ice or by swimming, and there are stories of these.

The main risk when travelling, besides the danger of encountering supernatural beings, is the weather. In many legends, bad weather, storms and mist can also work as a portal into the supernatural world. Many tell of people who take shelter from bad weather and are then found by supernatural beings. On other occasions they get lost in the mist and stumble upon farms they have never seen before and find themselves greeted by outlaws.

The Icelandic folk legends show men venturing into the wild for various purposes. There, people would risk running into trolls and ogresses, thieving outlaws and even polar bears.

Trolls appear in the Icelandic sagas and are also found in the Icelandic legends. In Jón Árnason's introduction to troll stories, he notes that the word "troll" is "extremely extensive because it symbolizes all those beings greater than humans in some way and all those who are in some way malevolent, such as ghosts and even sorcerers". [7] However, in the nineteenth century, when Jón was collecting his legends, the troll figure was a specific kind of supernatural being, best known for its size.

Icelandic trolls are figures that appear in human form but are more monstrous and animalistic. They are often huge – much larger than humans. In most Icelandic legends, much like those from the other Nordic countries, trolls are also shown to be primitive, ancient, dumb, greedy and cruel. [8] In some of the legends, however, they are said to be friendly, trusting and trustworthy.

The trolls are shown as being closely connected to nature. They live in the wilderness relatively far from human habitation, often in big canyons or caves. According to the legends, most trolls cannot stand the sunlight and turn to stone when the sun hits them. This results in many fossilized trolls being found in the Icelandic natural

Brian Pilkington (b. 1950) is an English-born Icelandic artist renowned for his illustrations, many of which are inspired by Icelandic folk stories. His illustrated books on trolls have been read to Icelandic children for many years, and it's safe to say that no one has had a greater influence on how Icelanders today imagine trolls. The illustration here is from his book *Trolls: Philosophy and Wisdom* (2011).

landscape. The trolls are also said to be heathens and to hate Christianity. Among other things, this is seen in the many Icelandic legends that tell of conflicts between trolls and priests, in which the priests more often end up victorious. When being chased by a troll, one's best option is often to find the nearest church and ring the church bells as loudly as possible, as that will send the troll running back to their cave.

While legends of the hidden people are still present in today's society and new stories are still being formed, folk stories of trolls are a thing of the past.[9] Jónas Jónasson, an Icelandic collector of folklore, states in his book that Icelanders stopped believing in trolls in the eighteenth century. The Icelandic folklorist Ólína Þorvarðardóttir

These rock formations in the Strandir area are said to be two of the three trolls who, according to legend, tried to separate the Westfjords from the rest of Iceland after the country converted to Christianity. Disturbed by the constant ringing of church bells, the trolls decided to dig through the land to create a separation, with the intention of turning the Westfjords into a troll paradise. Two trolls began digging in Gilsfjörður, while the third worked in Kollafjörður, planning to meet in the middle. They were so focused on their task that they didn't notice the sunrise and were turned into stone.

has reached a similar conclusion, noting that at the time the legends were collected, people no longer really believed in trolls and legends about them were mainly told for entertainment purposes.[10] In spite of this, they are set to happen in the Iceland of the past and are often connected to specific places or people. Even though they were told for entertainment, it is evident that, like the stories of the hidden people, they still reflect the society in which they were told.

It is interesting that more Icelandic legends tell of female trolls or ogresses (in Icelandic *tröllkonur* and *skessur* (female troll), *skass* (hag), *flögð* (shrew), *gýgur* (giantess) and *kerlingar* (crone)) than male trolls. According to the legends, these female trolls are more dangerous than male trolls. They sometimes steal men to keep as their husbands or lovers, or simply just to eat them. Although trolls mostly eat fish, meat and Icelandic moss, it is around Christmas that they want to treat themselves to human meat, and troll women are not very particular about the type of men they choose to kidnap or eat. They can pose a threat to anyone: workers, farmers and even priests, sometimes taking men while they are travelling in the wilderness or working outside, but also on occasion entering farm spaces and stealing men from their homes or the church, with the intention of taking them home. In some legends the trolls are even said to use magic to lure the men to them.

The literary scholar Helga Kress points out that these ogresses combine two elements that men have tried to tame through the years: women and nature.[11] The female trolls are powerful, and when they are hungry they take the men and swallow them, literally. All in all, the portrayal of female trolls in these legends is negative: they pose a threat not only to men but to society as a whole, by killing animals and stealing men. As Ólína Þorvarðardóttir concludes, these troll stories reflect society's fears: for example, the fear of the unknown.[12] However, an overarching theme in troll legends is that things do not end well for troll women. They are usually overcome and even killed by men. The men are shown to be clever, strong Christians, while the ogresses are devious but easy to fool. The trolls are then punished for their transgressions as they are turned into stone, defeated in a wrestling match or even beheaded by the men, something that essentially confirms men's power and position in society.

The legends of outlaws in Iceland are in many cases similar to those of trolls, and many of them can be said to be somewhere between legends and wonder tales in form. Most often the outlaws in these accounts are presented as dangerous, almost inhuman or supernatural figures, although they have roots in reality since outlawry was a form of punishment in medieval Iceland, whereby people were banished from society for three years or even permanently for breaking the law.[13]

The connection between the legendary outlaws and reality has been discussed by several scholars. In his introductory chapter on outlaws, Jón Árnason theorizes that there were three main reasons why people still believed in outlaws in the nineteenth century. First, there were so many legends told about them; second, a great deal of the Icelandic highlands had not yet been explored and it was therefore difficult to deny the possibility that they were hiding out there; and third, farmers often lost sheep as they roamed free on the mountains in summer, something that could be explained by outlaws having taken them.[14] The anthropologist Kirsten Hastrup notes that the outlaw figure became increasingly supernatural in Icelandic culture over the course of time. The Icelandic scholar Einar Ól. Sveinsson nonetheless argues that their relationship to the real world kept them from fully transforming into trolls.[15]

In some legends, outlaws are painted in a romantic light, such as the accounts showing people escaping the harshness of human society to settle in a valley far away, where they are their own masters. In some stories, the outlaws are even said to have formed their own societies. However, more often they are shown to live outside human society, the legends emphasizing how evil and inhuman they are, noting that they have bad manners and do not abide by the laws of society, not going to church, not having to harvest the land and often not having any sheep of their own. Since they still have to eat to survive, they are often described as having stolen sheep and being dangerous thieves, murderers and sometimes even cannibals. Unlike the trolls, the most dangerous outlaw is usually male.

While stories of trolls are said to have been told for entertainment, some scholars have argued that the stories of the horrible outlaws were also educational and meant to teach people how not to behave. Hastrup also suggests that outlaw legends reflect not only a fear of the unknown in the environment but the fears of what lives within people themselves.[16]

Yet another threat that could be encountered in the wilderness of Iceland, often bordering the limits of the natural and supernatural, was, as mentioned earlier, polar bears. Polar bears are not typical inhabitants of Iceland but can arrive on drift ice or even swim over from Greenland. All in all, roughly six hundred polar bears are said to have arrived in Iceland since its settlement. That number must be taken with some caution because those accounts are found in a number of older sources that are not as reliable as the accounts from the past two centuries, which state that seventy polar bears arrived in Iceland in the twentieth century. This number includes the 27 bears that came ashore between 1917 and 1918, in a winter that was considered to be one of the coldest in Iceland's history, leading to a great deal of drift ice being found in the Icelandic fjords.[17] Even now, polar bears that arrive in Iceland are usually killed, as they can be dangerous.

There are several stories in the legend collections in which the polar bears seem to have a supernatural sense about them. One story tells of a polar bear king who bears a horn on his head, like a unicorn, but this one has a golden ring on its end. In the legends, the bears also have various human-like qualities. In some accounts, it is even noted that a polar bear cub is human when it is born, but then the mother puts its paw over the cub and turns it into a bear. According to legend, the bears are also considered to be intellectual beings, and so wise that they can recognize both their killers and their namesakes: it is believed that the bears will not eat those called Björn, Bjarni, Birna or Bessi, names that all mean "bear".[18] This account, alongside other legends, indicates the belief that polar bears can understand human language.

As with many other supernatural beings in Iceland, and especially the hidden people or elves, the polar bears in legends demand respect. A good example of this is the idea that there is a limit to how many bears an individual can kill in their lifetime.

The danger posed by polar bears is the subject of numerous legends and stories that tell of Icelanders' interactions with the animals. Several tell of polar bears arriving on farms while the farmers are not at home and attacking the workers, women and children. Those legends often possess similar features, such as an "unexpected hero" like a blind man, the wife or children, and an unlikely weapon, such as scissors or dull knives.[19] Some legends also tell of men who are attacked by polar bears when travelling in the wilderness.

Troll's Stone

In the neighbourhood of Kirkjubær, in Hróarstunga, stand some curious rocks under which is a cave. In this cave, ages ago, dwelt a troll named Þórir, with his wife. Every year, these trolls contrived to entice into their clutches, by magic arts, either the priest or the herdsmen from Kirkjubær, and thus matters went on until a priest arrived at the place, named Eiríkur, a spiritual man, who was able by his prayers to protect both himself and his herdsmen from the magic spells of this worthy couple.

One Christmas Eve, the female troll had tried her incantations quite in vain, and went to her husband, saying, "I have tried my utmost to entice the priest or the herdsman, but to no purpose, for, as soon as ever I begin my spells, a hot wind blows upon me which forces me by the scorching heat to desist, as if it would consume all my joints. So you must go and procure something for our Christmas dinner, as we have nothing left to eat in the cave."

The giant expressed great unwillingness to trouble himself, being rather lazy, but was at length compelled to go, by the entreaties of his wife, and accordingly marched off to a lake in the neighbourhood which since was called by his name. There he broke a hole through the ice, and lying down on his face, cast in a line and caught trout. When he thought he had caught enough for the Christmas dinner, he wanted to get up again, in order to take them home; but the frost had been so hard while he was intent upon his fishing that it had frozen him tight to the ice, so that he could not rise from it. He struggled desperately to escape, but in vain, and the frost seized upon his heart and killed him where he lay.

The female troll finding her husband rather long in returning, and becoming very hungry, sallied out in search of him and discovered him lying dead upon the ice. She ran to him and tried to tear his body up from the ice, but failing in this, seized the string of trout, and placing it over her shoulder started off.

Before she went, she said, "A curse on thee, thou wicked lake! Never shall a living fish be caught in thee again."

Which words have indeed proved fatal to the fishery, for the lake since then has never yielded a single fish.

Then she went back homewards with great strides. As she came, however, to the edge of the neighbouring hill, she saw the day-break in the east, and heard from the south the sound of the Kirkjubær church-bells (two things, which, as everyone knows, are fatal to trolls), upon which she was instantly changed into the rock which now bears the name of Troll's Stone.

Told by an unknown storyteller to Jón Árnason,
translated by Eiríkur Magnússon and George E. J. Powell

Ólafur and the Trolls

Some people who lived in the south part of the country, at Biskupstungur, once went into the forest to cut wood for charcoal, and took with them a young lad to hold their horses. While he was left to look after the animals he disappeared, and, though they searched in every direction for him, they failed in finding him.

After three years had passed, the same people were cutting wood in exactly the same place, when the lost boy Ólafur came running to them. They asked him where he had been all this time, and how he had gone away.

He said, "While I was looking after the horses, and had strolled a short distance from them, I suddenly met a gigantic troll-woman, who came rushing towards me and seized me in her arms, and ran off with me until she came into the heart of the wilderness to some great rocks. In these rocks was her cave, into which she carried me. When I was there I saw another giantess coming towards me, of younger appearance than the former, but both were immensely tall. They were dressed in tunics of horse-leather, falling to their feet in front, but very short behind. Here they kept me, and fed me with trout, which one was always out catching, while the other watched me. During the night they forced me to sleep between them on their bed of horse-skins. Sometimes they used to lull me to sleep by singing magical songs in my ears, so that I was enchanted by wonderful dreams. They both were very kind to me, and watched me carefully in case I should wish to escape from them. One day when I had been left alone, I was standing outside the cave, and saw, on the other side of the wilderness, the smoke of the charcoal burners; so, as I knew that neither of the trolls was at home, I ran off in the direction of the smoke. But I had gone very few paces when one of the trolls saw me, and, running after me, struck me on the cheek, so that I have never lost the bruise, and seizing me in her arms, took me back again to the cave. After this, they looked after me diligently enough.

Once the younger troll said to the elder, 'How is it that whenever I touch the bare cheek of Ólafur, it seems to burn me like fire?'

The other replied, 'Do not wonder at that; it is on account of the prayer which Oddur the wry-faced [bishop] has taught him.'

In this way I passed three years; and when I knew that the season for charcoal-burning was come, and that there would be people on the other side of the wilderness assembled for the purpose, I pretended that I was sick, and could not eat any food. They tried every means in their power to cure me, but all in vain, I only became worse.

Once they asked me whether I could not mention any delicacy for which I had a fancy.

I said, 'No, except it were shark-flesh, which had been dried in the wind for nine years.'

The older one said, 'This will be very difficult to get you, for it is not to be found anywhere in the whole country, but at one farmer's house in the west, Ögur. At any rate, I will try to get it.'

Then she strode off in search of it. Directly I saw that she was gone, and that the younger troll was busily engaged in catching trout, I took to my heels, and never ceased running towards the smoke of the charcoal-fires until I arrived here safely."

When they had heard his story, the burners mounted their horses and took Ólafur as speedily as possible to Skálholt. On the way, when they had just crossed the Brúará river, whom should they meet but the ugly old troll herself, who came tearing down the rocks towards them, and crying, "Aha! There you are, you wretch!"

Ólafur, at the sound of her voice, went mad, and tried to break away from the men, so that it was all they could do to hold him back.

Then the troll seized hold of a horse which stood near her on the rocks, and tearing it apart, threw the pieces over her shoulder in her fury, and ran back to her cave.

When the news arrived at Skálholt, they took Ólafur to the bishop, who kept him by him for a few days, and then sent him into the east part of the country, out of the reach of the trolls, having cured him of his madness.

Told by an unknown storyteller to Jón Sigurðsson,
translated by Eiríkur Magnússon and George E. J. Powell

————

In the stories of the "Troll's Stone" and "Ólafur and the Trolls", the risk female trolls pose to men is quite apparent; several stories tell of ogresses who steal men either to eat or to keep as lovers. Stories similar to "Ólafur and the Trolls" are known in several variants in the Icelandic legend collections. Fermented shark meat formed part of Icelanders' diet in the nineteenth century. Based on the legends, it seems that the older the shark was, the better, much like wine and cheeses in other countries. The shark has a very strong taste and is today usually only eaten as part of Þorrablót, a festival in the early part of the year that is strongly connected with old Icelandic food traditions.

The Shepherd of Silfrúnarstaðir

A man named Guðmundur lived once upon a time at a farm called Silfrúnarstaðir, in the bay of Skagafjörður. He was very rich in flocks, and looked upon by his neighbours as a man of high esteem and respectability. He was married, but had no children.

It happened one Christmas Eve, at Silfrúnarstaðir, that the herdsman did not return home at night, and, as he was not found at the sheep-pens, the farmer caused a diligent search to be made for him all over the country, but quite in vain.

Next spring Guðmundur hired another shepherd, named Grímur, who was tall and strong, and boasted of being able to resist anybody. But the farmer, in spite of the man's boldness and strength, warned him to be careful how he ran risks, and on Christmas Eve bade him drive the sheep early into the pens, and come home to the farm while it was still daylight. But in the evening Grímur did not come, and though search was made far and near for him, was never found. People made all sorts of guesses about the cause of his disappearance, but the farmer was full of grief, and after this could not get any one to act as shepherd for him.

At this time there lived a very poor widow at Sjávarborg, who had several children, of whom the eldest, aged fourteen years, was named Sigurður.

To this woman the farmer at last applied, and offered her a large sum of money if she would allow her son to act as shepherd for him. Sigurður was very anxious that his mother should have all this money, and declared himself most willing to undertake the role; so he went with the farmer, and during the summer was most successful in his new situation, and never lost a sheep.

At the end of a certain time the farmer gave Sigurður a ram, a ewe, and a lamb as a present, with which the youth was much pleased.

Guðmundur became attached to him, and on Christmas Eve begged him to come home from his sheep before sunset.

All day long the boy watched the sheep, and when evening approached, he heard the sound of heavy footsteps on the mountains. Turning round he saw coming towards him a gigantic and terrible troll.

She addressed him, saying "Good evening, my Sigurður. I have come to put you into my bag."

Sigurður answered, "Are you mad? Do you not see how thin I am? Surely I am not worth your notice. But I have a sheep and a fat lamb here which I will give you for your pot this evening."

So he gave her the sheep and the lamb, which she threw onto her shoulder, and carried off up the mountain again. Then Sigurður went home, and right glad was the farmer to see him safe, and asked him whether he had seen anything.

"Nothing whatever out of the common," replied the boy.

After New Year's Day the farmer visited the flock, and, on looking over them, missed the sheep and lamb which he had given the youth, and asked him what had become of them. The boy answered that a fox had killed the lamb, and that the ram had fallen into a bog; adding, "I believe I shall not be very lucky with *my* sheep."

When he heard this, the farmer gave him one ewe and two rams, and asked him to remain another year in his service. Sigurður consented to do so.

Next Christmas Eve, Guðmundur begged Sigurður to be cautious, and not run any risks, for he loved him as his own son.

But the boy answered, "You need not fear, there are no risks to run."

When he had got the sheep into the pens about night-fall, the same troll came to him, and said:

"As sure as ever I am a troll, you shall not, this evening, escape being boiled in my pot."

"I am quite at your service," answered Sigurður, intrepidly; "but you see that I am still very thin; nothing to be compared even to one ram. I will give you, however, for your Christmas dinner, two old and two young sheep. Will you condescend to be satisfied with this offer of mine?"

"Let me see," said the troll; so the lad showed her the sheep, and she, hooking them together by their horns, threw them onto her shoulder, and ran off with them up the mountain. Then Sigurður returned to the farm, and when questioned, declared, as before, that he had seen nothing whatever unusual upon the mountain.

"But," he said, "I have been dreadfully unlucky with *my* sheep, as I said I should be." Next summer the farmer gave him four more rams.

When Christmas Eve had come again, just as Sigurður was putting the sheep into their pens, the troll came to him, and threatened to take him away with her. Then he offered her the four rams, which she took, and hooking them together by their horns, threw them over her shoulder. Not content with this, however, she seized the lad too, tucked him under her arm, and ran off with her burthen to her cave in the mountains.

Here she flung the sheep down, and Sigurður after them, and ordered him to kill them and shave their skins. When he had done so, he asked her what task she had now for him to perform.

She said, "Sharpen this axe well, for I intend to cut off your head with it."

When he had sharpened it well, he restored it to the troll, who bade him take off his neckerchief; which he did, without changing a feature of his face.

Then the troll, instead of cutting off his head, flung the axe down on the ground and said, "Brave lad! I never intended to kill you, and you shall live to a good old age. It was I that caused you to be made herdsman to Guðmundur, for I wished to meet with you. And now I will show you in what way you shall arrive at good-fortune. Next spring you must move from Silfrúnarstaðir, and go to the house of a silversmith, to learn his trade. When you have learned it thoroughly, you shall take some specimens of

silver-work to the farm where the dean's three daughters live; and
I can tell you that the youngest of them is the most promising
maiden in the whole country. Her elder sisters love dress and
ornaments and will admire what you bring them, but Margrét
will not care about such things. When you leave the house, you
shall ask her to accompany you as far as the door, and then as far
as the end of the grass-field, which she will consent to do. Then
you shall give her these three precious things – this handkerchief,
this belt, and this ring; and after that she will love you. But when
you have seen me in a dream you must come here, and you will
find me dead. Bury me, and take for yourself everything of value
that you find in my cave."

Then Sigurður bade her farewell and left her, and returned
to the farm, where Guðmundur welcomed him with joy, having
grieved at his long absence, and asked him whether he had
seen nothing.

"No," replied the boy; and declared that he could answer for
the safety of all future herdsmen. But no more questions would he
answer, though the family asked him many. The following summer
he went to a silversmith's house, and in two years made himself
master of the trade. He often visited Guðmundur, his old master,
and was always welcome. Once he went to the trading town of
Hofsós, and buying a variety of glittering silver ornaments, took
them to Miklibær, and offered them for sale to the dean's daughters,
as the troll had told him. When the elder sisters heard that he had
ornaments for sale, they begged him to let them see them first,
in order that they might choose the best of them. Accordingly
he showed them his wares, and they bought many trinkets, but
Margrét would not even so much as look at the silver ornaments.

When he took leave, he asked the youngest sister to accompany
him as far as the door, and when they got there, to come with him
as far as the end of the field. She was much astonished at this request,
and asked him what he wanted with her, as she had never seen him

before. But Sigurður entreated her the more the more she held back, and at last she consented to go with him. At the end of the field Sigurður gave her the belt and handkerchief, and put the ring onto her finger.

This done, Margrét said, "I wish I had never taken these gifts, but I cannot now give them back to you."

Sigurður then took leave and went home. But Margrét, as soon as she had received the presents, fell in love with their giver; and finding after a while that she could not live without him, told her father all about it. Her father bade her desist from such a mad idea, and declared that she should never marry the youth as long as he lived to prevent it. On this Margrét pined away, and became so thin from grief that the father found he would be obliged to consent to her request; and going to the farm at which Sigurður lived, engaged him as his silversmith.

Not long after, Sigurður and Margrét were betrothed.

One day the youth dreamed that he saw the old troll, and felt sure from this that she was dead; so he asked the dean to accompany him as far as Silfrúnarstaðir, and sleep there one night. When they arrived there, they told Guðmundur that Sigurður was betrothed to Margrét. When the farmer heard this, he said that it had long been his intention to leave Sigurður all his property, and offered him the management of the farm the ensuing spring. The youth thanked him heartily, and the dean was glad to see his daughter so soon, and so well provided for.

Next day Sigurður asked the farmer and the dean to go with him as far as the middle of the mountain, where they found a cave into which he bade them enter without fear. Inside they saw the troll woman lying dead on the floor with her face awfully distorted. Then Sigurður told them all about his interviews with the troll, and asked them to help him to bury her. When they had done so, they returned to the cave and found there as many precious things as ten horses could carry, which Sigurður took back to the farm.

Not long after, he married the dean's daughter, and prospered to the end of his life, which, as the old troll had prophesied, was a long one.

Told by an unknown storyteller to Jón Þórðarson,
translated by Eiríkur Magnússon and George E. J. Powell

---»»» «««---

A few Icelandic legends tell of friendships forming between humans and trolls, as is the case in the story here, something that usually turns out to be very valuable for the human. Trolls in Icelandic legends are sometimes shown to be very wise and may even possess the power of foresight. The idea of a predestined fate appears to be a potent one in Icelandic folk belief.

Up! My Six, in Jesu's Name!

One autumn, six men went on a search into the sheepwalks, with their leader, who was a strong man and dauntless withal. When they had reached the farthest point of their search, a storm came on with a heavy snowfall, and the men lost their way, not knowing where they were. After a long walk, they found that their path led downhill, and soon they found themselves in a small valley, and having by chance come across a house, they knocked at the door. There came out an old fellow, ugly and mighty rascally-looking, and said that it was a new thing for strangers to come and pry about his dwellings, and looked with ungleeful eye on his guests. The leader spoke for them all, and told him how they had happened to come thither: and having told the old fellow this he stepped inside the door with all his men, without waiting for the inhospitable man's leave or refusal. When they had sat for a while, meat was brought to them on dishes, by a young damsel of downcast mien.

She whispered to the guests, as she gave the meat to them: "Eat only the meat at the edge of the dish farthest from you."

They looked and were soon sure that all at that edge was mutton, but all at the other, human flesh.

When they had finished, the girl removed the meat from the table, and took the wet clothes of the strangers to dry them and said in a low voice: "Be watchful, do not take off your underclothes; neither sleep!"

It was a moonlight night, and the leader lay in a bed in the shadow, and told his comrades, that they should not move or speak aught, till he called them.

Shortly after they had gone to rest, the old man came in, and going to the bedside of one of his guests, touched his chest and said:

"Lean chest and craven."

And in the same way he felt them all muttering the like wellnigh, at every one, till at last, when he came to the bed of the leader and had felt his chest, he said:

"Fat chest and mettlesome."

And, in the same moment he turned to a nook in the room and seized an axe, and returned with it to the bed of the leader. But the latter, seeing what was to come, sprang nimbly down from the bed, wherein the old cannibal dealt him a blow, missing him, of course; but the leader now seized the axe, and wrung it from the wretch's hand, who roared out:

"Up, my twelve, in the Devil's name!"

Now the leader drove the axe into the old man's pate, so it stood in the brain, and he fell dead on the spot.

Then the leader said:

"Up, my six, in Jesu's name!"

When he had thus called upon his followers, a trap-door was opened in the floor and there came up the head of a man. But the leader was not long in cutting it off, and thus killed twelve of them in the open trap-door of a cellar which was under the floor.

After this they found the girl who had waited on them in the evening. She turned out to be a farmer's daughter from Eyjafjörður, whom the old man had stolen, and would force, against her will, to marry his eldest son. But she bore an untellable loathing towards them all, chiefly because they killed everyone that came to them, who had lost their way, and then ate their flesh.

Here the men found many precious things, and many sheep in the valley. They agreed that the leader should remain, and one man with him, to comfort the girl, and to watch the sheep during the winter, in order that they might not starve for want of care. But the others returned home.

Next spring, the leader brought the girl home, and afterwards, with the consent of her father, married her, and

moved everything that he found in the valley to the North:
began farming, and lived a long and happy life with his wife to
a high age.

Told by Gunnhildur Jónsdóttir to Skúli Gíslason,
translated by Eiríkur Magnússon and George E. J. Powell

⟶≫ ≪⟵

Ketilríður

In the days of yore, there lived, in a valley of the East-country, a man named Grímur. His wife was named Þórkatla, and his daughter, Ketilríður, and they had no other children than this daughter.

One autumn, it happened that, when the walks were searched, numbers of sheep were missing. Ketilríður's father was one who suffered most from this, as he lost nearly all his sheep. He, as well as others, was greatly annoyed, but there was nothing to be done. Early in the winter, Ketilríður came to her father and spoke thus to him: "I would, father, that you allow me to go and search the wildernesses for your sheep. I have a foreboding that, if you should give me your leave to go, my search will not be in vain."

Grímur answered: "I knew well, before now, daughter, that you had a man's heart in a woman's breast, but I cannot say I find this journey to be very promising. It is more than likely that trolls, mountain spirits, and robbers haunt the wildernesses and lie in wait for you, and will make you their prisoner, and either take away your life, or, at least, keep you in endless thraldom."

Ketilríður answered: "This, I believe, is more talk than truth, and in no way am I ready to put faith in it."

She begged her father thus, till at last he gave his consent to her going and bade his herdsman accompany her. To this she uttered no unwillingness; and now she prepared for a long walk, taking provisions and new shoes, and having bidden farewell to her parents, went off with the herdsman. But as soon as they were out of sight, she made the man go back again. This made Grímur, her father, very anxious about his daughter's safety, and he thought that surely Death had called her into this hazardous and strange undertaking.

Now Ketilríður walked for a long time, through the wildernesses, and, at last, the clouds began to gather up, and the weather became gloomy, and a snow-storm drew nearer and nearer. In the storm, she quite lost her way, but still went on for a long while, not knowing where she was, or whither she sped. At last, she came to the brow of a mountain, and stepping over it, went down the slopes, and a fearfully hard passage she found it, what with the precipices and the frozen snow. However, she got down to the level ground, and then the storm was so thick, that she could not see things before her, even at a span's distance. She deemed, nonetheless, that she was in a valley, and after a short while, she came to a river, covered with ice-edges along the banks, but open in the middle. She followed the course of this river, till she came to a pen of huge size and saw a man, with many sheep, at the door of it. Not finding the man evil-looking, she greeted him, and he answered curtly. Then Ketilríður recognized here, her father's sheep and those of other folk in their neighbourhood.

She asked the man his name, and he said it was Þorsteinn, adding moreover that there was but one cottage in the valley. He was letting the sheep into the pen, and Ketilríður helped him to do so, and said that she would ask for shelter at the farm, for the night.

The man said it was very unwise of her, if she cared for her life. "For here," he said, "no one's life is ever spared of those who ask for shelter. But I will, notwithstanding, undertake to guard against anything happening to you, if you will follow me. I know what your errand is, and I should wish it to succeed."

Now they went to the house, and through the door, and there, in a corner, the man, removing several things, lifted at last a trap-lid, under which a little underground cave opened. Down into this, he bade Ketilríður go, and not move, whatever she might hear, and however great noise was going on; for, if she moved, or uttered a sound, it would cost her her life. After this, he covered up the cave, and went away.

In a short while, the girl heard the sound of footsteps, and the voices of no less than six people, all asking about, and searching for the guest. She also heard Þorsteinn deny that anyone had gone there.

And now the noise waxed so loud, that every rafter cracked, and the earth trembled, and she was seized with an awful fear. After some while, all became still, and Ketilríður soon dropped into a deep sleep, being both drowsy and weary.

Early the next morning, Þorsteinn woke her, and bade her follow him. She was not long in getting up. He went with her to the pen, and gave her her father's sheep and those belonging to her neighbours; and afterwards accompanied her out of the valley, in fine and clear weather.

When they parted, Þorsteinn said to Ketilríður: "Now, I will lend you my dog, to follow you home. He will do the task of any active man, in driving sheep. He will leave you, at the enclosure wall of your farm. But I wish you would gather people round you, who should be in readiness whenever you wanted them. Do not come hither with them yet, till I have sent you Sörli, my dog, for then I shall be sorely in need of help. I will also beg you not to marry, till you know what becomes of me."

Thereupon, they parted, and Sörli drove all the sheep home to Grímur's farm.

Now Ketilríður went home, and her parents were wondrous glad to have their child back again, as they thought, from the very jaws of death. All folk got too, their missing sheep, and there was no end to their praise of Ketilríður's courage and activity. She then gathered together, to her, the stoutest and strongest men in the parish, twenty-four in all, and appointed a man named Ketill, to be their leader, and bade them to be ready whenever she might call them.

Once, in the winter, she dreamt that Þorsteinn came to her, saying that he was in sore need of her help. She got up early, and as she opened the door of the farm, at it stood Sörli, wagging his tail and caressing Ketilríður, as she stepped out. She went swiftly for her men, who all busked in a hurry, and started off with Sörli as their guide. They came into the valley, late in the day, and walked up to the farm, but there was no one to be seen outside.

Ketilríður said to the men: "Wait at the back of the houses, and do not betray yourselves, but if I call come then forth without delay."

They promised to do so, and now she went in, and into the living room, and took silently a seat on the dais. She saw in the room an old man and an old woman, and six young men, and all these people looked awfully fierce. The old woman spoke to Ketilríður and asked if she would have something to eat. Ketilríður said she would, and out went the old woman, and brought in a large dish full of meat. But as the damsel looked at the meat, she did not like it, for it was human flesh. She said she was unaccustomed to such food, and asked for other, and the old woman brought in mutton. But as soon as it had been set before the guest, the old man took a great knife and began to sharpen it, saying to his sons that it would be as well to kill Ketilríður, the sooner the better, and bidding them seize her. They stood up at once, but she asked to be allowed to sing first her death-prayer, for she was a Christian. The old man was not a devout person, and said that, of such twaddle, he would have none; but his sons were curious to hear the prayer, having never heard such a thing before, and therefore she was allowed to sing her prayer. She then asked them to take her to the threshold of the entrance-door, for God would never enter their cottage, to take her soul. This the old man would not allow, but his sons would have their own will, and took her to the threshold, the old man following behind, with his knife in his hand. And now Ketilríður began praying thus:

> Keta! Keta! Keta mine!
> Come thou hither, with followers thine,
> And fetch thou hence this soul of mine!

Then Ketill and his men jumped up, and rushed, with all their weapons, to the door, and thereat the lads let go their hold of Ketilríður, but could not escape, for Ketill and his men killed all the rascal-band, and burned them afterwards. Now began the search for Þorsteinn, whom they found, under Sörli's guidance, in a room locked off, with his hands tied to the back of the seat he was sitting on, and his legs in ice-cold water up to the knees. Before him was a dish with smoked mutton on it, but he could not reach it. Then he was untied from his chair and given refreshment. He told them whence he was, and that these wretches had stolen him, as he was a good herdsman. Now all that was of any value was taken away from the cottage, and itself burnt. There was an endless quantity of treasures, all of which became the property of Þorsteinn and Ketilríður. They brought all their riches to the damsel's home, and rewarded the men well for their trouble.

Now Þorsteinn wooed Ketilríður, and got her father's consent, and they married, and lived at Grímur's farm after his death. They loved each other tenderly till the end, and became the richest of farming folk in their days.

Told by Gamalíel Þorleifsson to Páll Jónsson,
translated by Eiríkur Magnússon and George E. J. Powell

Outlaws such as the ones in the stories "Up! My Six, in Jesu's Name" and "Ketilríður" are shown to live outside human society, in the sense that they live in the wilderness, away from civilization, and do not follow the rules of society, having bad manners and being thieves, murderers and even cannibals.

The Eagle

It is said that when the hook on the end of an eagle's beak grows too large, it cannot fend for itself and becomes as tame as a dog. Then the eagle shall be taken and the hook shall be filed off, as the eagle will bring a wishing-stone in return, which is a great boon. The eagle is the largest of all birds in this country and the one that flies the highest; it is wildly predatory and daring, so it is said that in olden times they often kidnapped children; from there comes the story of the place name Tregagil.

A widow lived in Klaustursel, in Jökuldalur Valley, and had an infant. She carried it out to the meadow while drying hay one summer. Before she knew it there glided down a great eagle; it took the child and floated with it eastward and up to the great river canyon which is at the edge of the heath. The eagle had a nest and younglings there. The poor mother followed the eagle to the canyon's edge and watched as it tore the baby apart for its young. The woman sat down and wept. And this canyon has since then been called Tregagil (Mourning Canyon), and the river is likewise of the same name. The canyon is strikingly deep and terrifying.

The eagle is a scavenger and hunts various aquatic animals. It is not afraid of any creature except the meadow pipit, who seeks to fly into its rectum and from there intends to come out of its mouth. But it is said that the meadow pipit will most often give up along the way, exhausting both birds. There are multiple stories of the eagle and its hunting tricks. In Nes, an eagle took a ram lamb, but then its skin ripped and the eagle lost its lamb. It became an old sheep, called Loddi. Another eagle carried a foal but landed with it in a creek and was killed. Once, an eagle carried a trout from a stream, but then another eagle came and wanted it too, and accidentally struck the first eagle so that both died.

Told by various storytellers to Sigfús Sigfússon,
translated by Sigurður Líndal

—»»»— ««««—

Various folk beliefs concerning birds can be found in Icelandic folk legends, many of which give them human-like attributes. In Icelandic legends, ghosts sometimes take the shape of an eagle, and they may be considered to be bad omens. The eagle in Icelandic folk legends often appears as dangerous, for other animals and even humans, as is the case here. In Iceland there are known instances of eagles stealing young children, as was the case with a woman called Ragnheiður Eyjólfsdóttir (born in 1877), who was stolen by an eagle when she was two years old, but as the child was too heavy to carry, the bird had to lower its flight and Ragnheiður was rescued. When Icelanders started focusing more on keeping eider ducks and collecting eider down, the eagle could be very troublesome as it is known to kill the ducks. This caused Icelanders to hunt the eagle quite aggressively in the nineteenth century. At risk of extinction, the eagle was protected by Icelandic law in 1913, and it is still protected today.[20]

The Bear on Breiðdalsheiði

One very harsh winter, it is said that bears walked onto land in
many places in northern and eastern Iceland. It is said that a large
polar bear settled down in the Breiðdalsheiði mountain pass, in
or near the area called Tjarnarflöt. The word got out in the two
districts that lay either side, Breiðdalur and Skriðdalur, and people
thought it ominous that the animal should stay there, where it
would have nothing to live on. People did not risk traversing the
mountain pass without weapons, and even then few would brave
it. Eventually one man set out on the journey, a great daredevil
with a high opinion of himself who was not particularly well liked.
He had a large pointed staff in one hand. The staff had a spike that
was long and sharp. Some say that this man's name was Bessi. He
went on his way up to the mountain pass, where there is little else
than a nesting ground for birds. When he emerged from a so-called
narrow, he saw the animal by his path. It observed him, and he
threatened it with the staff, insulting it and daring it to attack him.
He said that accounts of its intelligence, courage and strength must
have been exaggerated, seeing as it did not dare to respond to his
challenge. The bear looked down, as if ashamed. The man then
went along his way, over what is called Víðigróf in Þrep. There he
met a man from Hérað and told him all about the animal, sparing
no details about his encounter with it. The other man felt uneasy
about the situation and said that as there was such a short distance
left to Haugar, it should be safe for the first man to lend him the
staff. The man agreed, claiming to not fear the animal even without
the staff, and gave it to him. He then walked along the path that
lies eastwards by so-called Skriðuvatn lake. From there it is a good
distance over the hills that lie on the way, and onwards from there
to the farm Haugar.

It can now be said of the man who went south that he was not
aware of any presence until he came down to Tjarnarflöt, where

he saw the bear. It observed the man in great detail. The man kept the staff to hand should he need to use it, but did not interact with the animal. But it did not look for very long at him, as in an instant the bear became ferocious, dashing northwards along the mountain pass as if it had no time to lose. The man then came to suspect that it intended to find the man who had provoked it earlier, having seen that he had given away his staff and was left with no means of protection. He saw no way to chase the bear, as he thought that the other man would have reached the farms Stefánsstaðir or Haugar by the time that the bear caught up with him. And so the man continued on his way to Breiðdalur, where he told this story.

It is to be said of the man who had come from Breiðdalur that he was little on his guard until he had come far out in the Haugahólar hills, near so-called Háhóll, and had only a short way left to the farm when he heard something charge up behind him. There the bear had arrived. Defenceless, the man had no way to protect himself and no chance to flee. The animal attacked him and killed him, thereby repaying his provocation on Breiðdalsheiði, and then disappeared.

*Told by Árni Björn Arnbjarnarson to Þorsteinn M. Jónsson
and Sigfús Sigfússon, translated by Alice Bower*

The danger posed to Icelanders by polar bears is the subject of numerous legends and stories. As folklorists Alice Bower and Kristinn Schram point out, the animals are often given human-like attributes, as in the story here, where the bear "looked down, as if ashamed".[21] The man, whom some say was called Bessi, does not seem to have received protection by his name. In folk legends involving polar bears (as well as, for example, hidden people), respect is an important element in their interactions with humans. It seems that, since the man did not respect the bear, he got what he deserved.

Jón from the Farm Parthús

Three men and a girl were on their way from some town in the northeast. They were well equipped and had smoked lamb in their provisions. They also had around eight litres of *brennivín* (schnapps) with them. They had to cross a single heath on their way. The weather was dreadful as they made their way up. When they reached the high heath, a blizzard struck them. They walked for a long time, and the blizzard grew stronger and stronger. Finally, the girl gave up; the men buried her in the snow, and left with her the smoked lamb and schnapps, before fighting their way down the heath. They reached a farm late in the evening but were so exhausted that they could not go back for the girl. Besides, they probably would not have found her in the darkness and blizzard, even if they had tried.

Around midday the following day, the blizzard subsided. The men then set out to look for the girl. They carried staffs with them, as is customary for winter travel. When they were getting close to where they thought the girl should be, they heard a truly terrible sound. They were horrified but continued on their way. They now heard one sound after another, a sound so horrid and wild that they could not compare it to anything they knew. Shortly after, they saw a monster. It had a human shape, or rather it looked like a butter churn that had been turned upside down, with a head and hands. It had bulging eyes that were blood red. Its nose was black and blue and bleeding. Its tongue hung out of its mouth. Its face was blood-spattered, and blood vessels protruded from the corners of its mouth. The chest was nearly entirely blood-smeared. The hair stuck up on one side but hung down on the other, tangled and clotted.

The men were horrified by this sight and thought that this was the ghost of the girl. They all recoiled except for one, named Jón, who approached the monster and struck it through with his staff. It produced a wailing cry and fell down.

It was as the men had suspected: it was the girl. During the night, she had woken up, eaten the meat and drunk all the schnapps in a fit of despair. She then jumped to her feet, mad with fright and wine. However, she had not got far, because her skirts had frozen around her, halting her journey. This was how they found her, and Jón had killed her.

Jón's actions were not well received, but people understood that he was not to blame since he had killed her unintentionally.

After this incident, Jón never crossed the heath where the unfortunate event had taken place alone.

There was a friend of Jón's named Þórður who lived on the other side of the heath. Once, Jón went to visit him. It was midwinter. Jón had brought a travelling companion with him, as he was accustomed to. They reached Þórður's place without any trouble. Jón stayed with him for some time, but when they parted, Þórður told Jón that he had a bad feeling that Jón might soon die, and asked him not to travel alone across the heath. Jón told him that he still would go, as one cannot avoid one's fate; they then bade each other farewell.

Jón and his companion found lodgings in a farm below the heath. The next morning, Jón's companion fell ill. Jón waited for a day, but the morning after, the companion's condition had not improved. Jón thought that he could no longer be away from his wife and children. The farmer advised Jón to wait for his companion's recovery, but Jón decided to set out nonetheless.

The weather was fine, it looked like the journey would be good, and Jón was well equipped, so there was no likelihood of anything happening to him. Shortly after Jón left, his companion recovered completely.

Jón did not return. A search was organized and he was eventually found, torn apart piece by piece where he had killed the girl.

Told by Guðmundur Scheving Bjarnason to Ólafur Davíðsson,
translated by Dagrún Ósk Jónsdóttir

Here, the greatest danger to the travellers is shown to be the sudden changes of weather that can take place in the wilderness. The story reflects the very real fear of natural forces, as well as portraying folk belief concerning ghosts, which will be better explained in the next chapter.

Katla

Once it happened that the Abbot of the Monastery of Þykkvibær had a housekeeper whose name was Katla, and who was an evil-minded and hot-tempered woman. She possessed a pair of shoes whose peculiarity was that whoever put them on was never tired of running. Everybody was afraid of Katla's bad disposition and fierce temper, even the Abbot himself. The herdsman of the monastery farm, whose name was Barði, was often dreadfully ill-treated by her, particularly if he had chanced to lose any of the ewes.

One day in the autumn the Abbot and his housekeeper went to a wedding, leaving orders with Barði to drive in the sheep and milk them before they came home. But unhappily, when the time came, the herdsman could not find all the ewes; so he went into the house, put on Katla's magic shoes, and sallied out in search of the stray sheep. He had a long way to run before he discovered them, but felt no fatigue, so he drove all the flock in quite briskly.

When Katla returned, she immediately perceived that the herdsman had been using her shoes, so she took him and drowned him in a large tubful of curds. Nobody knew what had become of the man, and as the winter went on and the curds in the tub sank lower and lower, Katla was heard to say these words to herself: "Soon will the waves of milk break upon the foot-soles of Barði!"

Shortly after this, dreading that the murder should be found out, and that she would be condemned to death, she took her magic shoes, and ran from the monastery to a great ice-mountain, into a rift of which she leaped, and was never seen again.

As soon as she had disappeared, a fearful eruption took place from the mountain, and the lava rolled down and destroyed the monastery at which she had lived. People declared that her witchcraft had been the cause of this, and called the crater of the mountain "The Rift of Katla".

Told by an unknown storyteller to Runólfur Jónsson,
translated by Eiríkur Magnússon and George E. J. Powell

In comparative terms, not many Icelandic legends tell of natural forces and phenomena such as volcanoes, glaciers and the aurora borealis. Several stories, however, note the idea that people somehow become "part of" places such as mountains and waterfalls when they disappear into them, never to be seen again, as in the case of Katla in the story. Katla is one of the largest volcanoes in Iceland. Located in the south of Iceland, it is still active today. The last major eruption there took place in 1918.[22]

3

The Dark

> Stories were often told in the twilight . . . folk legends and wonder
> tales. Troll stories, stories of hidden people, and especially ghost
> stories, which held the biggest and most prestigious place. The
> children listened to some of the stories mesmerized, frightened,
> and with chills running down their spines. It of course depended
> a lot on how well the story was told. These stories often led to an
> extreme fear of the dark in teenagers, and there were cases where
> kids became so scared that they never recovered.[1]

This is how a man born in 1888 described his memories of the
stories told when he was growing up in the north of Iceland.
When looking at Icelandic folk stories, it becomes clear that the seemingly endless darkness of the Icelandic winter has affected them. During
the winter months, daylight lasts only a few hours. Of course, towns
and cities are well lit today, but as soon as one leaves those places it can
be pitch black, especially in the more rural areas. In the past, before the
arrival of electricity, this was all people knew during the winter, and on
farms that were surrounded by mountains the sun could be completely
absent for a couple of months. (This is, of course, still true in some
towns today.) As the folklore collector Sigfús Sigfússon describes it:

> How people missed [the sun] when it disappeared during the
> winter and darkness fell over the earth and the winter cold

took over. But then, when the sun looked up from the sea and ran its rays over the ocean floor, or when it peeked smiling over the mountains into the valleys, there was hardly a person that did not have a look of joy on their face.[2]

In the places where the sun disappears for a certain period of time, its return is usually a cause for celebration and festivities, including the drinking of coffee and the baking of pancakes, things that were considered great luxuries in the old farming society. This is a tradition still known in some parts of Iceland, for example in the towns of Siglufjörður and Ísafjörður.

According to Icelandic folklore, it is important to treat the sun with respect. It was strictly forbidden to point at the sun, speak negatively about it or curse it. Indeed, according to Sigfús it was not uncommon for farmers to cross their chests when they first saw the sun in the morning, as it was, among other things, a means of showing respect and gratitude.[3] This is quite understandable given how important the sun was: they needed it to grow their crops and for their livestock. The farm's livelihood depended on it.

The moon was a more common sight in the winter. However, while everything good was believed to be brought by the sun, the moon was said to bring mischief. When the moon was strong it was sometimes called *draugasól* (lit. ghost sun).[4] This is a fitting name seeing as most ghost stories take place during the night, and in some of them the moon has an important role. In these ghost stories, the supernatural and other dangerous creatures lie in the shadows and can pose a risk to people.

The darkness was found during the winter months not only outside but inside. Candles, lamps and animal fat were the main light sources at the time but had to be used sparingly as they were hard to come by. During the evening wakes, there would often be only one lamp burning for people to work by while one person read for the others. As the historian Guðmundur Hálfdanarson points out, the darkness was also important in the sense that it created privacy, a somewhat limited resource in the farmhouse. Most of people's time on the farm was spent together, and they would even sleep together in one room, often also sharing a bed. The darkness could thus be said to offer the only protection from prying eyes.[5]

Around 1870 the first oil lamps started to make their way to Iceland. At first they were rather expensive and an option only for the more wealthy families, but soon they became more common.[6] This was a great improvement on the earlier situation. However, it was still quite dark, and – as can be seen in the 1999 questionnaire sent out by the National Museum about the arrival of electricity – many people, especially children and teenagers, were afraid of the dark. As a woman born in 1913 in the north of the country describes it:

> The old turf houses had many shadowy areas. Long, dark and crooked with dirt on every side, projections and porches, no light and you could only feel your way into the living room and welcome the light from a small oil lamp that reached far too short a distance, perhaps only into the middle of the room, wearing a collar of darkness along the walls. Is it any surprise that many were frightened?[7]

Jónas Jónasson describes a method said to cure people of this fear, which involved boiling human blood and water together and then rubbing that onto one's face. Jónas nonetheless makes no mention of how well known this method was, nor whether he had ever heard of it being used.[8]

It was not until the early twentieth century that electricity became available on some of the farms, and not until after the middle of the century in some of the more rural areas. Many describe the light that electricity brought as one of the biggest and most important changes in Icelandic history. As a man born in 1923 who grew up in one of the most rural areas in Iceland, Árneshreppur, notes:

There was great joy in our large family (we were ten siblings) when the first lights were switched on and the light flooded the living rooms and corridors. Belief in ghosts faded, but before there had been a lot of fear of the dark, at least in children. This electricity was only enough for lights. Everyone praised the electric lights, but I remember my father saying that they brought no warmth like the blessed lamp lights had done.[9]

The darkness and the mysterious sounds coming from outside the turf houses would have made a perfect setting for the telling of ghost stories.

Death also had a strong presence in the Icelandic society of the past. It has been described as being almost a member of the household, its presence always hanging over it. Family members would often die at home, and their bodies would be kept indoors until it was possible to bury them. This is quite different to today, where hospitals are the more common place of death. In the past, people's bodies were often kept on wooden stretchers in the room in which they passed away, or they would be moved to an empty, cold room until it was possible to take them to church for burial.[10] Many Icelanders from earlier times remember being afraid of these bodies as children, not least because they were sometimes made to touch the body as a means to rid them of this fear.[11]

It was a tradition that people on the farm would watch over the body at night, something that could naturally be rather uncomfortable. Before a body was buried it was wrapped in linen, which would be sewn up by the head and feet. According to folk belief, those who did this work were forbidden to cut or rip the thread with their hands; they were supposed to use their teeth. The seamstresses thus had to bend down close to the body, something that people also believed would help them notice if the deceased was in fact still alive (at the time there was a great fear of being buried alive).[12] After a person died,

Auguste Étienne François Mayer (1805–1890) was a French painter who participated in
several Arctic expeditions, which is reflected in his collection of artworks. He travelled with
the ship *La Recherche* on its voyage to Iceland and Greenland in 1835–6 and created this
illustration, *A Way of Transporting the Dead*, published in Paul Gaimard, *Voyage en Islande
et au Groenland . . . Atlas historique* (1838), vol. ii.

measures would also be taken to make sure that they would not come
back to haunt family members. For example, it was common to open
the window right after someone died so that their soul could get out
and not remain at the farm. Similarly, in the nineteenth century in the
north of Iceland, before the burial of a body, people would turn
the coffin in three circles after leaving the church, in order to confuse
the possible ghost.[13] There were also various ways to get rid of a ghost,
some of which are shown in the legends found in this chapter. The
idea that ghosts are unable to tolerate a church or the sound of church
bells seems to be prevalent. According to some stories, protection
could be provided by various magic runes or staffs. Showing trolls and
ghosts your bare backside was also considered a powerful protection.

When George E. J. Powell and Eiríkur Magnússon published their translations of selected stories from Jón Árnason's folk tale collection, the illustrations were credited to Powell himself, Jules Worms (1832–1924) and Johan Baptist Zwecker (1814–1876). This illustration shows a young woman speaking to a ghost. In Icelandic folklore, ghosts are sometimes described as skeleton-like, as depicted in the later legend "The Skeleton in Hólar Church" in *Icelandic Legends* (1864).

Similarly, it seems evident that urine had a bad effect on them, something that could come in handy when people slept with chamberpots under their beds – one legend tells of a woman who is startled by a noise while asleep in the living room; she grabs her chamber pot and throws everything inside it at what she believes to be a ghost, which turns out to be the local sheriff.[14] Finally, the idea (also known in other neighbouring countries) that ghosts – like other supernatural beings – can be shot with silver bullets can be found in Icelandic folk belief.

Yet other methods focused on the body of the person who had been turned into a ghost. Since Icelandic ghosts have a very physical presence, one could also make sure that their bodies could not leave their graves. This could be done by putting nails down into the grave. In more extreme cases, people would dig up the body and put nails into the soles of the corpse's feet so that they would be unable to walk. Another recognized method was to remove the head from the body of the ghost and then place it in the ground in such a way that those who were being haunted by it could walk between the head and the body. If nothing else worked, people would burn the body of the ghost.[15] Interestingly, in one extant letter from the Danish king from 1609, he chastises Icelanders for their harsh treatment of bodies, showing little concern for the fact that this treatment was meant to get rid of ghosts.[16]

Icelandic ghosts, usually referred to as *draugar*, are typically described as taking physical or material shape, meaning that sometimes people could not tell the difference between a ghost and the living. Still, such ghosts would usually make visible the way in which they died: those who drowned might leave a puddle of water behind them, for example, while another might have open, bleeding wounds.

Various types of ghost exist in Icelandic legend, but the main categories are *afturgöngur* (revenants) and *uppvakningar* (the raised dead). The *afturgöngur* are those that cannot move on, either because they have unfinished business, often related to love or revenge, or because they passed away suddenly and have not been buried in a graveyard or consecrated ground (although there are exceptions to this, as can be seen in the final chapter). A specific type of *afturgöngur* are the ghosts of children who were left to die of exposure; they become ghosts because they have not been laid to rest in holy ground, and to seek vengeance on their mothers. Quite a few Icelandic legends tell of such ghosts, called *útburðir*, a supernatural being also well known in the other Nordic countries. Some stories relate place names to *útburðir*, as in Útburðargil (Útburðar Canyon) and Ýluskarð (Howling Pass); these are usually short and centre around the idea that in those places one can hear the terrible sounds of the *útburður* crying. As old Norse scholar Matthias Egeler has noted, such stories might serve as a reminder of an earlier injustice and thus as a reflection of the conscience of the Icelandic people.[17]

This 2020 illustration by Sunneva Guðrún Þórðardóttir (b. 1998) depicts a sorcerer bringing a ghost back from the dead. The sorcerer is inspired by Sigurður Atlason, who for many years ran the Museum of Sorcery and Witchcraft in Hólmavík, Iceland.

The *uppvakningar* are ghosts that are brought back from the dead to do a specific job, often the work of revenge by the sorcerer who has awakened the ghost.[18] In his collection, Jón Árnason describes how ghosts could be brought back from the dead but warns that it can be dangerous. He describes the process, saying that first a sorcerer must speak some magic rites over the grave of the deceased. After that, the head of the ghost will appear out of the grave and the sorcerer then has to lick the foam that comes out of its mouth. The ghost will then climb out of the grave and the sorcerer must wrestle with it to gain control over it.[19] It is interesting to note that the legend collections make no mention of people bringing back their loved ones from the world of death. Raising the dead is never done with good intentions. Arguably this reflects the idea that people felt their loved ones were better off in heaven than back on earth, something that was an important consideration when death rates were high.

It is appropriate to open this chapter about darkness with the story "The Darkness Is Delightful".

The Darkness Is Delightful

From ancient times until our present day, it has been a custom to watch over the deceased, and it was usually done by candlelight if the night was dark. Once, a sorcerer, old in demeanour and of ill repute, passed away. Few were willing to watch over his body, until a courageous and wholehearted man agreed to take on the task. He managed to keep watch well. Then, the night before the body was to be placed in the coffin, the light went out just before dawn. At the same time, the corpse suddenly rose and said, "The darkness is delightful." The watcher replied, "That won't benefit you." He then recited this verse:

> Outside the earth is shining bright,
> Outside the night has ended.
> There was a candle, but you are dirt,
> And it is about time, you shut right up.

Then he leaped upon the body and broke it across its back. After that, what remained was quiet for the rest of the night.

Told by Einar Bjarnason to Skúli Gíslason,
translated by Dagrún Ósk Jónsdóttir

⟶≫ ≪⟵

The Deacon of Myrká

A long time ago, a deacon lived at Myrká, in Eyjafjörður. He was in love with a girl named Guðrún, who dwelt in a farm on the opposite side of the valley, separated from his house by a river.

The deacon had a horse with a grey mane, which he was always in the habit of riding, and which he called Faxi.

A short time before Christmas, the deacon rode to the farm at which his betrothed lived, and invited her to join in the Christmas festivities at Myrká, promising to fetch her on Christmas Eve. Some time before he went out on this ride, there had been heavy snow and frost; but this very day there came so rapid a thaw, that the river over which the deacon had safely ridden, trusting the firmness of the ice, became impassable during the short time he spent with his betrothed; the floods rose, and huge masses of drift-ice were whirled down the stream.

When the deacon had left the farm, he rode onto the river, and being deep in thought did not perceive at first the change that had taken place. As soon, however, as he saw in what state the stream was, he rode up the banks until he came to a bridge of ice, onto which he spurred his horse. But when he arrived at the middle of the bridge, it broke beneath him, and he was drowned in the flood.

Next morning, a neighbouring farmer saw the deacon's horse grazing in a field, but could discover nothing of its owner, whom he had seen the day before cross the river, but not return. He at once suspected what had occurred, and going down to the river, found the corpse of the deacon, which had drifted to the bank, with all the flesh torn off the back of his head, and the bare white skull visible. So he brought the body back to Myrká, where it was buried a week before Christmas.

Up to Christmas Eve the river continued so swollen, that no communication could take place between the dwellers on the opposite banks, but that morning it subsided, and Guðrún, utterly ignorant of the deacon's death, looked forward with joy to the festivities to which she had been invited by him.

In the afternoon Guðrún began to dress in her best clothes, but before she had quite finished, she heard a knock at the door of the farm. One of the maids opened the door, but seeing nobody there, thought it was because the night was not sufficiently light, for the moon was hidden for the time by clouds. So saying, "Wait there till I bring a light," went back into the house; but she had no sooner shut the outer door behind her, than the knock was repeated, and Guðrún cried out from her room, "It is someone waiting for me."

As she had by this time finished dressing, she slipped only one sleeve of her winter cloak on, and threw the rest over her shoulders hurriedly. When she opened the door, she saw the well-known Faxi standing outside, and by him a man whom she knew to be the deacon. Without a word he placed Guðrún on the horse, and mounted in front of her himself and off they rode.

When they came to the river it was frozen over, all except the current in the middle, which the frost had not yet hardened. The horse walked onto the ice and leaped over the black and rapid stream which flowed in the middle. At the same moment the head of the deacon nodded forward, so that his hat fell over his eyes, and Guðrún saw the large patch of bare skull gleam white in the midst of his hair. Directly afterwards, a cloud moved from before the moon, and the deacon said:

> The moon glides,
> Death rides,
> Seest thou not the white place
> In the back of my head,
> Garún, Garún?

Not a word more was spoken till they came to Myrká, where they dismounted. Then the man said:

Wait here for me, Garún, Garún,
While I am taking Faxi, Faxi,
Outside the hedges, the hedges.

When he had gone, Guðrún saw near her in the churchyard, where she was standing, an open grave, and half sick with horror, ran to the church porch, and seizing the rope, tolled the bells with all her strength. But as she began to ring them, she felt someone grasp her and pull so fiercely at her cloak that it was torn off her, leaving only the one sleeve into which she had thrust her arm before starting from home. Then turning round, she saw the deacon jump headlong into the yawning grave, with the tattered cloak in his hand, and the heaps of earth on both sides fall in over him, and close the grave up to the brink.

The story of "The Deacon of Myrká" has inspired various artists due to its chilling nature. Ásgrímur Jónsson is among those who created images based on this tale. This 1952 illustration depicts the deacon riding with Guðrún on their way to the graveyard.

GHOSTS, TROLLS AND THE HIDDEN PEOPLE

Guðrún knew now that this had been the deacon's ghost, and continued ringing the bells till she roused all the farmworkers at Myrká.

That same night, after Guðrún had got shelter at Myrká and was in bed, the deacon came again from his grave and endeavoured to drag her away, so that no one could sleep from the noise of their struggle.

This was repeated every night for a fortnight, and Guðrún could never be left alone for a single instant, lest the ghostly deacon should get the better of her. From time to time, also, a neighbouring priest came and sat on the edge of the bed, reading the Psalms of David to protect her against this ghostly persecution.

But nothing availed, till they sent for a man from the north country, skilled in witchcraft, who dug up a large stone from the field, and placed it in the middle of the guestroom at Myrká. When the deacon rose that night from his grave and came into the house to torment Guðrún, this man seized him and by uttering potent spells over him forced him beneath the stone and exorcised the passionate demon that possessed him, so there he lies in peace to this day.

Told by Sigurður Guðmundsson and Ingibjörg Þorvaldsdóttir to Jón Árnason, translated by Eiríkur Magnússon and George E. J. Powell

—————»» ««———

The story of the Deacon of Myrká is one of the most famous ghost stories in Iceland.[20] It is interesting to note that the deacon cannot say Guðrún's name as a ghost, because it is too closely connected to Christianity, *Guð* meaning God. He therefore calls her Garún instead. It is also common for Icelandic ghosts to speak in verse, as can be seen here, as well as in the previous story "The Darkness Is Delightful" and "Mother Mine in the Pen, Pen".

Miklabæjar-Solveig

A young woman named Solveig lived at the Reverend Oddur Gíslason's farmstead at Miklibær [he served as a priest there from 1767 to 1786]. Whether the priest had been between wives or had recently lost his wife is not known, but it is certain that this young woman had feelings for the priest and wanted more than anything for him to marry her. The priest, however, did not want to. The young woman became disturbed and was determined to kill herself if she should have the chance. A woman named Guðlaug Björnsdóttir, the sister of Reverend Snorri at Húsafell, slept with her at night to prevent her from leaving the farmstead, and during the daytime everybody at the farm paid close attention to her.

One evening at twilight, Solveig was able to leave and charged towards some ruins that were on the field. The priest had a worker named Þorsteinn who was energetic and reckless. He noticed Solveig running from the farm and followed her, but she had such nimble hands that she had already severed her neck on the ruins when he arrived. It is then said that when Þorsteinn saw how the blood flowed endlessly from her neck, he let out the words: "There the Devil received her." Solveig did not reply to this, but he understood from what she did say to tell the priest to bury her in the churchyard. After that she bled to death. Þorsteinn came home with the news and passed on her greeting to the priest, along with her prayer to be buried in the churchyard. The priest asked for permission from his superiors, but this was rejected on the grounds that she had taken her own life. While this was happening, Solveig's corpse was kept at the farmstead, and the night after he had received the rejection the priest dreamed that Solveig came to him and said: "If you don't want to grant me a resting place in consecrated ground, then you will not benefit from one either." There was great anger on her face as she stormed out. Solveig's corpse was subsequently buried outside the churchyard and without a ceremony. Shortly after this, it started to happen that she haunted the Reverend Oddur when he was travelling alone, whether he rode to the "annexe" church at Silfrúnarstaðir or somewhere else. This soon became well known, and so every man let it become his duty to accompany him home, especially if he was travelling late or alone.

Once the Reverend Oddur rode to the annexe church, while some say he rode to Víðivellir, and as the day went by he still had not returned. The people at Miklibær were not worried about him, as they knew that the priest was generally accompanied if he was travelling late. This time, it was the case that the priest was accompanied only to a field on Miklibær's land. Usually, those who accompanied him did not leave him until he had joined the people at the farm. This time, he had told the person who accompanied him that they did not need to travel any further because he would now get home safely. According to the person who accompanied him, it was there that they parted ways. That evening as the inhabitants of the farm stayed awake, they heard something approach the door, but because they thought it to be a pretty strange knock they did not answer. They then heard somebody come up to the living room with great speed, but before the person who had come up had the chance to say "God be here", they were dragged back down, as if taken from behind or by their feet, and people even thought that they heard a noise when this happened. When people went outside for the last time that evening, they saw that the priest's horse stood in the farmyard and his whip and mittens were under the cushion of the saddle. People became very uneasy after all of this, as they saw that the priest had come home but had now completely disappeared. They then went looking for him and asked after him at all the farms he was thought likely to have come by, and that was how they found out that he had been accompanied to the boundary of the field that evening but had not wanted to be accompanied further. After that, a group was formed and a search carried out for many days. But it yielded no results.

The search was later called off, and most thought it certain that Solveig had kept true to her word and seen to it that he would not be put to rest in a churchyard, and that she had taken him to her burial site, although it was never searched.

Once all the searches were over, the priest's worker Þorsteinn resolved that he wouldn't stop until he knew what had happened to his master. Þorsteinn slept in a bed that was across from the woman who had slept with Solveig. She was both sharp and had second sight. Þorsteinn got himself ready one evening, collected clothes and other things that had been in the priest's possession, lay them under his head and intended to see whether he dreamed of him. He asked Guðlaug to stay awake in her bed that night, but not to wake him if he should act up in his sleep, and rather to take note of what unfolded before her. With that, he let a light burn by his bed. Then both settled down, and Guðlaug noticed that Þorsteinn was completely unable to sleep for the first part of the night, but it then came to pass that sleep overcame him. She then saw that slightly later, Solveig came and held something in her hand that she could not identify clearly. She walked in across the floor to a plank in front of Þorsteinn's bed, as the living room was built on a base of earth with wooden structures surrounding the beds, and crouched over him. She saw that she positioned her hands on Þorsteinn's neck, as if she wanted to get at his windpipe. At that moment, Þorsteinn started to act up in his sleep, thrashing around in his bed with great intensity. She felt that this should not be allowed to continue and went to wake Þorsteinn. Solveig's ghost retreated, unable to withstand making eye contact with her. Guðlaug saw that a red streak was on Þorsteinn's throat where Solveig had aimed to cut him. She then asked Þorsteinn what he had dreamed. He said that it was as if Solveig had come to him and said that this would not suffice, and that he would never know what had happened to the Reverend Oddur. With that, she had laid her hands on him and intended to cut his throat with a large knife, and he could still feel the pain when he woke up. After this, Þorsteinn abandoned his plans to investigate what had become of the priest.

Solveig has attracted little attention since then. However, the Reverend Gísli, who was last a priest at Reynistaðarklaustur (1829–51) and was the son of the Reverend Oddur, has said that the first night that he slept with his wife, Solveig had haunted him so greatly that he had needed to put all his energy into defending himself against her, and he was a strongly built man like his father had been. Other stories about Solveig have not been told.

Told by Guðríður Magnúsdóttir and Sigurður Guðmundsson to Jón Árnason, translated by Alice Bower

⟶≫≻ ≺≪⟵

A key part of this story centres around Miklabæjar-Solveig's desire to be buried within the graveyard. According to the Grágás, one of the oldest law collections in Iceland, preserved in a manuscript from the thirteenth century, it was forbidden to bury those who were unbaptized, those who had taken their own lives or criminals in a graveyard.[21] Even in the nineteenth century, it remained forbidden by law to bury in graveyards those who had taken their own lives or criminals who had received the death penalty. The families of these deceased would often bury their relative directly outside the graveyard walls in the hope that when the site was expanded, their loved one would be included in the sacred ground.[22]

Although the storyteller notes at the end of the story that there is nothing more to tell of Miklabæjar-Solveig, her story gains a surprising continuation. Apparently, people in the area were quite sure that they knew where Solveig had been buried after her death, and in 1910, when the local graveyard was expanded, the place that was considered her final resting place ended up being inside the churchyard. In 1914, when a few men were digging a new grave in that same yard, they found an unusual small chest. When they examined it closer, it broke apart, and inside were bones and some pieces of clothing. The men believed this to be Solveig but decided to do nothing but push the bones to the side, and then the person for whom the grave was intended was buried as planned. After that, there was no more news of Miklabæjar-Solveig until the spiritualist movement was established in Iceland. As elsewhere, spiritualism was on the rise in Iceland in the early twentieth century. The Sálarrannsóknarfélagið (Society for the Research of the Soul) movement was founded in the winter of 1918 after the Spanish flu had hit the country, leading to the sudden deaths of around five hundred people. In the spring of 1937, Solveig apparently appeared to a group of mediums and once again asked to be properly buried in holy ground, now in a different graveyard and with a marked grave. That same year, on Sunday, 11 July, people in the north of Iceland gathered to watch as her bones were moved to the graveyard at Glaumbær, where it is now possible to visit her grave.[23]

Pjakkur

The ghost Pjakkur emerged according to the tale we shall now recount:

A man by the name of Ásgeir lived at Rauðamýri, on the coast of Langidalur, in days of old. His wife was named Guðrún. They were a prosperous couple. One cold winter's day in a raging blizzard, a destitute traveller arrived at their farm, a poor lad in wretched condition who sought lodging. Ásgeir hesitated for a while because his wife was reluctant to grant the boy accommodation, and, driven by her urging, Ásgeir turned him away. The boy threatened to get revenge on them if he should die because of this, a fate he firmly anticipated. The lad then left in a sullen mood, and it goes without saying that he died from exposure to the cold weather.

After his death, it was noticed by some that he followed Ásgeir and his kin. The ghost was named Pjakkur, after the sound that was heard wherever he was seen. The sound came from the ghost thrusting his spiky staff into the ground and at times creating a creak when the ground was frozen.

Pjakkur is described as wearing a black woollen sweater with an old woollen hat. Ásgeir was haunted by Pjakkur his entire life, and so were his descendants as the ghost followed all of his kin. It is said that those with clairvoyance often saw Pjakkur, sometimes in broad daylight and even more so after dark.

Told by an unknown storyteller to Guðmundur Gísli Sigurðsson, translated by Dagrún Ósk Jónsdóttir

⟶≫ ≪⟵

As has been noted, in Icelandic farming society, hospitality was one of the most cherished virtues, a tradition that is evident in various historical accounts as well as folk legends. It was important as it offered protection from the unpredictable and harsh weather conditions, which could strike suddenly, and because of widespread poverty. The emphasis on being a good host was an integral part of the safety net that surrounded the common people in Iceland, for people never knew when they themselves might be in need of hospitality and shelter.

Mother Mine in the Pen, Pen

There was once a woman who worked on a farm. She had become pregnant, given birth to a child and killed it by exposure, which was not all that uncommon in Iceland at a time when having children outside of marriage could lead to harsh penalties set by the Church, fines and executions. Some time after that, a type of festive gathering that was popular in the past called *vikivaki* was to be held, and this young woman was invited. But as she was not rich enough to own the highly decorated clothes that would be appropriate for the kinds of affairs that *vikivaki* were in those days, yet was fond of such finery, it made her very upset that she should have to stay home and miss out on the festivities. Once at milking time, before the festivities, this working woman was milking a ewe in the pen with another woman. She was complaining to the other woman that she needed clothes to wear to the *vikivaki*, but just as the words escaped her mouth, they heard this verse from underneath the walls of the pen:

My mother in the pen, pen
Do not worry, worry
I will lend you my rags
To dance in,
To dance in.

The working woman who had exposed her infant seemed to know that this message was for her, as she responded to the verse by losing her mind, and stayed this way for the rest of her life.

Told by Sigurður Guðmundsson to Jón Árnason,
translated by Alice Bower

When Icelanders converted to Christianity in the year 1000, three exceptions were made: they could still eat horse meat, they could still worship the heathen gods in secrecy and they could still expose newborn children as the old laws had allowed.[24] However, the exposure of children soon became illegal. When Icelanders became Lutheran around 1550, a new set of laws made all forms of relations between unmarried people, as well as those considered incestuous, along with the birth of children from such relationships, illegal and punishable by law – something that resulted in some people deciding to leave their newborn children outside to die of exposure in the hope of escaping punishment.[25]

The importance of Christianity is a strong feature in many Icelandic legends concerning the *útburður*, like those from the other Nordic countries; however, it appears in a slightly different manner. In the Nordic countries the stories often focus on the child's wish for a name and christening (something especially common in eastern Sweden and Finland), which would offer a means of salvation.[26] While this also occurs in Icelandic legends, it is not as common. Here, the relations to Christianity can be seen more clearly through the way in which the women are punished for their crimes.

Stories of *útburðir* often tell of how the ghost of a child comes back to haunt their mother. It is interesting that the fathers of these children are rarely mentioned, as is the case in the changeling stories discussed earlier. It is not hard to imagine that these stories were intended as warnings to women not to expose their children, or rather to avoid becoming pregnant out of wedlock.[27] In many *útburðir* legends, the woman's punishment tends to be intangible. They are either chastised by the ghost of the child or made to suffer mentally or emotionally: they sometimes lose the ability to see the sun (as is the case in the next legend, "Did Not See the Sun") or lose their sight altogether. In Iceland legends of *útburðir* tend to deal with women of the lower classes, giving a powerful image of Icelandic reality from the seventeenth century to the beginning of the twentieth. As the Icelandic historian Már Jónsson notes about the legal cases dealing with exposed infants:

Descriptions of *útburðir* vary greatly. In this 2020 illustration by artist Sunneva Guðrún Þórðardóttir, a young mother is depicted being attacked by the ghost of her child in an act of revenge.

There is no question that when Icelandic cases dealing with the exposure of infants are examined as a whole, one can see poverty, oppression and need lying behind them. Almost all of the women who had children who were left out to die of exposure were young workers who owned little or nothing.[28]

The previous legend, "Mother Mine in the Pen, Pen", is still well known today and can be found in four variants in the Icelandic folk tale collections. In all of these the ghost of the exposed child seeks revenge on its mother and punishes her, not only for its murder but for worrying about something as superficial as clothes and dances, both of which were viewed as sinful by the Church.

Did Not See the Sun

In the east, in the olden days, a married couple lived in a remote valley in great comfort. They had one daughter, their only child. It is not known what her name was, but she was cheerful and playful and everyone's sweetheart. Once, people suspected that she was carrying a child, but since nothing came of it, that talk ended. But they observed that, since then, she had been very quiet and absent-minded. This was at the time when to have a child out of wedlock was punishable by death. Sometime later, the girl was given to a kind man on the advice of her parents, and their marriage was excellent.

One day, during haymaking, her husband was beating a scythe in the smithy. They had then been together for thirteen years. He asked her to give him a drink, and she did. But as she went out the door, he heard her pray earnestly and saw her throw out her hands to the sky. He was startled and put down the scythe, followed her and gently asked her to tell him what had happened. He promised not to blame her for anything, no matter what. Then she said, "I now see that God has forgiven me, so I would be happy to tell you about my error. Fourteen years ago, I became pregnant, but because such a thing was punishable by death, I killed the baby. There was a ridge above the farm, and a river ran by it. There I drowned it. The sunshine was hot when I birthed it at the foot of the ridge, and in my anguish I cursed the sun, and it disappeared from my sight. I have never seen it since, until today, and I praised God with a loud voice, as you heard, for I saw that he has forgiven me." That is how she ended her story, and their marriage was none the worse for the telling of this tale.

Told by Sigríður Pétursdóttir to Torfhildur Hólm,
translated by Sigurður Líndal

--->>>- -<<<--

Christianity plays an important role here. As mentioned earlier, *útburðir* legends tend to tell of lower-class women who could not get married. In those legends where the woman is eventually forgiven, as in the one told here, she tends to be of a higher class. Today, when thinking of the women's punishment whereby the sun disappears from their sight and endless darkness and unhappiness follow, one cannot help but interpret it as a metaphor for depression and regret.[29]

The Story of Ábæjar or Nýjabæjarskotta

A farmer called Ólafur lived at Tinnársel, in Austurdalur in
Skagafjörður. He was thought to possess magical knowledge.
He was once travelling in Svartárdalur, in the Húnavatnssýsla
district, and came to Bergsstaðir at night. As he rode past the
churchyard, he took a look in and saw a man wrestling with a newly
risen ghost, which had just overpowered him. Ólafur then called
to the man, "Bite at her left breast, damn it." Ólafur rode off on
his way, and it is said that the man made use of this advice and that
it had sufficed, but the man became full of jealous hatred towards
Ólafur for having known better. It is said that he prepared the ghost
for a journey and sent it to Ólafur, but Ólafur was ready with his
magical knowledge and contained the ghost inside a horse's leg
bone, which he put inside a compartment within a chest. He kept
it there for as long as he lived, and right before his death he asked
his daughter Guðbjörg to burn the leg after his passing, but to
avoid taking the stopper out.

After the man's death, Guðbjörg took the horse's leg out of
the chest. Out of curiosity, she removed the stopper. A fly flew
out and instantly took the form of a woman, who asked what task
she should carry out. "Go to Nýibær", said Guðbjörg, "and kill the
farmer Guðmundur Nikulásson." Guðbjörg's husband Jón wanted
to get Guðmundur off the farm so that he could move there.

The ghost went straight to Nýibær and came across the farmer
Guðmundur, but he was able to defend himself against the ghost.
That spring, he moved away to Krákugerði, as Skotta's [the ghost]
haunting had nearly driven him crazy over the winter. Jón and
Guðbjörg then moved to Nýibær, and the ghost has followed them
and their descendants ever since, and is known as Skotta from either
Ábær or Nýibær.

Told by unknown storytellers in Skagafjörður to Jón Borgfirðingur Jónsson, translated by Alice Bower

---»»» «««---

Uppvakningar are ghosts that have been woken up by a sorcerer, often one who is seeking revenge. Skotta is the name of a female family ghost and Móri of a male; both get their names from the way in which they dress. Like many other countries, Iceland went through a period of witch trials; the key difference in Iceland from what happened in most of the neighbouring countries is that here it was mostly men who were accused of witchcraft and burned alive. In Iceland twenty men in total died in this fashion while only one woman suffered the same fate. The first person to be burned at the stake for sorcery was Jón Rögnvaldsson (d. 1625), who was charged with having raised a ghost and sent it to harm his enemy.[30] The Icelandic legends reflect this gender difference by showing that men are the ones who control magic, while very few legends tell of witches, unlike in neighbouring countries. The story of Ábæjar or Nýjabæjarskotta continues in the collection of Jón Árnason, noting that people believed that the ghost killed Jón and proceeded to haunt and terrorize the family, among other things by killing farm animals. According to the story, Jón and Guðbjörg had a daughter named Guðrún, who was also said to have been haunted by the ghost and was eventually driven mad by it.

The Sorcerers in the Westman Islands

During the time when that dread pest, called the Black Death, raged through Iceland, eighteen sorcerers banded together, and went out to the Westman Islands, in order to escape, as long as possible, the scourge. When, after a while, by means of their magic arts, they discovered that the plague was abating its fury, they were curious to know how many people were left alive in the country.

So they agreed to send one of their company to land, that he might find how matters stood, and make his report to the others. They chose for this errand a man who was neither first nor last in the knowledge of their arts; and when they put him ashore they told him that if he did not return to them by Christmas Day next, they would dispatch a *Sending* [ghost] to him who would kill him.

Far and wide wandered the man, north, south, and east, without finding a single living soul. All the dwellings stood wide open, and from floor to roof, even on threshold and on hill, lay the dead. At last he came to a house which was shut up, and through his wonder at this half hoped to find there still some signs of human life. He knocked loudly at the door, which was instantly opened, and there came out a young and beautiful damsel, who, half-wild with joy to see again a living man, answered his salutation by falling on his neck, and embracing him; telling him at the same time with many tears that she had thought herself the only living creature in the whole land.

She begged him to stay with her some time, which he consented to do, and they went into the house and held a vast deal of talk together. She asked him whence he came, and what was the object of his journey. He told her all about the company of sorcerers, their desire to know how many people were left alive in the land, and their strict command to him to be back in the Westman Islands before next Christmas Day. But she begged for his company as long as he could possibly afford it her; and he, pitying her loneliness, agreed to stay with her some time. The girl told him that within many and many a mile not one soul was left alive; for she had made a week's journey from home in all directions, hoping to find someone still living, but quite in vain.

So the man abode there, and Christmas Day drew nearer and nearer, until, at last, he felt bound to tell the girl that he must leave her now, or suffer the punishment of death for his disobedience to the commands of the other sorcerers. But the girl would not hear of his going so soon, and coaxed him to stay yet a little longer, saying that surely his companions were not such unmerciful and heartless folks as to kill him for so slight a fault as staying with a poor lonely woman. By these words she quite overcame his determination to leave her till Christmas Eve came round. Then, said he, he truly must leave her as he valued his life. At first she tried to persuade him to stay with her by caresses and prayers; but finding him deaf to them, she changed her tone, and said, "Well, my good man, since you *will* go, go! And reach the Westman Islands by Christmas Day if you can. I wish you luck in your journey, and somewhat more than common speed!" Then the man suddenly bethought himself that more than common speed must indeed be his, if he would make the journey in time; and so, knowing that it was totally useless for him to start now for the Westman Islands, resolved to stay and await his death where he was. He passed the night in a sad state of mind; but the maiden, on the contrary, was as lively as lively could be, and asked him if he could now see what was going on among his companions. He said they had just rowed the *Sending* ashore from the islands. So she sat on the foot of the bed, which was near the door, and he lay behind her. After a while, he told her that he felt a strange heaviness come over him, which he knew to be owing to the magic arts of the sorcerers. Having told her this, he fell into a deep sleep.

By and by, the girl, who still sat at the bed's foot, woke him, and asked him if he knew now where the *Sending* was, or his way.

He said, "Within the bounds of the farm," and fell back again into a sleep so deep, that, shake him as she would, she could not rouse him from it.

When she had sat there a little while longer, she saw a brownish vapour enter the house through the open door. It glided softly towards her, and standing still before her, took the figure of a man. "Well," said the girl, "what do you want here?"

The *Sending* said to her, "I am sent hither by the sorcerers of the Westman Islands to slay this man, who has broken his word to them – as one who knows not what truth is. Move, therefore, from the bed, for while you sit there I cannot reach him."

"All in good time," replied she. "But, first of all, you must do me some services."

The *Sending* asked what service she would of it.

"Make yourself, for instance," she answered, "as large as you can."

This, it said, it would assuredly do, willingly enough.

Accordingly it made itself so large that it quite filled the house.

"That will do," said the girl. "Now, for instance, make yourself as small as you can."

So the *Sending* shrank down and down, till from a monstrous giant it became the smallest fly you ever saw.

"Aha," said she, and stuck it forthwith into an empty marrow-bone, which she had in her pocket, and corked it in.

Then putting the bone back in her pocket, she woke the man. He started up, wondering that he was still alive, and she asked him where the *Sending* was.

"I know not," said he; and she answered, "I thought your companions were no such great sorcerers as you made them out to be. Trouble yourself no more about them; they will not slay you just yet; but let us spend Christmas Day in mirth and joy." So they spent Christmas Day in such revel as befitted the time and a late escape from death, and laughed and sang, till the rafters had not heard the like of it for many a long year.

Now, as New Year's Day drew nigh, the man fell again into his old sadness, and became so gloomy that the girl noticed his strange manner and asked him what ailed him.

He answered, "The sorcerers on the Westman Islands are now preparing another *Sending*, and when that shall come here, it will be no easy task for me to escape from it."

"Oh," said the girl, "just wait till I have tried its strength, and then it will be time enough to be afraid of it. Meanwhile don't trouble your head about either your friends on the island or their threats."

And since the maiden was so light-hearted, he thought that surely he would be but a coward to be dull and sad, and accordingly put the brightest face he could upon the matter.

On New Year's Eve he spoke to the girl and said, "Now the *Sending* has been put ashore; and, gifted as it is with all the wrath of the sorcerers, it comes apace."

She begged him to come with her, and led him across the country till they came to a place where the grass was high and the shrubs were thick. In the midst of this, the girl stooped down, and removing a low mound of earth and grass which stood at her feet, came to a large slab of stone, which she lifted, and, by doing so, disclosed a passage, leading far below ground. They entered the passage, and after walking for a long time in darkness, greater than that of the blackest night, they came to a cavern, which was dimly lighted with some fat, burning in a human skull. Near this light, in a mean and wretched bed, lay an old man of the most horrible aspect. His eyes were red as blood, and his mouth reached from ear to ear; and as for his nose, no words can tell its length and colour. So frightful was he, that the sorcerer quaked at the very idea of going near him.

"Oho!" said this old fellow, "strange news you have to tell me, no doubt, foster-daughter. It is long enough since I saw you last. What can I do for you?"

The girl told him all about the sorcerer, and his friends in the Westman Islands, and how they had dispatched a *Sending* to slay him, and in what way she had treated the same. Upon which the old man waxed quite lively, and asked to see the marrow-bone. So she immediately took it out of her pocket and gave it to him.

As soon as he saw it, he waxed even livelier than before, and became at last so very brisk, that he was really quite another man. Taking the bone in his hand, with every appearance of pleasure, he turned it about and patted it and rubbed it all over.

While he was mumbling over the bone, the girl noticed the islander growing sleepier and sleepier, and, at length, said to the old man, "If you will aid me at all, aid me now, for I know full well that the *Sending* is near at hand."

Without more ado, therefore, the old fellow took the cork out of the bone, and out crept the fly, whom he patted and stroked, and to whom he said, "Go now. Receive all the *Sendings* from the sorcerers on the Westman Islands, and swallow them."

Immediately, with a loud roar like thunder, the fly flew from the cavern; and when it came to the upper world, behold! It became so large, that one jaw reached up to the heavens, and the other touched the earth; and when not only one *Sending*, but two or three came, it swallowed them all down; and so the islander was saved from the malice of his companions.

After thanking the old man for his timely help, the girl and the Westman islander returned to the farm, where, as the story goes, they became man and wife, lived to a good old age, and increased and multiplied. Thus was the land repopulated. As for the other sorcerers, mighty little more was ever heard about them; just enough indeed to amount to nothing.

Told by an unknown storyteller to Magnús Grímsson, translated by Eiríkur Magnússon and George E. J. Powell

⟶≫ ≪⟵

The story of the sorcerers in the Westman Islands is set during the pandemic of the Black Death. It is believed that this plague arrived in Iceland in the spring of 1402. It is not known exactly how many Icelanders lost their lives as a result of the disease, but some scholars have suggested that it was one-third or up to half of the population. Various legends tell of Icelanders' fight with the plague, which is often personified, for example in the form of a mist or smoke.[31] However, in this story the enemy is a ghost sent by sorcerers, called a *Sending* (literally, a Being Sent). The ghost appears as a fly, something that is common in Icelandic legends, and is then trapped in a hollow bone.[32]

The White Cap

A certain boy and girl, whose names this tale telleth not, once lived near a church. The boy being mischievously inclined, was in the habit of trying to frighten the girl in a variety of ways, till she became at last so accustomed to his tricks, that she ceased to care for anything whatever, putting down everything strange that she saw or heard to the boy's mischief.

One washing-day, the girl was sent by her mother to fetch home the linen, which had been spread to dry in the churchyard. When she had nearly filled her basket, she happened to look up, and saw sitting on a tomb near her a figure dressed in white from head to foot, but was not the least alarmed, believing it to be the boy playing her, as usual, a trick. So she ran up to it, and pulling its cap off said, "You shall not frighten me, *this* time." Then when she had finished collecting the linen she went home; but, to her astonishment – for he could not have reached home before her without her seeing him – the boy was the first person who greeted her on her arrival at the cottage.

Among the linen, too, when it was sorted, was found a mouldy white cap, which appeared to be nobody's property, and which was half full of earth.

The next morning the ghost (for it was a ghost that the girl had seen) was found sitting with no cap upon its head, upon the same tombstone as the evening before; and as nobody had the courage to address it, or knew in the least how to get rid of it, they sent into the neighbouring village for advice.

An old man declared that the only way to avoid some general calamity, was for the little girl to replace on the ghost's head the cap she had seized from it, in the presence of many people, all of whom were to be perfectly silent. So a crowd collected in the churchyard, and the little girl, going forward, half afraid, with the cap, placed it upon the ghost's head, saying, "Are you satisfied now?"

But the ghost, raising its hand, gave her a fearful blow, and said, "Yes; but are *you* now satisfied?"

The little girl fell down dead, and at the same instant the ghost sank into the grave upon which it had been sitting, and was no more seen.

Told by an unknown storyteller to Jón Bjarnason,
translated by Eiríkur Magnússon and George E. J. Powell

⟶⟫ ⟪⟵

A Naked Woman Deals with a Ghost

In times of past hardship, many impoverished wanderers traversed the land to survive. Some journeyed through counties, others through entire provinces or even across the breadth of the country, enduring months of nomadic existence. Among these wretches was an old woman named Sólveig. She travelled to the west, but where exactly Sigríður [the narrator] could not remember.

During June, the month of endless daylight, Sólveig arrived at a modest farm. While everyone else was busy with outdoor chores, the housewife allowed her to stay, and led her to the living room. Under the gable was a high platform. There a young woman sat crying profusely.

Sólveig made herself at home, walked over to the young woman, and asked her what was the matter. For a long time, the girl was reluctant to say what was going on, thinking that Sólveig would not be able to remedy her sorrow. Eventually, she told her that a young man from the area had become besotted with her, but when she turned him down, he had threatened to haunt her when he was dead. Now he had killed himself, and according to his oath, she could expect him that very night.

Troubled by the girl's plight, Sólveig volunteered to spend the night in the room with her. Despite initial protests, the girl eventually agreed, and Sólveig stayed with her during the night. But before she did, she borrowed a redwood-handled shaving knife from the farmer, as ghosts cannot stand the presence of red mahogany. She stuck this knife over the living room door and went to bed at the same time as other people, but took off all her clothes because it is believed that ghosts are afraid of nudity.

As the night progressed, the ghost appeared, rather ugly-looking. Sólveig was not alarmed but jumped up, seized the knife and pointed it at the ghost, which was already retreating. They continued in this manner two farms' distance, to the vicarage. There they came to the ghost's open grave, outside the church. Sólveig thrust the knife into the ghost as it plunged into the grave, never to be seen again.

Returning home, Sólveig found that her courage had waned, yet she suffered no ill effects despite her naked journey, the mildness of the night likely sparing her from catching a chill. The story was told to our storyteller by an older woman, who had seen this Sólveig herself.

Told by Sigríður Jónsdóttir to Torfhildur Hólm,
translated by Sigurður Líndal

⟶⟫—⟪⟵

This story is a variation of a legend type in which men who have been turned down by women return as ghosts to seek revenge on them and assault them while they sleep (as is the case in the story "The Son of the Ghost", which can be found in the next chapter). This variant is unique in the sense that the ghost does not manage to fulfil its intentions, as the young woman is saved by the older one, while in all other versions the girl becomes pregnant with the son of the ghost.

4

The Church

The settlers who first came to Iceland were of various religions. Many of them were pagan and worshipped old Norse gods or goddesses, but as Terry Gunnell identifies, old Norse religious beliefs and practices varied by time and place, largely in accordance with the social practices and environments of the people, as well as their class and social status, and their contact with people outside the immediate Nordic area.[1] Other settlers were Christian, and some did not believe in any god. In the years after the settlement, several attempts were made to spread Christianity within the country, but this was met with mixed results as the Norse religion was relatively well established. Around the year 1000, the Icelandic people officially accepted Christianity, with the condition that pagan practices could continue privately, something that allowed the coexistence of old and new beliefs and a gradual transition. The main decision was made at the Icelandic parliament, Alþingi, by the law speaker at the time, Þorgeir Ljósvetningagoði, who declared that Iceland should officially adopt Christianity as the country's religion.[2]

In the middle of the sixteenth century, Icelanders became Lutheran. At the time, Iceland was still ruled by Denmark and the religious reform was formally imposed by the Danish king, although Luther's influence had already reached Iceland via German fishermen.[3] The Reformation was met with some resistance, which ended with the execution of Jón Arason, the Catholic bishop of Hólar, and his two sons in 1550.

According to a legend in Jón Árnason's collection,[4] a church bell at Hólar started ringing without being touched when Jón's body was brought back to Hólar after his execution, ringing three times before it broke. Since Jón had been very popular and well liked in his diocese, this legend suggested that even inanimate objects in the north of Iceland objected to his death.

At first glance, it might seem as though Christianity and folk belief were two completely different things, but this is not the case. The Christian faith was deeply integrated into Icelandic society and culture, and it is clear that folk beliefs and superstitions coexisted with Christian practices. Conflicts between the old paganism and Christianity are nonetheless a common theme of Icelandic legends. Evil supernatural beings such as ghosts, trolls and outlaws were often said to be heathen or unchristian, and Christianity was often thought the best protection against them. The hidden people, on the other hand, were believed to

Ásgrímur Jónsson grew up hearing stories of the hidden people living in the rocks near his home. This 1905 watercolour depicts the church of the hidden people and provides a glimpse into how he imagined the homes and churches of the elves.

be Christian and to have their own churches and masses, something that reflects how similar they are to humans. In Jón Árnason's collection, the hidden people are also seen as having a Christian origin in a legend called "Huldumanna Genesis" (The Genesis of the Hidden People), which tells of God visiting Adam and Eve and meeting their children. In the story, Eve has not managed to clean all her children, so she hides those who are still dirty. God is aware of this and announces that what is hidden from him will not be seen by others, and so turns the dirty children into the hidden people.[5] Similar stories can be found in other places of the world (see ATU 758, "The Various Children of Eve", where this is used to explain class division). Similar legends about the hidden people's relationship to either Adam or Eve also appear in other Icelandic collections. Although the hidden people are said to be Christian, some legends nonetheless say that they had difficulty taking part in Mass in a human church. All in all, Icelandic legends are deeply affected by Christian ideas, something that is not strange considering the omnipresence of religion and the Church in Icelandic society of the past.

In the early nineteenth century, the Church was still the centre of both culture and education in Iceland. The clergy held an important position within Icelandic society, and religious practices played a major part in people's everyday lives. As the theologian Hjalti Hugason points out, the religious life of Icelanders in the early nineteenth century can be divided into two categories: people's official religious life and their private one.[6] The former refers to those practices that took place in church. At the beginning of the nineteenth century, most Icelanders would visit church every Sunday for Mass and ceremonies such as baptisms, confirmations, weddings and funerals. Going to church was important, and many churches were built all over the country to make them more accessible to the people. Nevertheless, many still had to travel quite a distance to attend Mass. As with houses, many of the churches were made of turf and stone. As Jónas Jónasson notes, they were often small and without riches: "In general, churches could hardly be distinguished from the best sheds, if it was not for the fact that bells hung in the front of the building and the cemetery surrounded them."[7] It was not until the nineteenth century, when other building materials became more common, that people started building churches from wood.

At the time, services would not be cancelled if the weather was poor, despite the distances people had to travel.[8] As a woman born in 1908 notes, going to church was both a religious and a social event:

> People went to church, even if it meant walking quite a distance. Church outings were, for many years, journeys that people did not want to miss, because in addition to listening to the priest, coffee was often available afterwards. Both the young and the old gathered there for enjoyment, and many news and updates were shared among acquaintances during these church outings.[9]

However, not everyone was allowed to leave the farm at the same time to go to church, especially during the winter. Someone had to stay at home and look after the farm, the children and the animals. This was usually a task for women, housewives or housemaids.[10] Many Icelandic folk legends tell of the risks faced by the person who stayed behind to take care of things at the farm while the others went to church, as can be seen in some of the earlier legends.

Priests had various roles in society: they were religious leaders, were responsible for primary education and often had political influence, holding positions of local authority. They were responsible for gathering information and making assessments of their congregations, their finances, status and medical condition.[11] Many of them were the sons of priests, meaning that the office often stayed within the same family for generations (34 per cent between 1850 and 1900).[12] Not everyone was happy with them, and they could be controversial figures. Those vagabonds who travelled the country in the nineteenth century would

Many Icelandic legends recount conflicts between priests and female trolls, who were considered extremely heathen. This 1949 drawing by Ásgrímur Jónsson illustrates the story of "The Troll of Mjóifjörður", depicting a female troll trying to lure a priest to the gulf of Mjóifjörður.

often perform small satirical sketches in which they would mock the local priest as a figure of power and authority.[13] Despite this, the portrayal of priests in legend collections is mostly positive, but one also needs to bear in mind that many of the stories were collected by the priests themselves.[14] Even though some of the priests in question originally belonged to the same communities as the people they were collecting from, it is important to take into account the power relations involved in their work. As the French philosopher Michel Foucault notes, people often censor themselves when talking to the authorities or someone of a higher standing. Folklorist Gísli Sigurðsson comments that it is likely that people at the time chose carefully which stories to tell the folk tale collectors, and there is also a chance that they changed or censored the legends when telling them.[15]

In the legends, priests are often shown to straddle the border between Christianity and the supernatural. Some stories tell of them having hidden women as mistresses, and they are often also said to be sorcerers, as in other Nordic countries and as will be seen here.[16] Nevertheless, this does not seem to have a negative effect on their portrayal. The Church and priests are presented as figures of authority and safety that offer protection, even from supernatural beings.

People's more private or unofficial religious lives took place outside the church and at home. They would pray, with specific prayers often recited in the contexts of seafaring and travelling, and at meals. Older people on the farms were strongly encouraged to teach the young those Christian values that were approved by authorities. The evening wakes were particularly important in this regard. They were often held on farms in winter evenings and usually ended with *húslestur* (readings), in which the Bible, homilies and sermons would be read out loud. Before the *húslestur* took place, there would often be a quick break while people did their last chores of the day, such as milking the cows before nightfall or cleaning up in the *baðstofa* to bring a certain solemnity to the room. When everything was ready, the reading of the religious texts could begin, and during this part of the wake people would also say prayers and sing verses. Commonly this was done every evening throughout wintertime but only once a week during spring and summer. This was because of the longer daylight hours, which allowed people to work outside for longer periods of time.[17] The purpose of the readings was to both entertain people and educate them about Christian values. While this was important for the home, many still remember being bored by the religious readings as children. Guðbjörg Jónsdóttir (1871–1952) writes in her memoirs:

> I cannot say that all of these readings had a positive impact on me. There are few things so great that habit doesn't diminish its value. Often, I would sit and pay no attention to what was being read, my mind wandering elsewhere. Most things are easier than restraining a little bird that longs to reach out from the darkness, to expand its cramped cage into the

sunlight and life. However, if I knew that I would be questioned about the content of the readings, I would not dare not to pay attention.[18]

Like others, Guðbjörg remembers enjoying the stories, legends and sagas that were told at the evening wakes prior to the religious reading.

As has been mentioned, the Icelandic legends are highly influenced by Christianity, and the messages they convey often align with Christian morality and values. They emphasize the importance of being good to those in need, of being obedient towards both the secular and spiritual authorities, and of practising one's faith. The legends thus played a role in people's religious upbringing, as the historian Þórunn Valdimarsdóttir points out:

> Folk tales serve to enhance religious devotion when the guidance of priests and household readings fall short. They contain images of that frightening world that existed outside Christian society, where the only defence against those creatures lay in true faith, thereby strengthening both the folk belief and the Christian spiritual life of people.[19]

In the latter half of the nineteenth century, church attendance started to decline, and the readings became fewer and fewer, mostly disappearing in the early twentieth century. There are many reasons for this, but chief among them was that a certain change in religious ideas came about as people started moving away from the farms into newly formed towns, and as people got jobs outside the farm. The tradition of everyone gathering at the farm to listen to a reading started to fade and was eventually replaced by radio.

While the common beliefs of people in the nineteenth century were closely linked to official Christian belief, people nonetheless seem to have interpreted Christianity in a way that was somewhat different from what the Church intended. For instance, common belief was

often materialistic, with certain objects being seen as being holy or magical. People also believed in the power of words to protect them from evil and keep away danger. This was based on a belief in a higher power that could be affected by people and their actions.[20] This is understandable, since at the time people were powerless to fight dangerous diseases, hunger or bad weather and would use every tool in their arsenal to try and improve their harsh reality. In these matters, it is safe to say that the line between prayer, sorcery and superstition could become quite blurred.

At the same time, the idea that everyone's destiny was already decided remained strong in the old farming society. This is something that can be seen, for example, in people's strong belief in the meaning of dreams, which is still prevalent today, as evidenced by the following figures from the surveys sent out by Erlendur Haraldsson and Terry Gunnell concerning Icelanders' folk beliefs.[21] Here, we have the

This 1950 drawing by Ásgrímur Jónsson depicts a story in which a young girl must pass through a graveyard after dark. She hears a ghost but escapes thanks to her bravery and quick thinking.

responses of Icelanders to the question of whether they believe dreams can have prophetic qualities, figures that have decreased in recent years but which are still relatively high:

	1974	2006	2007	2023
Impossible	1%	3%	5%	11%
Unlikely	2%	5%	7%	16%
Possible	40%	42%	38%	35%
Likely	31%	26%	26%	22%
Certain	26%	24%	23%	16%

The idea that no one can escape their destiny is also prevalent in many legends, as can be seen, for example, in the previously recounted tale "Jón from the Farm Parthús", in which a man heads into the wilderness even though he has been told that it will lead to his death. This belief offered people a certain serenity, allowing them to believe that whatever difficulties they faced, they had all been something God had intended, and were for the best.

The church as a setting in legends also underlines the Christian values of the time. It is usually a place that offers protection from supernatural beings, but, because of its closeness to the graveyard, it is also a great setting for ghost stories.

The Dance at Hruni

A long time ago there was a priest at Hruni, in the Árnessýsla district, who was very much inclined towards festivities and merriment. It was generally the custom of this priest that when people came to church on Christmas Night, he would not officiate during the first part of the evening, instead holding a large dance in the church with the parishioners, with drinks and games and other improper festivities long into the night. The priest had an old mother called Una. She was very much opposed to this conduct displayed by her son and often criticized him for it. But he did not pay her much heed and continued as he had for many years.

One Christmas Night, the priest was occupied with this dance for a longer time than was usual. His mother, who was both prescient and had second sight, then went to the church and asked her son to stop his games and hold Mass. But the priest said there was still enough time and said: "Just one more circle, mother." His mother then went back in from the church. Three times Una went out to her son and asked him to be cautious of God and to stop before the situation became any worse. But he answered in the same way as he had done before. But as she walked forth on the church floor away from her son for the third time, she heard this verse spoken and took note of it:

> There is noise in Hruni,
> Whole courts rush over there
> So the dance will resound
> That boys may remember it
> Still there is Una
> And still there is Una.

When Una exited the church, she saw a man outside the entrance. She did not know him, but she did not like the look

of him and thought it certain that he had said the verse. She reacted
very badly to all this. It seemed to her that this was a very bad state
of affairs and that this was the Devil himself. She then took her son's
horse and rode in a hurry to the next priest and asked him to come
and try to remedy this trouble, and to free her son from the danger
that he faced. The priest went there with her and was accompanied
by many, as regular church goers remained loyal to him. But when
they came to Hruni, the church and its churchyard had sunk with
the people inside, and they heard howls and yells in the ground
below.

Evidence can still be seen of a building having stood at Hruni,
which is the name of a hill from which the farm takes its name.
But after this happened, the story goes, the church was moved
from Hruni down to its current site, as it is said that there was
never again a dance on Christmas Night in Hruni church.

*Told by an unknown storyteller to Jóhann Kristján Briem
Gunnlaugsson and Jón Norðmann Jónsson, translated by Alice Bower*

While the church is often seen as a place that offers protection, it
can also appear as a threatening place. This becomes clear in legends
based on the motif of a church that sinks into the ground with all the
people at Mass still inside it. Usually this is associated in some way
with the Devil and indicates either that something evil has found its
way into the role of the priest, or that the people in the church are
not behaving in accordance with Christian ideology. In the case here,
people are dancing in the church, something that was frowned upon
by the Icelandic Church in the eighteenth century.[22]

The Son of the Ghost

The farm Bakki (now called Prestbakki, in Hrútafjörður) once stood further north than it does now, and the reasons of its being moved from its ancient to its present position are as follows.

It happened that a certain farmer's son courted the daughter of the priest that lived at Bakki, but met with refusal of his offers, which grieved him so sorely that he fell sick and died, and was buried at the church near the priest's house. This had happened in summer. The winter following, people noticed a certain strangeness in the demeanour of the priest's daughter, for which they could not account.

One evening, it happened that her foster-mother, an old woman and a wise withal, went out to the churchyard with her knitting, as it was warm enough, and the moon had but few clouds to wade through.

Some time before this, her foster-child had told her that since his death her old lover had often been to see her, and that she found herself now with child, whose father had assured her that the infant would prove an ill-fated one; and the unfortunate girl had asked the old woman to try to prevent, from that time forth, her ghostly lover's visits; and it was for this purpose that the good dame had gone out into the churchyard. She went to the grave of the young man, which was yawning wide open, and threw her ball of thread down into it, and having done so, sat down on its edge to knit. There she sat until the ghost came, who at once begged her to take up the ball of thread from the grave, so that he might enter his coffin and take his rest.

But the old woman said, "I have no mind to do so, unless you tell me what you do out of your grave thus at night."

He answered, "I visit the priest's daughter, for he has no means of preventing my doing so. Ere long she will be delivered of a boy."

Then the old woman said, "Tell me this boy's fate."

"His fate," replied the other, "is, that he will be a priest at Bakki, and the church with all its congregation will sink down to hell the first time he pronounces the blessing from the altar, and then my vengeance will be complete, for the injury the priest did me in not allowing me to marry his daughter during my lifetime."

"Your prophecy is, indeed, a great one, if it meets with a fulfilment," answered the old woman; "but are there no means by which so horrible a curse can be prevented?"

The ghost replied, "The only means are for someone to stab the priest the moment he begins to pronounce the blessing; but I do not fancy that anybody will undertake that task."

When she had gathered this information, the old woman said to him, "Go now into your grave, and be sure never again to come out of it."

After this the old woman drew up her ball of thread, and the corpse leaped into the grave, over which the earth closed itself. Then she recited over the grave some magic spells, which bound the corpse in its last rest forever; and returning home, told nobody what had passed between her and the ghost-lover.

Some time afterwards, the girl was delivered of a fine and healthy boy, who was brought up at Bakki by his mother and his grandfather (though the latter did not know who its father was). In his early youth people saw that he excelled all his companions both in mind and body; and when his education was complete, and he had arrived at the proper age, he became his grandfather's curate.

Now, the old woman saw that something must be done to prevent the approaching ill-fate, so she went to her son, who was a man of great courage, and one who did not shrink from trifles, and told him the whole story of her interview with the ghost, and begged him to stab the young priest directly as he began to pronounce his blessing from the altar, promising herself to take all the consequences of the deed. He was at first very unwilling to do this, but when she pressed him with the earnest entreaties, he at last made the promise she required, and confirmed it with an oath. At length the day came on which the young curate was to perform service for the first time, and the large congregation assembled in the church were struck with his eloquence and sweet voice. But when the youth stood at the altar and raised his hands for the benediction, the old woman signed to her son, who rushed forward and stabbed him, so that he fell dead on the spot. Horror-struck at this fearful act, many rushed forward and seized the murderer, but those who went to the altar to raise the priest found nothing of him but the top bone of his neck, which lay where he had been standing. Everyone now saw that what had happened was no every-day murder, but that some ghost had had to do with it; and the old woman, standing in the midst of them, told them the whole story.

When they had heard it they recovered from their panic, and thanked her for her foresight and her son for his quickness and courage. They then perceived that the east end of the church had sunk down a little into the ground, because the priest had had time to pronounce the first few syllables of the blessing.

After this, the farm of Bakki was so haunted by ghosts that it was removed from its old to its present situation.

Told by an unknown storyteller in Hrútafjörður to Magnús Grímsson, translated by Eiríkur Magnússon and George E. J. Powell

In this legend, the main emphasis is placed on the heroic acts of the man who rescues the church and the people in it. However, when reading the account in today's context, one also notes the sexual violence inflicted on the woman in the legend. Several variants of this legend are found in Iceland, all of which tell of women who turn down men, who then die, return as ghosts and rape the women in their sleep so that they become pregnant (with the exception of "A Naked

Woman Deals with a Ghost" in the previous chapter). Sexual violence in Icelandic legends is admittedly not very common. When it does occur, it is rarely the focus of the legend, and usually the abuser is someone from outside the local community. Although in this story it is a ghost, it is important to remember that, as has been noted, supernatural beings in legends are commonly used as a means of acting out everyday human conflicts, making it easier for people to discuss them and deal with them mentally. It is interesting to note that in Iceland, many variants of the legends in question were indeed told by women, and while the legends do not take a strong position against violence and might thereby not have offered women much comfort, it is possible that they engendered the feeling that women were not alone, and that other women had experienced similar things and feelings, thereby giving them the opportunity to discuss such difficult topics.[23]

Who Built Reynir Church?

A certain farmer once lived at Reynir, in the district of Mýrdalur. He was ordered by the bishop to build a good church hard by his farm-house but had so much difficulty in getting enough timber before the haymaking season, and then so much trouble in finding proper builders, that he feared he should be unable to finish the work before the winter.

One day as he was walking in his field, thinking sadly over the matter, and how he should excuse himself to the bishop for failing to obey his bidding, a strange man, whom he had never seen before, met him, and stopping him, offered him his services in building the church, declaring that he should require the services of no other workman. Then the farmer asked him what payment he would think fitting of such labour, and the man made the following condition – that the farmer should either find out his name before he had finished the church, or else give him his son, who was then a little boy six years old. The farmer thought these easy terms enough, forsooth, and laughing in his sleeve, gladly consented to them.

So the strange builder set to work, and worked with a will, by day and by night, speaking but little to anybody, until the church rose beneath his hands as quickly as if by magic, and the farmer plainly foresaw that it would be finished even before the haymaking was over.

But by this time he had rather changed his mind about the payment he had before thought so easy, and was very far from feeling glad that the end of the church-building was so near; for do what he would, ask whom he would, and search the country round as he would, and had done, he could not, for the life of him, find out the name of his quick-handed mason. Still the church went on not a whit slower for his anxiety, and autumn came, and a very little more labour would finish the building.

One day, the last day of the work, he happened to be wandering outside his field, brooding, in deep grief, over what now seemed to be the heavy price he would have to pay to his master-builder, and threw himself down upon a grass-mound which he came to; he had scarcely lain there a minute, when he heard someone singing, and listening, he found that the voice was that of a mother lulling her child, and came from inside the mound upon which he had flung himself down. This is what it said:

> Soon will thy father Finnur come from Reynir,
> Bringing a little playmate for thee, here.

And these words were repeated over and over again; but the farmer, who pretty soon guessed what they meant, did not wait to hear how many times the mother thought fit to sing them, or what the child seemed to think of them, but started up and ran with all speed, his heart filled with joy, to the church, in which he found the builder just nailing the last plank over the altar.

"Well done, friend Finnur!" said he, "how soon you have finished your work!"

No sooner had these words passed his lips that friend Finnur, letting the plank fall from his hand, vanished, and was never seen again.

Told by an unknown storyteller to Skúli Gíslason,
translated by Eiríkur Magnússon and George E. J. Powell

→→»» «««←

The idea that there is power in a name is well known in folklore all over the world, and Iceland is no exception. This can certainly be seen in the polar bear legends discussed earlier, in which those who have names referring to bears are protected from them, and the way in which mentioning whales is said to summon them. It is also seen in a common legend type, "The Name of the Supernatural Helper" (ATU 300), in which parents have to guess the true name of a magical being or creature in order to protect their children from being taken away or harmed, as witnessed in well-known fairy stories like the Brothers Grimm's "Rumpelstiltskin". A number of legends of this kind can be found in the Icelandic corpus, one of them being the story "Who Built Reynir Church?"[24]

Murder Will Out

Once upon a time, in a certain churchyard, some people who were digging a grave found a skull with a knitting pin stuck through it from temple to temple. The priest took the skull and preserved it until the next Sunday, when he had to perform service.

When the day came, the priest waited until all the people were inside the church, and then fastened up the skull to the top of the porch. After the service the priest and his servant left the church first, and stood outside the door, watching carefully everybody that came out. When all the congregation had passed out without anything strange occurring, they looked in to see if there was anyone still remaining inside. The only person they saw was a very old woman sitting behind the door, who was so unwilling to leave the church that they were compelled to force her out. As she passed under the porch, three drops of blood fell from the skull on to her white head-dress and she exclaimed, "Alas, murder will out at last!" Then she confessed, that having been compelled to marry her first husband against her will, she had killed him with a knitting-pin and married another.

She was tried for the murder, though it had happened so many years back, and condemned to death.

Told by an unknown storyteller to Skúli Gíslason,
translated by Eiríkur Magnússon and George E. J. Powell

→→→ ←←←

In the story "Murder Will Out", the main theme is the idea that dishonesty and deception cannot remain hidden forever and that the truth will eventually be exposed. As folklorist Jacqueline Simpson notes, similar stories in which a murder mystery is solved by the bleeding skull of the victim are known from a number of other places in Europe, such as England and Scotland.[25]

The Skeleton in Hólar Church

Once, on a winter evening, it happened that Jón Arason, Bishop of Hólar, wanted a book which he had left lying on the altar in the church, so he called his household folk together, and asked which of them would do him the favour of fetching the book for him. They all shuddered at the idea, and all drew back, except one maid, who declared herself quite willing to go, and not in the least afraid.

Now the bishop having enemies – as who has not? – had made a tunnel from his own house, which was called the Palace, underground to the church, with a view to being able, if need should ever be, to take sanctuary at a moment's notice, and unobserved.

Through this tunnel the maid went, having procured the keys of the church; but when she had taken the book from the altar, she determined not to go back through the tunnel, which she had found dismal and ghostly, but rather round the other way. So she walked down the church with the keys to the outer door; and looking towards the benches where the women were usually sat, she saw there a human skeleton with long yellow hair! Amazed at this, but in no way frightened, she went up to the figure and said, "Who are you?"

Upon which the skeleton said, "I am a woman, and have long been dead. But my mother cursed me so that I can never corrupt, and return to the dust whence I sprung. Now, therefore, my good girl, I entreat you to release me from this ban, if it lies in your power."

"But," answered the girl, "it does *not* lie in my power, as far as I know. Tell me how I can help you."

The skeleton replied, "You must ask my mother to forgive me my faults and to annul her curse; for she may very likely do for the living what she refuses to do for the dead. It is a rare thing indeed for the living to ask favours of the dead."

"Where is your mother, then?" asked the maiden.

"Oh," said the other, "she is here, there, and everywhere. Now, for example, she is in the choir."

Then the maiden went through the door into the choir, and saw sitting there on one of the benches a wondrous ugly old woman in a red hat, to whom she addressed herself, asking her to be good enough to forgive her daughter, and remove from her the curse. After pausing a while, plainly unwilling, the old hag answered – "Well! It is not often that you living people ask favours of me, so for once I will say to you: Yes!"

Having thanked her for her goodness, the maiden went back towards the outer door, but when she came to the place where she had seen the skeleton, found there only a heap of dust. So she went on towards the door, and as she opened it she heard a voice from the inner part of the church, which cried after her, "Look at my red eyes, how red they are!" And without looking round, she answered, "Look at my black backside, how black it is!"

As soon as she had shut the door behind her, she found that the churchyard seemed to swarm with people who were shouting and screaming direfully, and who made as if they would stop her. But she, summoning up the courage, rushed through the middle of them, without looking either to the right or to the left, and reached the home-building in safety.

As she delivered the book to the bishop, she said:

> So loud were the voices of the ghost band,
> That five echoes for each were found.
> In the mountain-rocks, though far they stand,
> From Hólar burying-ground.

Told by an unknown storyteller to Magnús Grímsson,
translated by Eiríkur Magnússon and George E. J. Powell

This legend can be found in several variations in Iceland and usually tells of brave girls (and in one case a boy) who are sent into the church after dark to retrieve a book for the local priest. However, inside the church they are greeted by a ghost and must use their wits to escape.[26]

More Dirt, More Dirt

Once, there lived a priest's son who was known for his wild and irresponsible behaviour, despite numerous warnings to mend his ways. One day, during a burial, a multitude of bones surfaced in the churchyard, including large leg bones. The boy seized one of the leg bones and began jesting about the strength of the deceased, mocking his diminished state. Though others cautioned him against such disrespect, he paid no heed and continued to jest.

There is no more to tell until Christmas. Then the priest hosted a Christmas party. Everyone had entered the house on Christmas Eve and the sun had set. Tables were laden with food; then came a knock. All were startled, and no one dared come out; yet one man went to the door and saw no one. He went back in and said that no one had been there. Then came the knocking again. Now someone else walked out, but they didn't see anyone. The son of the priest had an old foster father. He told the boy, "Go outside, they'll probably want to meet you. If there is anything there at all, take him by the hand silently and lead him in." The boy went out half-heartedly. When he came to the door, a large man stood outside, his hair white. He took his hand, led him in and seated him at the table. The guest had held the boy's hand firmly, such that a chill swept through him.

Now the guest sat at the table and would not eat food, even when invited to do so. No one spoke to him, and he to no one. Then the foster father of the priest's son told the boy, "Now take a plate and go out to the last of the excavated graves; put some dirt on the plate and bring it to the guest." The boy did this, and when the dirt arrived, the guest started to eat. When finished with the plate, he said quietly, "More dirt, more dirt!" The boy took the plate and retrieved more dirt from the grave. The guest ate nearly everything and then set the plate aside.

Then the foster father of the priest's son ordered him to offer the guest altar wine. The boy did so, and the guest took two shots; then he stood up, took the boy firmly by the hand, and led him outside. He walked out into the cemetery and they came to a small house; the large man went inside, where there was a bed made up. There he directed the boy to lie down. He did not dare to do otherwise. Then the man said, "Look up!" He did so, and there hung a naked sword, terribly large and sharp looking, hanging by one hair. The point was aimed directly at the boy's heart. This made him so afraid that he nearly panicked. He did not dare stir, and a cold sweat ran all over him. After he had been there for some time in this fear of death, the great man said, "You have shaken my bones and said how powerless I am, but now look how little your power is when you see a deadly sword hanging over you. So it hangs over all of you, and you know it not until it pierces your heart, and the whole world's greatness perishes. Remember this, and do not mock the dead any more; be careful and expect that the sword of death will pierce your heart without notice." Now the great man took the boy's hand, raised him from the bed and led him out. The boy fainted.

The boy was searched for in the evening and next morning and was not found. At the height of Mass on Christmas Day, the priest's son awoke from his stupor. He did not see the house, but he was still in the cemetery. He went to church and listened to Mass, but without leaving as he had always done before. His father thought it a good change, and after this, his son was the most civilized and happy young man. He never forgot the night when he lay under the sword that hung over him, suspended from only a single hair.

Told by an unknown storyteller to Jón Árnason,
translated by Sigurður Líndal

The idea that the dead must be shown respect is very common in Icelandic folk legends and belief, as elsewhere in the world.[27] Several

Icelandic legends tell of young people (often men) who mock bones that are found when digging. Often the joke revolves around the size of the bones as they are unusually large. Those who make such jokes are usually punished by the owner of the bones.

The Troll of Mjóifjörður

In the east of Iceland, a bay runs into the land between two steep mountains, which is called Mjóifjörður. In one of the mountains is a deep rocky gulf called Mjóafjarðargil. This gulf was inhabitated by a troll, who used to draw into her power by magic spells the priests living at the farm Fjörður. She was accustomed, while the priest was preaching, to lay one of her hands upon the window over the pulpit in the church. As soon as the strange hand prevented the light from falling on the paper on which the sermon was written, the priests became mad, and used to cry out to their congregation:

"Take my bowels out, for I must be off to the gulf, to the gulf of Mjóifjörður."

With these words the priests disappeared from the church in the direction of the gulf and were never heard of again. A traveller, happening to pass the gulf, once saw the troll sitting on a ledge of rock, kicking her heels and holding something in her hand.

He said to her, "Well, old hag, what have you there?"

"Oh," replied the other, "I am gnawing the last piece of the skull of Snjóki, your late priest."

After this, no priest would take the charge of the church, until one intrepid man declared that he would do so in spite of the troll and all her tricks. The first time he had to perform service in his new church, he told the boldest of his parishioners to look out for him changing his demeanour in the pulpit and then to act as follows:

"Six of you," said he, "must run and catch hold of me and not let me go, however much I struggle; other six of you shall ring the bells as loud as you can; and ten more of you shall run to the door and place your backs against it."

Shortly after the priest had mounted the pulpit, the hand of the troll was seen moving backwards and forwards outside the window, and at the same moment the priest went mad and said:

"Out with my bowels, out with my bowels, and I must away to the gulf, to the gulf of Mjóifjörður."

With these words he endeavoured to rush out of the church.

But the six men, whom he had previously selected, seized him and held him back; six others rang the bells with all their might; and the remaining ten ran to the door and set their backs against it. When the troll heard the bells ring, she took to her heels and jumped from the church on to the wall of the churchyard. When she touched this her foot slipped back, and she cried:

"May you never stand again."

From the churchyard she ran to the gulf, and was never more seen.

But the gap in the churchyard wall which her foot had made could never be mended perfectly, however well the workmen worked, and however good the materials.

The troll's iron shoe, which had tumbled off, was found there, and used by a farmer for an ash-scuttle.

Told by an unknown storyteller to Skúli Gíslason,
translated by Eiríkur Magnússon and George E. J. Powell

In the story about the troll of Mjóifjörður, one sees the conflict between trolls and priests common to many Icelandic legends, as the troll tries to lure the priest out of the church with magic. The idea that the troll ruins the wall of the graveyard is also a common theme, and such stories can be found all over Iceland and elsewhere in Europe.[28]

Tungustapi

In the olden times, many years ago, a rich farmer lived at Sælingsdal-stunga. Of his children, two were sons, by the names Arnór and Sveinn. These brothers were both full of promise, though as different in character from one another as day and night. Arnór was a brave, stirring, and active youth; Sveinn, a quiet, gentle, and timid one.

Arnór, who was full of life and spirits, spent all his time in out-door sports and games, in company with the other young men who lived in that valley, and who used to meet together at a rocky hill standing near the farm Tunga, which was called Tungustapi. Their favourite amusement in the winter was to slide in sleighs down the snowy sides of the hill, and in the evenings, the rocks used to echo again with their shouts and merriment, Arnór being always the ringleader.

Sveinn scarcely ever took part in their sports, but was wont generally to pass his time in the church, and to wander alone about the foot of the hill, when the rest were not playing there. People used to point at him, and to say that he had to do with the elves who dwelt in the mountain.

Certain it was that, without fail, every New Year's Night, he used to disappear, and nobody knew where he went to. He often warned his brother not to make such riot on the hill, but Arnór always laughed at him for his pains, and said that "no doubt the elves were none the worse for it. As for stopping their sports on the hill, he saw no fun in that, and go on he would." And go on he did, just the same as ever, though Sveinn assured him, over and over again, that harm would come of his folly.

One New Year's Night Sveinn had disappeared as usual, but stayed much longer away from home than was his custom. Arnór offered to go and look for him, saying in joke, "He is certainly enjoying the company of his friends the elves." So starting out, he took his way to the mountain.

The night was dark and stormy. When he had arrived at that side of the hill which faced the farm, the rock opened suddenly before him of its own accord, and he saw, within, endless rows of the brightest lamps. At the same time he heard the sound of music, and bethought himself that this must surely be the time for the elves' public worship. And drawing nearer he came to an open door, through which he looked, and saw vast crowds of people assembled within. One, who seemed to be a priest, stood, dressed in splendid robes, by an altar, round which were placed numberless burning candles. Arnór then went further in still, and saw his brother Sveinn kneeling before the altar, while the priest, laying his hands on his head, was speaking some words over him. Round about him stood many others, all in sacred robes, so that Arnór guessed at once that they were making his brother an elfin-priest.

Then he cried aloud, "Sveinn! Come! Come with me! You are running the risk of death!"

Whereupon Sveinn started up, and, turning towards the door near which his brother stood, made as if he would hurry to him. But the priest, who stood before the altar, said:

"Shut instantly the door! And let us wreak vengeance upon the man who has dared to place his feet within our holy place. But thou, Sveinn, must go from among us for thy brother's fault; and in as much as thou wert willing to go to him, and loved more his shameless call than these our sacred rites, thou shalt fall down dead whenever thine eyes see me standing in my robes before this altar."

Arnór now saw those who had been standing round the altar lift his brother in their arms and vanish with him through a distant arch of rock. At the same moment the sound of a bell rang out above him, and all the assembled crowd rushed with one accord to the doorway. He himself ran through it first, back into the outer night, and sped towards his home. But soon he heard behind him the sound of following feet, and the weird trap of fleet elfin horses. And one of the foremost riders cried with a loud voice –

Ride! Ride! Ride on!
For the slopes are dark and the path is dim;
He flees before, ride after him!
Let us, with fell enchantment, spread
Confusion over his feet and head,
In order that he
Many never see
To-morrow's sun! Ride! Ride! Ride on!

Then the whole troop rode between Arnór and the farm and
drove him back. On they went over hill and rock and morass, Arnór,
whose dread clogged his feet, knowing not whither he fled. At last
he came to some slopes far east of his home, and there, his strength
forsaking him, he fell down fainting, and the whole elfin-troop rode
over him, bruising him with the hoofs of their horses, till he was
more dead than alive.

As to Sveinn, he came home just when the household, tired of
waiting, were going to bed. He did not utter a word about himself
or his own long absence, but bade them at once make search for his
brother Arnór. All the workers, therefore, went out and spent the
rest of the night in vainly trying to find him. But he was found at
last by a farmer who lived to the eastward, and who, as he rode to
early worship, at Tunga, next morning, stumbled across him lying
at the foot of the slopes. Arnór was sensible, but dying, and so weak
that he only found strength and words to tell the farmer what had
happened, and to beg him not to take him home again, but leave
him, before he fell back dead.

Ever since that those mounds have been called "the slopes of
death!"

Sveinn was never himself again, but became more sullen, silent
and strange than he had been before. And it was noticed from
that time forth he neither went near nor looked towards the rocky
mountain, Tungustapi. He seemed to care no more for worldly

things, and at last gave them up with their interests for ever, by
becoming a monk, and shutting himself up in the monastery of
Helgafell. He was so learned that none of the brethren were by
any means a match for him, and he sang the Mass so sweetly that
the like of it – they said – had never been heard before. So they
looked on him with awe, and as on one who is not of this world,
and he was, as it were, head over them all.

Now, after a while, his father, at Tunga, being far on in years,
fell sick for the last time, and yearning to see his son before he died,
sent for Sveinn to come to him. Sveinn at once obeyed the bidding,
but, as he departed, said sadly to the monks who had assembled to
wish him God-speed:

"May it fare well with you all for ever, for perchance I may never
come back with life again."

He arrived at Tunga the Saturday before Easter, and found his
father so void of strength as to be scarcely able to speak. But the old
man made it understood that he wished his son to sing the Mass on
Easter day in the church, whither he himself would be carried to
die. Sveinn, strangely loth, consented, but only on condition that
the church door should be kept firmly shut during the whole service,
for upon the fulfilment of this something told him that his life
depended.

Easter morning has arrived, and the dying man is borne by his
workers into the church. Then Sveinn, attired in his priestly robes,
stands upon the steps of the altar and sweetly sings the Mass. So
sweetly, that all there present think that never before have they heard
a voice like this, and they kneel with the very breath hushed upon
their lips to listen to him the better.

But when, at the close of the service, the priest turns from the
altar, and with outstretched hands pronounces solemnly the blessing,
suddenly a strong wind from the west strikes the church, and the
door, bursting from its fastenings, falls heavily inwards. All turn to
look, and they see through the empty frame that the rocky hill near

at hand yawns open, and that within it gleam countless rows of burning lamps. And when they turn again towards the altar, Sveinn has fallen down and lies dead where he has just pronounced the blessing. And his father has fallen also from his couch, his face likewise white with death.

Then the people knew whence the west wind came, and how Sveinn has been slain by the revengeful elves.

For the farmer, who had found Arnór at the foot of the slopes, has long ago told them the story; and they whisper to one another that Sveinn has seen the elfin-priest standing robed at his altar.

So the father and son were buried on the same day.

But the church at Tunga now stands elsewhere, that it may be out of sight of the elfin temple, whose altar is to the west and whose door to the east.

Told by an unknown storyteller to Jón Þorleifsson,
translated by Eiríkur Magnússon and George E. J. Powell

The setting of the legend "Tungustapi" is both a human church and that of the hidden people, who, as mentioned, are often noted to be Christian. In many legends it is shown to be dangerous to visit and interact with the hidden people; if one is not careful, things may not end well.

The Black School

Once upon a time, there existed somewhere in the world, nobody knew where, a school which was called the Black School. There the pupils learned witchcraft and all sorts of ancient arts. Wherever this school was, it was somewhere below ground, and was held in a strong room which, as it had no window, was eternally dark and changeless. There was no teacher either, but everything was learnt from books with fiery letters, which could be read quite easily in the dark. Never were the pupils allowed to go out into the open air or see the daylight during the whole time they stayed there, which was from five to seven years. By then they had gained a thorough and perfect knowledge of the sciences to be learnt. A shaggy grey hand came through the wall every day with the pupils' meals, and when they had finished eating and drinking took back the horns and platters. But one of the rules of the school was that the owner should keep for himself that one of the students who should leave the school the last every year. And, considering that it was pretty well known among the pupils that the Devil himself was the master, you may fancy what a scramble there was at each year's end, everybody doing his best to avoid being last to leave the school.

It happened once that three Icelanders went to this school, by names of Sæmundur the learned, Kálfur Árnason and Hálfdán Eldjárnsson; and as they all arrived the same time, they were all supposed to leave at the same time. Sæmundur declared himself willing to be the last of them, at which the others were much lightened in mind. So he threw over himself a large mantle, leaving the sleeves loose and the fastenings free. A staircase led from the school to the upper world, and when Sæmundur was about to mount this, the Devil grasped at him and said, "You are mine!" But Sæmundur slipped out of the mantle and made off with all speed, leaving the Devil the empty cloak. However, just as he left the school the heavy iron door was slammed suddenly to, and wounded Sæmundur on the heels. Then he said, "That was pretty close upon my heels," which words have since passed into a proverb. Thus Sæmundur contrived to escape from the Black School, with his companions, scot-free.

Some people relate that, when Sæmundur came into the doorway, the sun shone upon him and threw his shadow onto the opposite wall; and as the Devil stretched out his hand to grapple with him, Sæmundur said, "I am not the last; do you not see who follows me?" So the Devil seized the shadow, mistaking it for a man, and Sæmundur escaped with a blow to his heels from the iron door.

But from that hour he was always shadowless, for whatever the Devil took, he never gave back again.

Told by unknown storytellers from Borgarfjörður to Magnús Grímsson, translated by Eiríkur Magnússon and George E. J. Powell

Sæmundur Gets the Living of Oddi

As Sæmundur, Kálfur, and Hálfdán were returning from the Black School, they heard that the living of Oddi was vacant. So they all hurried to the king, and each asked it for himself. The king, well knowing with whom he had to deal, promised it to him who should be the first to reach the place. Upon this Sæmundur immediately called the Devil to him and said, "Swim with me on your back to Iceland; and if you bring me to shore without wetting the skirt of my coat, you shall have me for your own." The Devil agreed to this, so he changed himself into a seal and swam off with Sæmundur on his back. On the way Sæmundur amused himself by reading the book of Psalms of David. Before very long they came close to the coast of Iceland. When he saw this, he closed the book and hit the seal with it upon the head, so that it sank, and Sæmundur swam to land. And as, when Sæmundur got to shore, the skirts of his coat were wet, the Devil lost the bargain, but Sæmundur got the living.

Told by unknown storytellers from Borgarfjörður to Magnús Grímsson, translated by Eiríkur Magnússon and George E. J. Powell

→→»→ «←←←·

Numerous legends tell of priests who are also said to be sorcerers. One of the most famous is Sæmundur fróði (Sæmundur the Learned), who was a real person mentioned in the *Íslendingabók* (Book of Icelanders), written in 1122–33. There he is described as having been an educated man and a minister who was born in 1056 and died in 1133. In the nineteenth and twentieth centuries, Sæmundur was still a prominent figure in Icelandic legends,[29] where he is said to have been a great sorcerer as well as a priest. As noted earlier, in Iceland sorcery tended to be associated with men rather than women. It was also commonly linked with learned knowledge and formal education, and the sorcerers in these legends were often clerics, a role that was not available to women.[30]

In the stories of Sæmundur, he goes abroad to study sorcery at the Black School, run by the Devil. However, this does not negatively affect the portrayal of Sæmundur; the legends are usually concerned with conflicts between Sæmundur and the Devil, with Sæmundur fighting evil on behalf of the good.[31]

5

The Ocean

People have always feared the unknown. In the past (and still today), a great deal of the ocean was uncharted and unfamiliar, so it is perhaps no surprise that it inspired tales of sea monsters. Such stories have been told for generations all over the world, and Iceland is no exception. The country is surrounded by the North Atlantic Ocean, and the sea has therefore played a significant role in shaping Icelandic culture and the Icelandic way of life. In the past, many Icelanders believed that the ocean surrounding the island was inhabited by mysterious and dangerous creatures.

Sea monsters are mentioned in many old Icelandic sources, such as the Icelandic sagas and old maps with illustrations of monsters in the ocean surrounding the island. In records from the winter of 1601–2, one of the harshest winters in Iceland's history, written by Jón lærði Guðmundsson (Jón the Learned, 1574–1658), the author notes that "the year has been so awful that even the monsters living in the oceans have disappeared."[1] Jón was a respected self-taught scholar who wrote a great deal about topics such as nature and folklore. This harsh winter was called *Lurkur* (lit. bludgeon) owing to the frost and cold weather, and the year as a whole was known as *Kynjaár* (The Year of Oddities, or *annus mirabilis*). In the same source, Jón writes that while

Overleaf: Various medieval maps depict Iceland surrounded by sea monsters. The map seen here comes from a collection of maps published *c.* 1585 by the Dutch map-maker Abraham Ortelius. The map has been attributed to Anders Sørensen Vedel, although it has also been suggested that it may have been created or at least influenced by an Icelandic source, the bishop Guðbrandur Þorláksson.

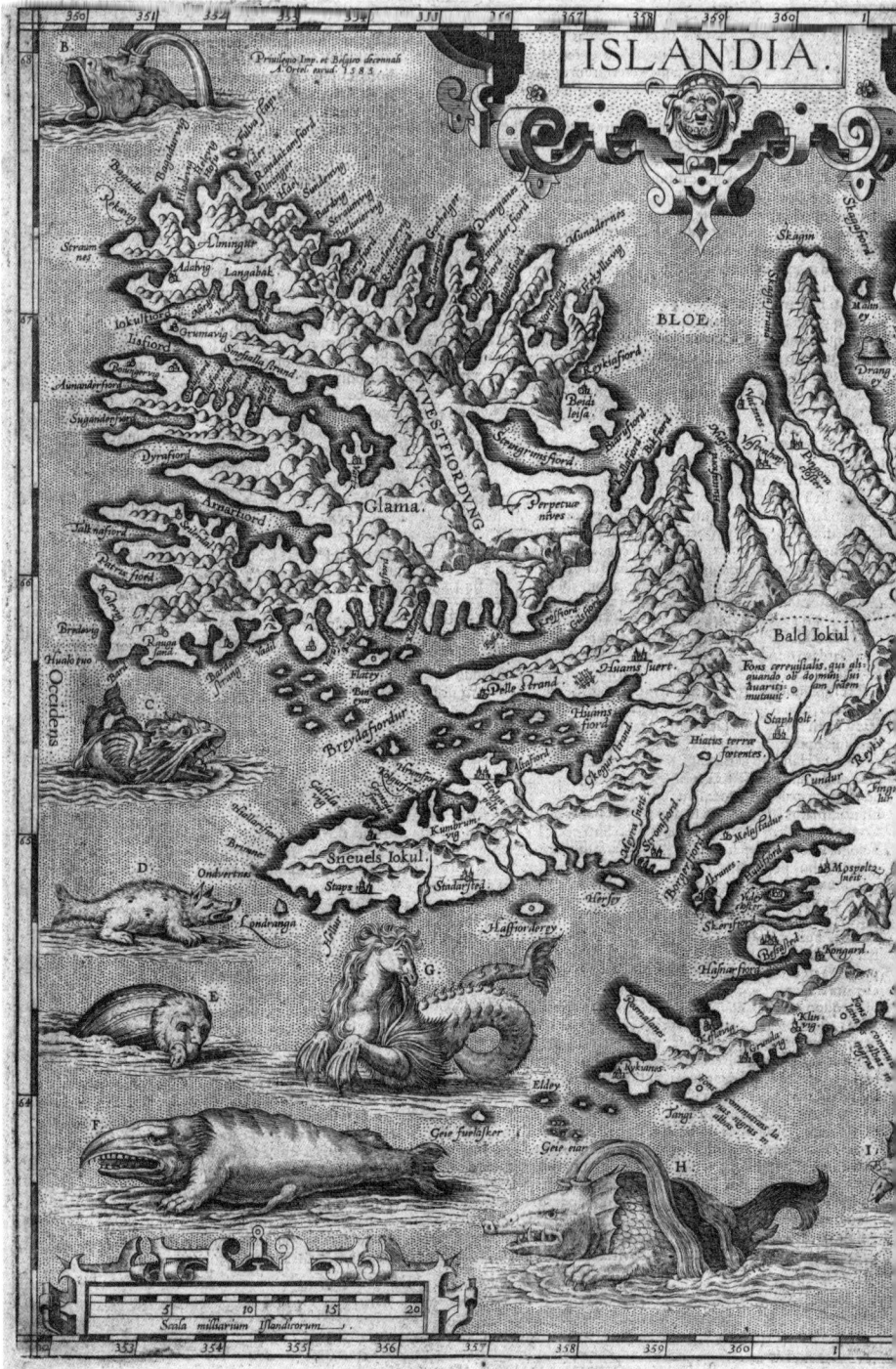

ISLANDIA.

B

Privilegio Imp. et Belgico decennali
A. Oriel. excud. 1585.

BLOE

68

Straum
nes

Reikta

Liminghe
Adalvig   Langabak
Iokulfiord
Grumavig
Isfiord
Dominguevig
Aunandirfiord
Sugandenfiord
Dyrnfiord

VVESTFIORDVNG

Glama.

67

Perpetuæ
nives

Skagin

Malm
ey

Drang

Arnarfiord

Valkinafiord
Dirrefiord

Brialavig

Huolsruo

66

Occidens

C

Brydafiordur

Flatey

Pelle strand   Huams fiort

Huams
fiord

Bald Iokul

Fons corruscalis, qui ali-
quando ob dominu[m] in-
Suarcis[m] tam fædem
mutauit.

Stapholt

Hiaris terræ
fætentes

Lundur

65

D   Ondverenes

Londranga

Sneuels Iokul.

Stape   Stadarfiord

Herfey

Mossfelts
Insiet

Borgarfiort

E

G

Haffiordurey

Hafnarfiora

Bongard

64

F

Eldey

Gnefurlasker   Gnes eiar

Dyckranes

Tangi

H

I

5   10   15   20
Scala milliarium Islandicorum.

Septemtrio

4 5 6 7 8 9 10 11 12 13 14 15

68

A

Grims ey

Rauda gnupur

Langanes prom.

Skallanes fiord

Roloker

Flat ey

Lundey

Sion

Kollafiord

Fulmanzuig

Suningauig

Husley

Surpak dalur

Eyafiorden

Straumsfiord

Robia heydur

Grimels fiord

Nidsfiord

Eunafiord

Q

Modur valler closter

Holgur dalur

Huseuig

Husauig

Sandury

Digranes

67

NORDLEN DINGAFIOR DVNG.

Munke tuere closter

Mokrufeld

Bardur dalur

Grenefiord

Muli

Mrnaes

Hof.

Strand

Kurbur

Balanes

66

Sand Iokul.

Swartur notn.

Fodinæ sulphureæ præstantissimæ

Iokul a

Skirdu closter.

Reydar fiord

Garauig

Arnafelds Iokul.

His notis distinguitur limes inter vtramq dioecesim

Florbdalr

AVSTLENDIN GAFIORDVNG.

Bern fiord

Pap ey

65

Oriens

Rauma brygger

Langedal

Aradal

Hierskeyd

Mocau

Horn

SVNDLEN DINGAFIOR DVNG.

Hekla perpetuis damnata piceis et sub horrendo boatu lapides euomit

Fiske notn.

Sfiabi

Almenhou

Langanstiord.

bur lon

Breid a

Stin ouer

Brolangs eyer

SKALHOLT sedes episco palis, cui adiun cta est schola.

Oddi

Equorum tanta hic velocitas, vt continuo cur su 20. milli arq con ficiunt

Brenkholl Shabat

Eyafialla Iokul.

Solheima Iokul.

Mydals Iokul.

Kirka bar closter.

Medalland

Astuta vulpecularum, vrsicum nisu volu crum suppligandi atque diripiendi

Ingolt hofdul.

N

O

P

Eyrarbach

Vaccæ marinæ

Corui, et falcones albi.

Adal a.

O

K

Eldor

M

HVLDRAVNA EIAR.

L

ILLVSTRISS. AC POTENTISS. REGI FREDERICO II DANIAE, NORVEGIAE, SLAVORVM, GO THORVMQVE REGI, ETC. PRIN CIPI SVO CLEMENTISSIMO, ANDREAS VELLEIVS DESCRIBEB. ET DEDICABAT.

64

4 5 6 7 8 9 10 11 12 13

he has not read a lot about monsters himself, he saw quite a few until they all disappeared that harsh winter. It is safe to say that there was a living folk belief in sea monsters during his time.

Despite Jón's declaration, stories of such monsters continued to circulate, some people in Iceland still believing that these fearsome creatures lurked in the ocean. The Danish historian Peder Hansen Resen (1625–1688) travelled to Iceland in 1684–7 and published a book about his travels. It contains a list of animals found in Iceland, including sea creatures such as whales, and among them several supernatural whales.[2] It is therefore clear that when it came to the sea, the borders between the natural and the supernatural were not always clear.

Roughly two hundred years later, in 1852, a farmer named Jón (which was, and still is, a very common name in Iceland) wrote in his diary about an encounter with one sea monster:

> June 19: Northerly winds and dry weather. Keli and I attempted to fish near Oddagrunnur, without success. We spotted the *stökkull* just behind us, so we quickly headed towards the shore. We put down our lousy net near Steinbogi and caught four trout.[3]

The diary writer, Jón Jónsson, was often called Jón the Old. He was born in Strandir, an area in the Westfjords, in 1795, and kept a diary from when he was 51 years old until his death. His diary is unique because it gives a detailed description of poverty in the old farming society, Jón himself having been very poor. The quote above is typical of diary writing in many ways, the daily accounts being often quite similar, short, with notes about the weather and the work done that day.[4] What is interesting here is his encounter with a *stökkull*, a whale noted in the folk tale collections as being a sea monster or an *illhveli* (monstrous whale), a creature that would be extremely dangerous to fishing boats. The folk tale collector Sigfús Sigfússon gives a more detailed description of a *stökkull* in his collection:

It comes nearly straight up from the sea and rises so high above the ocean's surface that a multitude can easily be seen beneath its arches. Consequently, there are tremendous crashes and clamours when it falls back into the sea; it then proceeds to dive down onto the boats or whatever else is above the water.[5]

Fortunately for the fishermen, according to legend a *stökkull* has a flap that covers its eyes while underwater so it can hardly see, making it difficult for it to find boats. It is hard to state with any certainty that Sigfús and Jón shared the same conception of what a *stökkull* was, as Jón's description is rather short. It nonetheless seems that Jón was not surprised to see such a creature; indeed, the fact that he wrote that they hurried back to land shows that he knew stories of the creature and feared it.

Fishing was, and still can be, a dangerous job. "The sea gives, and the sea takes" is an old Icelandic adage, reflecting the idea that the ocean can be both generous, providing sustenance and livelihood through fishing, and unpredictable, posing risks and challenges to those who depend on it. The saying is also a reminder of the dynamic and sometimes unforgiving relationship that existed between coastal communities and the sea.

Fishing was particularly important in Icelandic society in the nineteenth and twentieth centuries, as it had been in the centuries before. While some farmers and workers were able to fish along the coast by the farms they lived on, others would gather at specific fishing stations to carry out their activities.[6] Fishing seasons varied in different parts of the country, but hardly any fishing would take place between the months of July and September because it was the haymaking season, when all hands were required for harvesting the hay for the coming winter. It is not until the latter part of the nineteenth century, after villages began to develop, that one can speak of a summer fishing season, involving rowing boats without decks.[7]

During the nineteenth century, most Icelanders used open rowing boats to fish, boats that would usually take only two to four people, although some were bigger, with six or eight oars. At the beginning of the twentieth century, a number of decked vessels began to be imported, ships that were manned by a large number of fishermen. In 1902 the first fishing boat equipped with a motor appeared for the first time, and after that most new fishing boats would have an engine.[8]

Disasters at sea were not uncommon in Iceland, and many lives were lost there. This was also in part because in the early nineteenth century a significant proportion of the Icelandic population did not know how to swim. It was not until approximately 1880 that there was an increased interest in learning to swim. Indeed, some people thought that the ability to swim would only prolong the suffering of those who found themselves in perilous situations at sea, believing that drowning was an inevitable fate. In the spring of 1884, a man called Björn Blöndal started teaching Icelanders how to swim. Tragically, later that same year, three young men perished in a boating accident when their vessel capsized. This disaster sparked an increasing interest in swimming lessons, as many believed that the ability to swim might have made a difference in that case. Regrettably, this enthusiasm was short-lived, as Björn himself met a watery grave only two years later. Those who opposed swimming lessons saw this as confirmation of their earlier views. Swimming was still taught, but not many participated. Decades later, another man, named Páll Erlingsson, taught swimming classes that were specifically aimed at fishermen, but here, too, interest proved to be lacking at first. Once again, it is possible that many of the fishermen believed that a quick death would be preferable to a prolonged struggle. A significant change in this perspective nonetheless occurred in autumn 1902, when 44 fishermen in Reykjavík enrolled in Páll's swimming courses.[9]

The dangers of the ocean are reflected in a great many folk beliefs in Iceland that were associated with the sea, sailing and boatbuilding. Many of these are similar to beliefs found elsewhere in the world, and they would have given people the sense that they could have some influence on circumstances that in reality were beyond their control, as, for example, with the idea that our actions can somehow affect the weather. This is a recurring theme within Icelandic folk belief in general as well as regarding seafaring and has shaped the way in which Icelanders perceive and interact with the ocean. As has been noted, the weather in Iceland can be very unpredictable and change rapidly, posing particular danger when one is out at sea on an open boat. Fishermen therefore had to be good at making weather forecasts, especially in the nineteenth century when there was nothing to rely on but experience and judgement.[10] In the folk tale collection of Jón Árnason, certain specific weather conditions and types of waves are known as *náöldur* (death waves) and *náskellur* (death breaker), both of which were supposed to predict disasters at sea. In that kind of weather, it was better to stay home than to venture out. People also believed that the weather would become tranquil for a while when a ship had sunk, a period that was called *dauðalag* (death calm). This allowed the other ships at sea to return to land safely, as the sea was seen as having already taken its share.[11]

This 1820 illustration by Poul De Løvenørn (1751–1826), a Danish map-maker who visited Iceland in 1786, shows fishermen dividing their catch on the shore. The illustration is featured on one of his maps.

Dreams were also thought to be a means of predicting the weather and disasters at sea. A dream of a red-coloured ship, for example, was believed to indicate that a ship would sink and that everyone on it would perish. To dream of instruments playing music meant that a storm was coming, while to see one's boat broken or a seal circling it signified bad luck.[12]

Fishermen were often suspicious about beginning the season on one of the first days of the week, especially Mondays, which would cause bad luck; in a similar way, fishermen's clothes should not be sewn on Sundays. At sea there were also many precautions that had to be maintained; for instance, one should not whistle or curse. At home, people also had to be careful to protect those who were out at sea. It was believed, for example, that one should not make the bed of a fisherman until he had been away for three nights, otherwise he would not return.[13] Beliefs varied according to time and place, and some are still known among sailors today. As the Icelandic folklorist Símon Jón Jóhannsson notes, superstition, by its nature, is usually conservative and seeks to maintain a firmly established order. As long as everything remains within strict confines, all will go well, but if things stray from the norm, the outcome may be uncertain.[14] While it is hard to say whether people believed in all of these superstitions, it is not difficult to imagine that people would not wish to tempt fate or take unnecessary risks when dealing with the lives of their loved ones. It is sometimes easier to follow a superstition than take the risk of not doing so.

Icelanders had no qualms about mixing Christianity, which formed an important part of people's lives, with various folk beliefs. Many fishermen would cross themselves while getting dressed in their seaman's clothes, and at many fishing stations a specific seafaring prayer would be recited before the fishermen headed out, the men praying for a good catch, protection against disasters and a blessing for their boat and fishing equipment. Some would keep a written copy of this prayer in their pocket or have it sewn into their clothes. Crosses were also not uncommon at sea and were often kept on the boats. All of this was

Fishing in the past was dangerous due to unpredictable weather and open boats, leading to many fatalities. Various folk beliefs and superstitions revolved around the safety of fishermen. This 1953 drawing by Ásgrímur Jónsson depicts a man navigating the treacherous sea.

meant to keep the boat safe or make sure the fishing would be successful.[15] Such seafaring prayers and accompanying rituals slowly began to diminish at the beginning of the twentieth century, around the same time that other religious activities started to fade.[16]

By some accounts, the ocean around Iceland was considered to be the equivalent of "hallowed ground", meaning that those who were lost at sea would not return as ghosts, even though they had not been buried in a graveyard. (Exceptions to this rule were when bodies were washed ashore, something that will be further discussed in the next chapter.) This belief nevertheless reflects how common it was for people to lose their loved ones at sea and offered some consolation to those who remained.

The ocean thus inspired many legends, usually focusing on its unpredictable nature and its dangers. A number of legends tell of fishermen's conflicts with hidden people who were also fishermen, and trolls who sometimes lived in cliffs close to the shore. Other stories tell how magic was used to help one fish well or to spoil the fishing for one's enemies. Yet others tell of specific supernatural beings that live in the ocean, such as the monstrous whales mentioned above. Interestingly, many Icelandic legends of this kind take place in the Westfjords and Eastfjords of Iceland. For that reason, many of the legends in this chapter, and in the next one dealing with the shore, come from collections other than those of Jón Árnason, such as that of Sigfús Sigfússon, who mainly collected stories in the east and included a great number telling of sea creatures. Sigfús divided his legends of sea dwellers into three main categories: those dealing with merpeople, those dealing with monsters and those dealing with animals that are shown to be supernatural.

The merpeople seem to live in societies at the bottom of the ocean, and legends of people's interactions with them are often quite short. In the Icelandic legends, it is more common to find mermen than mermaids; ideas of seductive, singing mermaids are rare, although they can be found.[17] As Sigfús Sigfússon notes in his introduction to such legends: "The poets have depicted mermaids as beautiful and gentle beings, but these types of wonder tales are few here."[18] The merpeople are usually considered dangerous to humans.

When it comes to Sigfús's second category, the monsters, the line between the natural and the supernatural often seems to be blurred, something that raises the question of what really constitutes a monster. Is it their unrecognizability, their unnatural appearance or behaviour, their size and the danger they pose, or is it their evil intentions that make them a monster? Sigfús Sigfússon describes monsters as follows:

> Monster is a term referring to a supernatural or unknown creature that is exceedingly ugly, fierce, and of a malevolent nature ... Belief in such monsters in Iceland has been highly diverse, intricate, and a rich source of folklore, presenting an inexhaustible wellspring of tales.[19]

Some of these stories are personal narratives told in the first person, and many are quite short. They often describe people seeing something mysterious and strange, but do not go into much detail about the encounter. Because of this, descriptions of monsters vary greatly; many of the creatures have no specific names and are simply called "monsters", sometimes with a reference to the places where they were seen.

On the border of the supernatural and natural are stories of whales, to which Sigfús dedicates a whole chapter in his collection. As he writes:

The narratives are gradually moving into the familiar realm
of existence, which also bears much that is mysterious and
unique about it . . . There are various tales about whales, the
voracity of some and the rescue efforts of others, in other
words, about both malevolent and harmless whales.[20]

It is not hard to imagine how whales might have come to be categorized as monsters, huge as they are compared to the small rowing boats used by Icelandic fishermen. The whales in Icelandic legends often possess supernatural abilities, much like the polar bears discussed earlier. As can be seen in the quote from Sigfús above, they are commonly given human-like abilities and intentions, and may even be characterized as good or bad. Their association with the supernatural is also seen in the idea that one should not utter the word *hvalur* (whale) while at sea and instead use the word *stórfiskur* (big fish). It was thought that if one was not careful, whales could be summoned by the sound of their name and might emerge to destroy the ship.[21]

Other legends bordering on the supernatural are those that tell of monstrous mothers, such as the *Selamóðir* (mother of seals), *Flyðrumóðir* (mother of halibut) and *Skötumóðir* (mother of skates).[22] These beings were believed to be enormous, monstrous versions of the animals they are associated with, and were often seen as being protectors of their kind. They are powerful beings that affect nature and

This 1976 painting by Finnur Jónsson (1892–1993) depicts two men battling the monstrous red-comb whale. Finnur was a prominent figure in Icelandic art history. As he was a fisherman himself from 1905 to 1919, his work often reflects life at sea, sometimes incorporating supernatural elements.

should not be offended. This idea can be seen, for example, in the belief that if people hunt too many seals, the mother of seals will appear and take revenge. The legends of these protective monsters emphasize the necessity of respecting the ocean, presenting a caution to the fishermen by warning them of what can happen if they overfish or overhunt.

Before the nineteenth century, it was not uncommon for women in Iceland to venture out to sea, but around the turn of the century this changed.[23] Owing to the fact that it was more commonly men who went to sea in the nineteenth and early twentieth centuries, many Icelandic legends that take place at sea revolve around men, much like those legends that take place in the wilderness. Some of these tell of awful accidents, while others are heroic tales of men who defeat a sea monster. For logical reasons, the ocean is portrayed as a dangerous and unpredictable place. It represents the unknown, inhabited by immense and foreign creatures, and was indeed a place where many fishermen's lives came to an end.

Rauðkembingur (Red-Comb)

What some call the horse-whale is said to be one of the toothed
whales, and the most ferocious and difficult whale one can come
across. It is the largest of all of the toothed whales and, according
to stories, keenly seeks to run boats ashore. It is said that it travels in
circles around the whole of Iceland on two different currents, so that
it moves quickly. It is then generally above the surface and is so difficult to overcome that white breaker waves froth around its breast.
It is said that it takes its name from the red mane or fin spine placed
prominently on its back. When it is sighted or heard on the horizon,
most fishermen consider it time to row to shore. It is said that an
American whaler once harpooned one near Norway but thanked his
lucky stars that he was able to escape it and resolved to never mess
with it again. Many know the story of when the red-comb came and
chased the brothers from Höfn in Héraðsflói Bay and kept them
for many days on the sands. "There red-combs are often knocking
about," said Hjörleifur. Runólfur in Fagridalur, a champion and
sorcerer, once caught a shark's head on a contraption used for shark
fishing towards the north of Fjallaendi. Then a red-comb came
towards him. Runólfur let another person row and showed it the
shark's head. The whale did not like this, and so Runólfur let the
head dangle from the side of the ship as they rowed back to land.

Generally, red-combs are followed by narwhals (or beluga
whales), which clean up the men from the ships that the other
destroys. The red-combs are more productive, while the others
are slower and reap the benefit of the red-combs' hard work.

One day, a red-comb could be seen from Grindavík, in the
Gullbringusýsla district, swimming along the shore with white
breaker waves frothing alongside it. It was followed by a beluga
whale, which are generally slow. Nobody thought it wise to row
from anywhere in that whole area, as people thought it certain that
those companions would be out to prey on boats. It turned out that

they could be seen from far across the land, all the way to Mýrar in the east. There they finally came across a boat, which the red-comb destroyed around noon that same day.

Told by an unknown storyteller to Sigfús Sigfússon,
translated by Alice Bower

⸙

The *Rauðkembingur* (red-comb) was said to be one of the most dangerous monsters in the ocean. Red-combs will not be found in any natural-science book today, but in the story it is accompanied by a beluga whale, a well-known species, highlighting the thin line between the natural and supernatural with regard to the ocean.

The Mermaid in Grindavík

It was in the days of Sigurður Eyjólfsson, the priest at Staður in Grindavík, around 1705, that a boat that the priest owned set out to sea for fishing at the fishing grounds called Þórkötlumið. Ormur, the steersman and the next in command to the captain, was a skilled singer and the lead vocalist at the church at Staður. There was no wind and the sea was calm. They began to catch a fair number of fish when, suddenly, they saw a woman with flowing hair emerge from the sea. They realized she was a mermaid. She rested on the sea's surface and gazed at the boat.

"Look, lads! She is preparing herself to sing," said the captain, "but it is not good to leave good fishing so soon. What do you say, lads?" Another replied: "Everything is fine as long as she remains silent." And the men continued to pull the fishing nets with all their might.

Suddenly, the mermaid began to sing a bewitching melody, and her song possessed such enchanting magic that it compelled the fishermen to stop pulling. Slowly, one by one, they succumbed to a drowsy stupor until all were asleep except for Ormur, the singer. He decided to join in the singing, and when she ended her song he started another, which the mermaid sang with him. This went on for a long time, one song after another, until Ormur started to fear he would exhaust all the songs he knew.

Then he came up with the idea to sing the paternoster (Lord's Prayer). He began to recite it, and at last the mermaid fell silent. She raised her hand and sank straight into the sea. Ormur called out to the other crew members and told them to row back to shore, explaining that the beautiful mermaid had finally been defeated and that she had disappeared back into the sea. By now, the fishermen had been asleep for a long time, and everyone else who had been out at sea was already safely on land and had put their boats in the boathouses. The crew members rowed quickly back to shore.

They thanked Ormur for saving them and praised his skill, knowledge and courage, he became well known for his singing skill that day, and was thanked by the clergy for rescuing the other men.

The following year, an epidemic known as *Stórabóla* (smallpox) struck Iceland and claimed many lives. It was believed that the mermaid had been an omen for it, as merfolk often surface before significant events. Several years later, the priest Sigurður, who owned the boat, passed away. At the same time, the boat sank at sea and the entire crew was lost, including Ormur, which was considered a great loss.

Told by Sigurður Árnes Jónsson to Sigfús Sigfússon,
translated by Dagrún Ósk Jónsdóttir

→→»→ «←←·

In Icelandic legends, the merpeople are divided into several categories, all of which can be dangerous. One type is the *hafmeyja* or *hafgúa* (mermaid or mertroll). As elsewhere in the world, this being is known for luring sailors to their deaths by singing.[24] However, as noted above, these kinds of legends are relatively uncommon in Icelandic folklore. In this tale, we once again see the protection that the Christian faith provides.

The Merman's Laughter

Long ago a farmer lived at Vogar, who was a mighty fisherman, and, of all the farms round about, not one was as well situated with regard to the fisheries as his.

One day, according to custom, he had gone out fishing, and having cast down his line from the boat and waited awhile, found it very hard to pull up again, as if there were something very heavy at the end of it. Imagine his astonishment when he found that what he had caught was a great fish, with a man's head and body! When he saw that this creature was alive, he addressed it and said, "Who are you and where do you come from?"

"A merman from the bottom of the sea," was the reply.

The farmer then asked him what he had been doing when the hook caught his flesh.

The other replied, "I was turning the cowl of my mother's chimney-pot, to suit it to the wind. So let me go again, will you?"

"Not for the present," said the fisherman. "You shall serve me awhile first."

So without more words he dragged him into the boat and rowed to shore with him.

When they got to the boat-house, the fisherman's dog came to him and greeted him joyfully, barking and fawning on him, and wagging his tail. But the master's temper being none of the best, he struck the poor animal; whereupon the merman laughed for the first time.

Having fastened the boat, he went towards his house, dragging his prize with him, over the fields, and, stumbling over a hillock, which lay in his way, cursed it heartily; whereupon the merman laughed for the second time.

When the fisherman arrived at the farm, his wife came out to receive him, and embraced him affectionately, and he received her salutations with pleasure; whereupon the merman laughed for the third time.

Then said the farmer to the merman, "You have laughed three times, and I am curious to know *why* you have laughed. Tell me, therefore."

"Never will I tell you," replied the merman, "unless you promise to take me to the same place in the sea wherefrom you caught me, and there to let me go free again." So the farmer made him the promise.

"Well," said the merman, "I laughed the first time because you struck your dog, whose joy at meeting you was real and sincere. The second time, because you cursed the mound over which you stumbled, which is full of golden ducats. And the third time, because you received with pleasure your wife's empty and flattering embrace, who is faithless to you, and a hypocrite. And now be an honest man and take me out to the sea whence you have brought me."

The farmer replied: "Two things that you have told me I have no means of proving, namely, the faithfulness of my dog and the faithlessness of my wife. But the third I will try the truth of, and if the hillock contains gold, then I will believe the rest."

Accordingly he went to the hillock, and having dug it up, found therein a great treasure of golden ducats, as the merman had told him. After this the farmer took the merman down to the boat, and to that place in the sea whence he had caught him. Before he put him in, the latter said to him:

"Farmer, you have been an honest man, and I will reward you for restoring me to my mother, if only you have skill enough to take possession of property that I shall throw in your way. Be happy and prosper."

Then the farmer put the merman into the sea, and he sank out of sight.

It happened that not long after, seven sea-grey cows were seen on the beach, close to the farmer's land. These cows appeared to be very unruly, and ran away directly when the farmer approached them. So he took a stick and ran after them, possessed with the fancy that if he could burst the bladder which he saw on the nose of each of them, they would belong to him. He contrived to hit out the bladder on the nose of one cow, which then became so tame that he could easily catch it, while the others leaped into the sea and disappeared. The farmer was convinced that this was the gift of the merman. And a very useful gift it was, for better cow was never seen nor milked in all the land, and she was the mother of the race of grey cows so much esteemed now.

And the farmer prospered exceedingly, but never caught any more mermen. As for his wife, nothing further is told about her, so we can repeat nothing.

Told by Guðrún Guðmundsdóttir to Páll Jónsson,
translated by Eiríkur Magnússon and George E. J. Powell

Icelandic legends tend to tell of encounters with mermen rather than mermaids. *Landnámabók* (Book of Settlements), from the twelfth century, contains a mention of a type of merman called *marmennill*, a creature later referred to in legends as a *marbendill*. In the nineteenth-century legends, these mermen are said to have enormous heads and to be incredibly wise, and are even said to know the future. According to the legends, when people caught a *marbendill* in their net it was important to release it immediately, otherwise those who caught it might hear something that was best left unknown.[25]

The Fisherman of Götur

It is told that long ago, a peasant living at Götur in Mýrdalur, went out fishing round the island of Dyrhólar. In returning from the sea, he had to cross a morass. It happened once, that, on his way home, after nightfall, he came to a place where a man had lost his horse in the bog, and was unable to recover it without help. The fisherman, to whom this man was a stranger, aided him in freeing his horse from the peat.

When the animal stood again safe and sound upon the dry earth, the stranger said to the fisherman, "I am your neighbour, for I live in Hvammsgil, and am, as you, returning from the sea. But I am so poor, that I cannot pay you for this service, as you ought to be paid. I will promise you, however, this much – that you shall never go to sea without catching fish, nor ever, if you will take my advice, return with empty hands. But you must never put to sea without having first seen me pass your house as if going towards the shore. Obey me in this matter and I promise you that you shall launch, at no time, your boat in vain."

The fisherman thanked him for this advice, and sure enough it was, that for three years afterwards, never putting to sea till he had first seen his neighbour pass his door, he always launched his boat safely, and always came home full-handed.

But at the end of the three years, it fell out that one day, in the early morning, the fisherman looking out from his house, saw the wind and weather favourable and all other fishermen hurrying down to the sea, to make the best of so good a time. But though he waited hour after hour, in hope of seeing his neighbour pass, the man of Hvammsgil never came. At last losing his patience, he started out without having seen him go by. When he came down to the shore, he found that all the boats were launched and far away.

Before night the wind rose and became a storm, and every boat that had that day put to sea was wrecked, and every fisherman drowned, the peasant of Götur alone escaping, for he had been unable to go out fishing. The next night he had a strange dream, in which his neighbour from Hvammsgil came to him and said, "Although you did not yesterday follow my advice, I yet so far felt kindly towards you, that I hindered you from going out to sea, and saved you thus from drowning; but look no more forth to see me pass, for we have met for the last time." And never again did the peasant see his neighbour pass his door.

Told by an unknown storyteller to Runólfur Jónsson,
translated by Eiríkur Magnússon and George E. J. Powell

Many stories tell of hidden people owning their own boats and using them for fishing, once again mirroring human society in the nineteenth century. The boats of these people are nonetheless seldom seen, but Jón Árnason describes how they leave light streaks called *álfarákir* (elf streaks) on the surface of the ocean, which he notes people described as a magical sight. In some stories, hidden people appear to others on boats, something that was usually considered a sign of luck, as the hidden people are said to be very good fishermen.[26]

Anna in Bessastaðir

A short walk from the farm of Bessastaðir is a fishing station called Skansinn. There were three crews at anchor there, and they rarely went home, but a maid named Anna was there providing them with coffee in the morning before they went fishing and other things like that. One of the captains was Eiríkur, a longtime worker at Bessastaðir and a man of sorcerous temperament.

One morning before the break of day, Anna came out and was going to heat coffee for the sailors. She then saw sixteen men coming to meet her, all drenched in seawater. She thought it strange and called out to them, "Have you come ashore, lads?" But they did not answer. Then Anna went inside and saw all the boys there; they had not gone to sea and were not wearing their skin clothes.

She then begged them, "Do not row today, lads, as I have seen your guardian spirits." But they laughed at her, and all three crews rowed out. That day, Anna came home to Bessastaðir and said it would not go well for the boys today and described what she had seen, but the people asked her not to spout such nonsense. Later that day a violent storm struck, claiming the lives of many sailors. Two of the crews Anna had seen the guardian spirits of were lost, but Eiríkur, one of the captains, managed to survive and save many ships that day. Anna shared her premonition the day before the storm hit, so this story surpasses others as it is true.

Told by Grímur Thomsen to Jón Árnason,
translated by Sigurður Líndal

⸺⤜⤛⸺

In Icelandic legends, meeting someone who is not really there is usually a sign of their impending death. Various legends tell of people who foresee tragedies and accidents, often at sea. Belief in clairvoyance in Iceland appears to have been relatively high in the past but is decreasing today, according to the surveys on folk belief first sent out by Erlendur Haraldsson and later Terry Gunnell. The surveys show that in 1974 only 7 per cent of people were prepared to say that clairvoyance was impossible or unlikely, while 93 per cent deemed it possible, likely or certain. In 2023 around 37 per cent deemed it impossible or unlikely, while 63 per cent believed it to be possible, likely or certain.[27]

The Man-Whale

In ancient times, in the south part of the country, it was the custom to go in a boat, at a certain season of the year, from the mainland to the cliffs, Geirfuglasker, to procure sea-birds and the eggs which they were in the habit of laying there. The passage to these rocks was always looked upon as an unsafe one, as they stood some way out at sea, and a constant and heavy surf beat upon them.

It happened once that some men went thither in a boat at the proper season for the purpose, as the weather seemed to promise a long calm. When they arrived at the rocks, some of them landed, the rest being left to take care of the boat. Suddenly a heavy wind came on, and the latter were forced to leave the island in haste, as the sea became dangerous and the surf beat furiously upon the cliffs. All those who had landed were enabled to reach the boat in time at the signal from their companions, except one, a young and active man, who, having gone in his zeal higher and further than the others, was longer in getting down to the beach again. By the time he did get down, the waves were so high that though those in the boat wrought their best to save him, they could not get near enough to him, and so were compelled for their own lives' sake to row to shore. They determined, however, when the storm should abate its fury, to return to the rocks and rescue him, knowing that unless they did so and the wind were soon spent, the youth could not but perish from cold and hunger. Often they tried to row to Geirfuglasker, but the whole season through, they were unable to approach them, as the wind and surf always drove them back. At last, deeming the young man dead, they gave up the attempt and ceased to risk their lives in seas so wrathful.

So time passed, until the next season for seeking sea-birds came round, and the weather being now calm, the peasants embarked in their boat for the Geirfuglasker. When they landed upon the cliffs, great was their astonishment at seeing come towards them a man, for they thought that no one could live in so wild and waste a spot. When the man drew near them, they recognized him as the youth who had been left there the year before and whom they had long ago given up as lost. Their wonder knew no bounds, and they guessed that he had the elves to thank for his safety. They asked him all sorts of questions. What had he lived upon? Where had he slept at night? What had he done for fire in the winter? And so forth, but he would give them none but vague replies, which left them just as wise as they were before. He said, however, he had never once left the cliff, and that he had been very comfortable there, wanting for nothing. They then rowed him to land, where all his friends and kin received him with unbounded amazement and joy, but, question him as they would, could get but mighty little out of him concerning his life on the cliffs the whole year through. With time, the strangeness of this event and the wonder it had awakened passed from men's minds, and it was little if at all more spoken of.

One Sunday in the summer, certain things that took place in the church at Hvalsnes filled people with astonishment. There were large numbers there, and among them the young man who had passed a year on the cliffs of the Geirfuglasker. When the service was over and the folk began to leave the church, what should they find standing in the porch but a beautiful cradle with a baby in it. The coverlet was richly embroidered, and wrought of stuff that nobody had ever seen before. But the strangest part of the business was that, though everybody looked at the cradle and child, nobody claimed either one or the other, or seemed to know anything whatever about them. Last of all came the priest out of the church, who, after he had admired and wondered at the cradle and child as much as the others, asked whether there was no one present to whom they belonged. No one answered. Then he asked whether there was no one present who had enough interest in the child to desire him to baptize it. No one either answered or came forward.

At this moment the priest happened to cast his eyes on the young peasant, concerning whose sojourn on the Geirfuglasker rocks he had always felt particularly suspicious, and calling him aside, asked him whether he had any idea who its father was, and whether he would like the child baptized. But the youth, turning angrily from him, declared that he knew nothing whatever about the child or its father.

"What care I," he said, "whether you baptize the child or not? Christen it or drown it, just which you think fit; neither it, nor its father, nor its mother, are aught to me."

As these words left his lips there suddenly appeared in the porch a woman, handsomely apparelled, of great beauty and noble stature, whom no one had ever seen before. She snatched the coverlet from the cradle, and flinging it in through the door of the church, said:

"Be witnesses all, that I wish not the church to lose its dues for this child's baptism."

Then turning to the young peasant, and stretching out her hands towards him, she cried, "But thou, O faithless coward, disowner of thy child, shalt become a whale, the fiercest and most dreaded in the whole wide sea!"

With these words, she seized the cradle and disappeared.

The priest, however, took the coverlet which she had flung into the church, and made of it an altar-cloth, the most beautiful that had ever been seen. As for the young peasant, he went mad on the spot; and rushing down to the Hólmur Cliffs, which rise sheer from the deep water, made as if he would throw himself from them. But while he hesitated for a moment on the brink, lo and behold, a fearful change came over him, and he began to swell to a vast size, till, at last, he became so large that the rock could no longer bear him, but crumbling beneath him hurled him into the sea. There he was changed into a great whale, and the red hat he had been wearing became a red head.

After this, his mother confessed that her son had spent the year
with the elves upon the Geirfuglasker. On his being left on the rocks
by his companions (so he had declared to her), he had at first wandered
about in despair, filled only with the thought of throwing himself into
the waves to die a speedy death rather than suffer all the pangs of hunger
and cold; but a lovely girl had come to him, and telling him she was an
elf, had asked him to spend the winter with her. She had borne him a
child before the end of the year, and only allowed him to go to shore
when his companions came again to the cliffs, on the condition that
he would have this child baptized when he should find it in the church-
porch, threatening him, if he failed in the fulfilment of this, with the
severest punishment and most unfortunate fate.

Now Redhead, the whale, took up his abode in the Faxafjörður,
and wrought mischief there without end, destroying boats
innumerable, and drowning all their crews, so that at last it became
unsafe to cross any part of the bay, and nothing could either prevent
his ravages or drive him away. After matters had gone on like this
for some time, the whale began to haunt a narrow gulf between
Akranes and Kjalarnes, which is now called after him, Hvalfjörður.

At that time there lived at Saurbær, in Hvalfjarðarströnd, an
aged priest, who, though hale and hearty, was blind. He had two
sons and a daughter, who were all in the flower of their youth, and
who were their father's hope and stay, and, as it were, the very apple
of his eye. His sons were in habit of fishing in Hvalfjörður, and one
day when they were out they encountered the whale, Redhead, who
overthrew their boat and drowned them both. When their father
heard of their death, and how it had been brought about, he was
filled with grief, but uttered not a word at the time.

Now it must be known that this old priest was well skilled in
all magical arts.

Not long after this, one fine morning in the summer, he bade
his daughter take his hand and guide him down to the sea-shore.
When he arrived there, he planted the end of the staff, which he had

brought with him, in the waves, and leaning on the handle fell into deep thought.

After a few minutes he asked his daughter, "How looks the sea?"

She answered, "My father, it is as bright and smooth as a mirror."

Again, a few minutes, and he repeated, "How looks the sea?"

She replied, "I see on the horizon a black line, which draws nearer and nearer, as it were a shoal of whales, swimming quickly into the bay."

When the old man heard that the black line was approaching them, he bade the girl lead him along the shore towards the inland end of the bay. She did so, and the black surging sea followed them constantly. But as the water became shallower, the girl saw that the foam arose, not from a shoal of whales, as she had thought at first, but from the swimming of a single huge whale with a red head, who came rapidly towards them along the middle of the bay, as if drawn to them by some unseen power. A river ran into the extreme end of the gulf, and the old priest begged his daughter to lead him still on along its banks. As they went slowly up the stream, the old man feeling every footstep before him, the whale followed them, though with a heavy struggle, as the river contained but little water for so vast a monster to swim in. Yet forward they went, and the whale still after them, till the river became so narrow between its high walls of rock, that the ground beneath their feet quaked as the whale followed them. After a while they came to a waterfall, up which the monster leaped with a spring that made the land tremble far and wide, and the very rocks totter. But they came at last to a lake, from which the river rose, whose course they had followed from the sea; the lake Hvalvatn. Here the heart of the monster broke from very toil and anguish, and he disappeared from their eyes.

When the old priest returned home, after having charmed the whale thus to his death, all the people from far and near thanked him for having rid their coasts of so dread a plague.

And in case anybody should doubt the truth of this story of the Redhead, the man-whale, we may as well say that on the shores of the lake Hvalvatn, mighty whale-bones were found lying long after the date of this tale.

Told by Jón Ásmundsson and Gunnhildur Jónsdóttir to Skúli Gíslason, translated by Eiríkur Magnússon and George E. J. Powell

⟶≫ ≪⟵

Similar legends are found in several Icelandic legend collections. The common message in all variants is the importance of men acknowledging their children who are born out of wedlock, the narrative serving as a warning to those who did not. These legends highlight the man's responsibility towards both the child and the mother, as the men are punished for not keeping their word.

The Girl in Álftamýri Parish

In Álftamýri parish in the west, a few years ago, there lived three
siblings, two brothers and a sister, who managed a farm alone.
The farm was situated in such a way that it required a journey
across a fjord or cove to reach the meadows by the sea. One night,
after returning from the meadows, the siblings loaded their boat
with hay, packing it so densely that the only space left for the girl
was at the stern amid the trimmings. Oblivious to her presence due
to the obstructing hay, the brothers rowed from the only available
spot midship. Upon reaching their destination and beginning to
unload the boat, they realized the girl was missing, and did not
know what had become of her except what they imagined: she
had gone overboard. Because it was dark that night, and nothing
could be seen, they made no effort to search for her, being certain
that she would not be found alive. They went home and slept
through the night.

One of the brothers dreamed of her that night; he felt her
presence directing him to where she could be found. The next
morning, both brothers set out in a boat and discovered her exactly
where she had indicated in the dream. They retrieved her body,
performed the last rites, and laid her to rest in a cemetery.

The girl had harboured feelings for a local man who did not
reciprocate them. After her burial, the man began experiencing
unsettling dreams about her and complained about her. Shortly
thereafter, he disappeared so that no one knew what had become
of him. A search ensued, and his lifeless body was eventually found
by the sea under high cliffs, all battered and bruised. People believed
that the girl had come back as a ghost, plunged him off the cliffs, and
thus killed him. When this story started doing the rounds, the girl's
brothers dug her up. Upon opening the coffin, they discovered her
turned face-down. Disturbed by this sight, they turned her around,
and drove sharp steel nails into the soles of her feet before resealing

the coffin and restoring the grave to its original state. Since then, the ghost of their sister has not been sighted.

Told by an unknown storyteller to Jón Árnason,
translated by Sigurður Líndal

The practice of driving nails into the soles of people who are believed to be ghosts is found in other legends and folk belief as well. With each step, the ghost has more difficulty walking, underlining the extent to which the ghost is bound to its body.

Priest Hálfdán and Ólöf of Lónkot

A certain old woman, named Ólöf, lived at a farm called Lónkot, in the parish of Fell, of which Hálfdán was the priest. She was very wise, and very well skilled in magic, but by no means amiable, and rather given to quarrelling. She and Hálfdán never got on well together, and many were the high words that passed between them whenever they met.

One day in the autumn, the priest and some of his workers were out fishing, and had had the luck to catch a large halibut. As, however, the weather was sharp and frosty, the rowers paid little enough heed to the fish, but blew ruefully on their chilled fingers and grumbled at the cold. Seeing this, Hálfdán said to them, "What would you give me, my lads, if I caught a good large hot sausage for you now?" They shook their heads, and said that he could not do so, skilful as he was, and looked more wretched than before. But the priest threw out a line over the edge of the boat, and in an instant dragged up on the end of it a large sausage, so hot that it bubbled and sputtered again. The rowers could hardly believe their eyes, but spent a mighty short time in wondering, finding that the best way to test the reality of the sausage was to eat it; which they forthwith did. But when they had finished their meal, the halibut was no more to be seen.

"Aha!" said the priest, "something the old woman must have for her hot sausage."

The truth was that Hálfdán had enchanted the sausage from Dame Ólöf; but she (like many other good folk we could mention) was not disposed to give a thing away when she could sell it at a price, so she paid herself by enchanting the halibut from Hálfdán.

Told by an unknown storyteller to Jón Árnason,
translated by Eiríkur Magnússon and George E. J. Powell

→→→≫ ≪←←←

Several Icelandic legends tell of the sorcerer and priest Hálfdán. The stories have been connected to a man called Hálfdán Narfason (d. 1568), who served as a priest at Fell in Sléttuhlíð, in the north of Iceland. In legends he is usually portrayed in a positive light, doing harmless magic (such as stealing sausages from old women) or helping others.

The Grímsey Man and the Bear

Once, in a winter, it happened in Grímsey, that the fire died out, and not in any one hut could fire be got. At this time it froze hard, but continued calm, so that the channel between Grímsey and the mainland was frozen over, and the ice thought strong enough to bear men.

The people of Grímsey had mind, therefore, to send to the mainland for fire, and to this end they chose the three briskest and strongest men on the island. They went away early one morning, in calm weather, and a great many of the island-folk went with them out on the ice, and bade them farewell and God-speed. Nothing is told of their travels, till, at about the middle of the channel, they found the ice open; the rift was so long that they could not see out, over the end of it, and so broad that only two of the messengers could jump over it, to do which the third would by no means trust himself. The others bade him, therefore, get back to the island, they themselves continuing their journey towards the land. He stood on the edge of the ice, unwilling to return to the island, and looked a long look after his companions; then he decided to go along the water, till he might find perchance, a point where the opening was narrower. When the day passed on, clouds gathered quickly, and a southern gale sprang up with rain and sleet; the ice suddenly began to melt, and at last the man was left on a piece of floating ice, drifting towards the main ocean.

In the evening, this piece of ice drifted against a large floe, up which the man went, and walked over it until he found a she-bear, resting over her young ones. The man was as cold as he was hungry, and in agonies of fear for his life. When the she-bear saw the man, she gazed at him for some time, and then, rising from her lair, went towards and round him, making him signs to come into her lair and lie down beside her cubs. This he did with but half a mind. After this, the animal laid herself down upon him, spreading herself out over him and her young ones, covering them all as well as she could, and by her signs, managed to make him take her teat into his mouth, and suck, together with her cubs. Thus passed the night.

The next day, the animal rose up from her lair and gave the man signs to follow her. When they came to the ice, not far thence, the bear flung herself down, giving the man to understand that he was to mount on her back. When the man had mounted, she shook herself till he could no longer hold himself on, and tumbled off. No more attempts were made by her, this time, but the man deemed this play of hers strange enough. Now three days passed in this way; at nights the man rested in her lair and sucked her, but every morning, she repeated the same exercise, making the man sit on her back and always shaking him off again. The fourth morning, the man could hold himself on her back, shake and twist herself as she would. This day, in the afternoon, she started from the floe, with the man on her back, and swam to the island. When they came to shore, the man beckoned his bear friend to follow him, and they went home, and he ordered his best cow to be milked, and gave of the teat-warm milk to the weary bear, as much as she would have. Then he went before her, to his pen, and took forth from it two of his best rams, tied them together by their horns, and flung them across the back of the bear, who swam away again, with her charge, to her young ones, and had a goodly feast of it.

This was a day of great rejoicing in Grímsey; for, while the islanders gazed in wonder after the bear, a boat was coming, sailing from the land, towards the island, having on board both the messengers, and the sorely-needed fire.

Told by an unknown storyteller to Sveinbjörn Hallgrímsson, translated by Eiríkur Magnússon and George E. J. Powell

⤙⤙⤙ ⤚⤚⤚

Grímsey is a small island north of Iceland's mainland that straddles the Arctic Circle, where there have been sightings of polar bears: for example, the largest polar bear ever killed in Iceland was in Grímsey in 1969 and can now be seen at the Húsavík museum. In Icelandic legends, polar bears are often said to show human-like qualities; in this story, the bear is noted to be a mother and shown as a caretaker.

The Nixie

There was once a girl who had been charged by her master to look after some ewes which were lost. She had gone a long way after them, until she was quite tired, when suddenly she saw before her a grey horse. Much delighted at this, she went up to it and bound her garter into its mouth for a bridle, but just as she was going to mount she said, "I feel afraid, I cannot be bothered to mount this horse." As soon as the animal heard these words it leaped into some water that stood near, and disappeared.

Then the girl saw that this was a river-horse.

Now the nature of this animal is that it cannot bear to hear its own name "Nennir", which can be translated to "bothered", and is the reason why it jumped into the water when the girl said, "I feel afraid, I cannot be bothered to mount this horse."

The same is the effect on the river-horse if it hears the name of the Devil.

Listen to another story.

Three children were playing together on the shingly bank of a river, when they saw a grey horse standing near them and went up to it to look at it. One of the children mounted on its back and after him another, to have a ride for pleasure, and only the eldest one was left. They asked him to follow, "for," they said, "the horse's back is surely long enough for all three of us."

But the child refused, and said, "I cannot be bothered." No sooner were the words out of his mouth, than the horse leaped into the river with the two other children, who were both drowned, while only the eldest survived to tell us this story of Nennir the grey river-horse.

Told by Hallgrímur Hannesson Scheving and people from Borgarfjörður to Magnús Grímsson, translated by Eiríkur Magnússon and George E. J. Powell

⟶⟫ ⟪⟵

The *nykur* (Eng. nixie; Nor: nøkken) is an underwater horse, often seen by lakes or rivers or even in the ocean. According to legend, it can sometimes be recognized by the fact that its hoofs and ears point backwards. The *nykur* is said to be dangerous for farm animals as well as people, for it can mate with horses on land and tries to get children to sit on its back and then takes them off into the water, drowning them.[28]

6

The Shore

The seashores of Iceland are often covered in black or grey sand, ground down from the black volcanic rocks that form when lava has cooled and solidified. The coastline is interspersed with narrow fjords, bays and coves. In Iceland the shore holds an important place both geologically and in the body of folk legend.

In earlier times, many farms were located close to the shoreline as the ocean was both an important resource for fishing and one of the main means of travelling. People would also go to the shore to collect eggs and eider down, seaweed, plants and mussels. They would check their fishing nets and sometimes hunt the seals that were resting close to the shore or collect the driftwood that had travelled with the currents from places such as Siberia. Due to a general lack of forests in Iceland, such driftwood was especially important in past centuries. It absorbs salt from the ocean on its way to shore, making it great building material as the salt protects it from fouling.[1]

People would also make use of other things that washed ashore. Those whales that got stranded on the shore were a particular stroke of luck for people who did not have enough food, something seen in the legend "The Marked Whale".[2] The legend in question takes place during spring after an especially harsh winter when ice had surrounded the country, livestock had died and famine was expected. That winter, one farmer had two whales wash up on his shore along with the ice. He decided to share the meat with everyone, so the people from nearby farms came over to get some of the whale meat. The man's wife and his friends were somewhat surprised by his generosity, but the man believed that God had chosen the whales to wash up on his land because he knew that the farmer would share them with others. According to the legend, this saved the people in the area from dying of hunger. The following spring, a blue whale marked with the farmer's initials washed ashore, and the farmer believed that this was God's reward for him sharing the previous two whales. Once again, this legend underlines how the act of helping others in need is rewarded.

According to Icelandic law at the time, those tenant farmers who lived on farms had no rights to what washed ashore unless they paid compensation to the landowner, and until shortly after the middle of the nineteenth century, those landowners tended to be wealthy farmers, the Church or the king. The law also stated that everything man-made that washed ashore was the property of the king of Denmark.[3] All the same, the existence of such laws does not necessarily mean that they were enforced in reality. It is not hard to imagine that people of the time would have used everything useful that washed ashore to make their lives easier or to survive, something else that is often reflected in the legends.

In nineteenth-century Iceland the shore was a threshold, and it can therefore be considered a liminal space, an ever-changing place where anything can happen.[4] As Terry Gunnell notes:

> In many senses, the shoreline was the ultimate liminal space: between here and there; between above and below; between clarity and opaqueness; between life and death. It was not even constant, changing in shape and size by the hour as the tides came in and went out, and the winds rose and fell.[5]

The shore was the threshold between Iceland and the rest of the world, and, because of the very real dangers of the ocean, sometimes also a threshold between life and death. Liminal spaces, such as the shore, often attract legends. Since it was an ever-changing place, ordinary rules and even the laws of nature do not seem to apply here, and the veil between the natural and supernatural is thinner, something that also makes the shore a place of danger.

The connection between the shore and death was reflected in the hazards of the ocean not only for fishermen but for those who travelled on the shore. Places that go underwater during high tide are called *flæðisker* (tidal skerries), and it was extremely dangerous to get trapped there. It was against the law to trap someone innocent in the high tide or to leave them on a tidal skerry. Some Icelandic legends depict how evil and cruel such an act was, such as in the legend of the skerry Sesselja,[6] named after a young girl who was very poor and dependent on help from the county. In Iceland the poor were seen first and foremost as being the responsibility of their families. When that was not possible, they became the responsibility of the county. Sesselja had been provided for by the parish of Tungusveit, where she was born, but she later moved on to another parish called Selströnd. The sheriff at Selströnd was unhappy about having to take care of the girl and decided to send a few workers on a boat across the fjord to return the girl to her home parish. When the workers arrived, the sheriff of her old county refused to take her back and ordered them not to come ashore. Since the workers did not dare return with the girl, they decided to leave her on a small skerry, hoping that the men of Tungusveit would hear her cries for help as the tide came in and rescue her. They never came, and the young Sesselja was drowned when the tide came in. The skerry now bears her name as a stark reminder of how badly people could treat the poor and the dangers of the tidal skerries.

Places on the shore that the ocean reached during high tide were sometimes chosen as places for executions and burial sites for those who could not be put to rest within the graveyard. As mentioned earlier, those who had broken the law or taken their own lives could not be buried in the graveyard. In Norwegian laws from the fourteenth century (a time when Iceland was still under Norwegian rule), it is stated that such people should be "buried on the shore, where the ocean and the green grass meet".[7] However, as previously mentioned, some people considered the ocean to be the equivalent of the graveyard, meaning that the shore was somewhere in between. This idea has roots in the Christian idea that after Jesus was baptized in the River Jordan, all rivers and waters became infused with his blessing.[8]

Sometimes, large rocks along the shore were used for executions by hanging, and during the witch hunts in Iceland, three men were burned on the shore in Árneshreppur, one of the most rural parts of Iceland today. This was done for practical reasons, as driftwood could be used to make the stake, and the ocean would take care of cleaning the site when the tide later came in.[9]

Sometimes the bodies of fishermen who had been the victims of shipwrecks would also wash ashore, and many people feared the possibility of stumbling upon such a dead body while walking along the shoreline. A man born in 1912 notes that young children were taught how to react if they found a body on the shore.[10] According to Icelandic folk belief, it was important to tend to such bodies, people being expected to "give them their last rites, adjust the body accordingly, and cover their face". If this was not done, the consequences were dire: "otherwise the dead could possibly come back to harm you or haunt you for the rest of your life."[11] The person who found a body was also responsible for ensuring that it was transported to a churchyard by informing the local authorities of its whereabouts. Numerous legends in the legend collections talk about such washed-up bodies, underlining the importance of showing the body respect. They also underscore the degree to which the shore was seen as being the threshold between Iceland and the rest of the world. As Terry Gunnell comments, in those stories one can observe an interesting division based on whether the body was Icelandic or foreign. Legends that tell of Icelanders who were lost at sea and washed up on the shore often relate how the deceased appeared to their friends or family back home in a dream. They tell them where their bodies can be found, asking to be given a Christian burial and be laid to rest alongside their family members. Those stories rarely say anything about the state and appearance of the body when it is found; rather, they provide a powerful reflection of the anguish of those waiting at home for news and their need for closure. In the case of foreign bodies, things are more complicated as they have not returned home, having been washed up in Iceland; instead, they have in a sense invaded the border and are unknown and possibly dangerous.[12]

This sense of the shore as a liminal space is further reflected in other legends. Some legends also say that one can find various magical stones and plants along the shore. According to Jón Árnason, the *óskasteinn* (wishing stone) could be found on the shore when the tide came in during a waxing moon, and this would allow anyone who possessed it to make a wish. Another stone that could be found on the shore was a *lausnarsteinn* (release stone), which had the ability to help women who were giving birth. Inside such stones were smaller stones, together representing a mother and her child. Those midwives who had a

This 1917 watercolour by Ásgrímur Jónsson depicts a body washed ashore with a woman beside it. In the old farming society, respecting the dead was of great importance, and children would learn how to react if they found a body when walking along the shore.

lausnarsteinn in their possession were considered to be very fortu-
nate.[13] A few such stones that have been preserved have in fact turned
out to be seeds that have washed ashore from foreign places.

Various legends also tell of people encountering monsters on the
shore. Some tell of monsters that are a particular threat to animals,
something that applies in particular to those stories of the *fjörulalli*
(beach creep). The beach creep is said to target sheep during the lambing season, when it troubles the ewes, causing mutations in newborn
lambs. Other farm animals have counterparts in the ocean. This includes
the so-called *sækýr* (sea cattle), which were said to have big bladders
on the front of their noses and to pose a risk to other cattle until the
bladder had been popped, at which point the animal became a great
milking cow. The *nykur* (nixie), meanwhile, is a sea or water horse as
seen in the previous chapter.[14]

In other legends, people are shown to be the direct targets of
monsters. It is interesting to note that many legends of this kind are
set on the shore and take place during the night, something that adds
to the ambiguity of the shoreline.

The artist Arngrímur Sigurðsson (b. 1988) published *Museum of Hidden Beings* in 2014, featuring 34 illustrations of supernatural creatures from Icelandic folklore, including sea monsters. Here we see his depiction of a merman, which was considered to be quite a dangerous being, standing on the shore.

A Ghost Doffs His Cap

Once, a man was strolling along the seaside late at night. Suddenly, he found himself confronted by a ghost, dripping with seawater. The man felt forced to enter the sea where he waded, although he knew it was not the wisest choice. So, in a fit of rage, he brandished his staff and fiercely attacked the ghost, causing it to recoil, so he could get out of the sea. But he had not travelled far when he met a man.

Politely, he tipped his cap and greeted the man, intending to seek directions, as he was disoriented. But the other man removed not just his cap but his entire head. Thinking quickly, the man wedged his staff between the ghost's neck and head, preventing it from reattaching. The ghost, unable to reclaim its head, spun aimlessly while the man regained his bearings and made his way home.

The same is true of sorcerers and ghosts: if they seem to take their heads off, they won't be able to put them back on if something is inserted between the head and the neck.

Told by Einar Bjarnason to Jón Árnason,
translated by Sigurður Líndal

⇢⟫ ⟪⟵

Here, once again, the physicality of the ghost is clear, as the man does not realize that he is meeting the ghost for a second time until it removes its head. Unfortunately, today, with decreasing numbers of people carrying a hat and staff, defeating ghosts might prove to be more challenging.

The Story of the Man with the Lantern and the Sea Monster

One time, not that long ago, a man was travelling alone late in the evening along the seashore near Reykjavík. Since it was dim, the man had a lantern to light up the way that lay before him. He continued along the shore. All of a sudden, he found the strength drain from his body so that he started to feel tremors in his bones without any explanation. He was hardly able to continue on from where he was standing but managed to drag himself slightly further with a little strength, limp and weak yet not ill. It was then that he became vaguely aware of the presence of something unpleasant. He cast his light upon the area that was ahead of him. He saw a large being close before him, and it seemed to him that it was a sea monster. He then realized that the closer that he got to it, the more he lost his strength. At this point he wanted to escape but was so powerless that he could hardly totter. He then tried to gradually drag himself along past it and was able to do this. All of a sudden, it crossed his mind that it could have been the lantern that attracted the sea monster to him. He threw it away from himself and was simultaneously able to move past the monster. It then happened that he slowly regained his strength and became quicker and quicker, until he could run. The last that he saw of the monster, it was taking the lantern. But the man was able to reach other people, exhausted.

The following day, the lantern was found smashed to pieces in the place where the man had left it.

Told by an unknown storyteller to Sigfús Sigfússon,
translated by Alice Bower

➤➤➤ ⟨⟨⟨⟨

Jón at Stokkseyri and the Monster

During the early seventeenth century, a man named Jón lived
in Stokkseyrarhverfi. He was extremely hardy but poor, so he
often walked the beach to see if he could find something useful
that had washed ashore. Once, Jón went beachcombing, as often
before, and found nothing but a small roller. Dusk was falling
when Jón started for home. He saw something lying right next
to him on the shore, and it first occurred to him that it was a
dead sheep.

Jón began to look more closely, but when he reached
the pile, he saw that it could not be a sheep, for it was both
somewhat larger and so different from a sheep in shape. The
head was extremely large, and the ears were so long and drooping
that they fell below the head. This creature was similar in size to
a young colt, but its legs were so short that Jón could not see
whether there were several or none. This animal was all covered
with shells on the outside, and it rattled with a sound like when
one walks on dry shells, but its eyes glowed as if they were the
eyes of a cat.

Jón now thought himself in an unfortunate situation,
as he had come upon a terrible monster, and he expected that
it would kill him there and then. The monster did indeed attack
him, but Jón hit it with the roller with all his might, and he
was able to defend himself for a long time in this way. Still, the
monster showed no signs of fatigue, despite the heavy blows
dealt to it by Jón. After a long fight, the monster began to ease
up and shake its head, because all its skin had slid off. However,
it still pressed Jón, who kept hitting it, until it jumped off and
into the sea; by then Jón was exhausted and so short of breath
that he laid down where he was, and lay there until daybreak;
then he got up, very tired still, and went home, but Jón was
for a long time afterwards bedridden. At first Jón would not

tell anyone what had befallen him, but his wife was finally able to get it out of him.

Told by Símon Gíslason to Ólafur Davíðsson,
translated by Sigurður Líndal

---»»» «««---

A Man from Sea and a Man from Land

In ancient times there lived a man on a coastal farm named Jón. During the day, he let his livestock graze by the seashore, but at night he housed them in a seaward shelter a short distance from his farm. Jón had long been a solitary farmer and managed this way of life quite well until he reached an old age. He had been a robust and diligent worker; however, as time went on he had to employ a farmhand and entrusted him with the care of the livestock.

As the farmhand took over the flock, Jón told him never to remain near the sea after sunset, as the shores were dangerous. He instructed the farmhand to shelter the sheep before nightfall and return home. The farmhand agreed to these conditions, and some time passed without any incident.

One evening, the farmhand did not return home at the usual time, and the night passed without his arrival. In the morning, Jón set out to search for him and discovered the farmhand's remains scattered in the ocean. Jón believed that a sea monster had killed the farmhand and torn his body apart. This saddened Jón greatly, for the farmhand had been a good smith.

After the farmhand's death, Jón decided to take matters into his own hands. He crafted a great and sharp knife and attached it to his arm in a way that allowed him to keep his hand free but also reach the knife whenever he wanted and needed. After that he ventured down to the shore, allowing his sheep to graze the shoreline well past sunset.

Suddenly, a merman emerged from the sea and attacked him. A fierce struggle ensued, with Jón desperately trying to secure his grip on the merman, who was covered in seashells. They wrestled all night, the merman continually attempting to drag Jón into the sea, but he resisted skilfully, knowing that only death awaited him in the deep waters.

Eventually, they both grew exhausted, especially the merman, and Jón continued to grapple with him until he noticed an exposed spot on the merman's chest where no seashell protected him. Seizing the opportunity, Jón quickly grabbed the knife and drove it into the creature's chest.

The creature reacted vigorously, freed itself from Jón's grasp, abandoned their fight and leaped back into the sea. Jón dragged his tired body home and was bedridden for a while after his encounter with the merman, as he had been severely wounded and battered. However, he eventually recovered and regained his health.

Told by an unknown storyteller to Sigfús Sigfússon,
translated by Dagrún Ósk Jónsdóttir

⟶≫ ≪⟵

The three stories "The Story of the Man with the Lantern and the Sea Monster", "Jón at Stokkseyri and the Monster" and "A Man from Sea and a Man from Land" all tell of men who go down to the shore for various purposes and encounter a sea monster, which they fight, managing to get back home despite being wounded. In the first story, the sea monster is not specified as being any particular kind of monster, nor is it said to be similar to any other animal. The second story describes a monster found in other legends and often referred to as a *skeljaskrímsli* (lit. shell monster), and in the last one the man fights a merman, which in Icelandic legends is a dangerous, horrifying creature.

Naddi

In ancient times there was a main road from Njarðvík to Borgarfjörður [in the east of Iceland], which passed over a very steep mountain, sloping down to the sea. But this road became unfrequented because a monster, half-man, half-beast, took up his abode upon it, and after nightfall used to destroy so many travellers that the way was at length considered impassable. This creature hid itself in a rocky gulf on the sea side of the mountains, which has since been called the gulf of Naddi [lit. creak]. This name arose from the fact that as people passed, a strange rattling was heard among the stones at the bottom.

It happened once, in autumn, that a certain man stopped at a farm in the neighbourhood, who intended late in the evening to cross this part of the mountain, and was not to be dissuaded from his determination by the entreaties of the farmer and his family. So he started off with the words "as long as I fear nothing, nothing can harm me."

When he came to the gulf he met with the monster, and at once attacked it, and they had a long and fearful struggle together. In their fight they came together to the verge of a precipice which has been since called Krossjaðar. Over this the man hurled the monster. Afterwards upon this very spot was raised a cross, with this inscription:

"Effigiem Christi, qui prodis, pronus Honora."

The man came to Njarðvík, black and blue with his struggle, and, after having kept his bed for a month, recovered.

Never was this fearful sea-monster seen after it had been vanquished by a human being. The man soon forgot his bruises in the glory of having rid his country of such a plague.

Told by an unknown storyteller to Jón Sigurðsson,
translated by Eiríkur Magnússon and George E. J. Powell

→→》 《←←

The story of the sea monster Naddi takes place in the eastern part of Iceland. The creature was considered to belong to the sea and to live in a cave somewhere on the shore, so people travelling over a nearby mountain path were at risk of running into it. While it is less common in the Icelandic legends that sea monsters are defeated by Christianity, that is what happens here, since a cross is raised where the man defeated the monster. That cross can still be found today and is regularly repaired. It is said to offer protection to those who travel there and keeps the story alive in the area. The Latin writing on it translates to "You who pass, kneel and honour the image of Christ".

Stories of the Beach Creep

In the Westfjords, there are many stories of strange creatures coming ashore from the sea. Some believe them to be sea otters, but others call them beach creeps. People describe them as closely resembling sheep in size and shape. They claim that the beach creeps primarily come ashore during the lambing season and try to trouble the ewes. People argue that this is proven by the fact that they cause mutations in newborn lambs, causing them to look similar to the beach creeps.

One incident occurred in the late nineteenth century in Bjarnarhöfn, in the Breiðafjörður region, early in the winter. Six men went out during the evening wake to see whether any missing sheep had returned to the farm. Then they saw something moving quickly near one of the houses. They thought it was a sheep and ran over to shelter it. However, when they got closer, they saw that it was alone and not a sheep at all. They surrounded it, but then the creature darted towards the sea, and they all followed it. One of the men later described it to me, saying, "It moved as quickly as a dog. It had a short, round head and looked more like a dog than a sheep, except for the hump on its back." It moved by jumping.

Another story tells of a farmer in Stapadalur, in Arnafjörður, who was travelling along the shore after dark, carrying an unloaded shotgun, when he came across an animal. It seemed to him to be about the size of a sheep, and quite similar to it. However, it appeared to stand on its front legs, while the hind part dragged in the sand. The farmer struck the back of the animal with his gun with such force that the butt of the gun broke off. The animal dragged itself back into the ocean and disappeared. The farmer told of this when he returned home, and people believed that it was a beach creep.

The third story tells of Jón Jónsson from Refsmýri, in northern Múlasýsla, when he was almost at the age of confirmation. He was once searching for cattle in bad weather. When he came south to the so-called Landamótstangi, he saw a strange creature emerging from the sea, roughly the size of a year-old calf. It slowly came up to the shore and stopped there, sniffing the air. Jón saw that it had short, cub-like legs and a long tail. Both Jón and his dog stared at it for a while; the dog's eyes were sharp and its ears perked up, but no sound came from it. Then Jón went home.

Told by unknown storytellers to Sigfús Sigfússon,
translated by Dagrún Ósk Jónsdóttir

⟶≫─≪⟵

This illustration, which accompanied the translations of Eiríkur Magnússon and George E. J. Powell, illustrates the story "The Troll in the Skrúður" in *Icelandic Legends* (1864). Notably the troll is depicted wearing rings on every finger, reflecting the idea in some Icelandic folk legends where trolls are portrayed as wealthy and in possession of various treasures.

The Troll in the Skrúður

Long ago, the priest's daughter at Hólmar, near Reiðarfjörður, was lost from her father's house, and though search was made for her in all directions, both by sea and land, was not found again.

At the mouth of Reiðarfjörður there is a high rocky island called Skrúður, upon which the priest used to graze his sheep, from the end of the autumn till the spring. But after he had lost his daughter, it happened that every winter, for several years, his best rams always disappeared.

Once, in the winter, some fishermen were caught in a storm at sea, and were compelled to take shelter under this rocky island. When they had fastened their boats, they sat down near the beach, drenched as they were, and to while away the time, sang songs about the Virgin Mary, when suddenly the rock opened, and a gigantic hand came out, with a ring on each finger, and the arm clad in a scarlet velvet sleeve, which thrust down towards them a large bowl full of stir-about, with as many spoons in it as there were fishermen.

At the same time they heard a voice saying, "My wife is pleased now, but not I."

When the men had eaten the stir-about, the bowl disappeared into the rock in the same way as it had appeared. The next day the storm had abated, and they rowed safely to the mainland.

At the same season in the year following, the fishermen were again driven to seek shelter on this island by violent winds; and while they sat near the beach, they amused themselves by singing songs about Andri the Hero; when the same hand appeared from the rock, holding out to them a great dish full of fat smoked mutton, and they heard these words, "Now am I pleased, but not my wife."

So the fishermen ate the meat, and the dish was taken back into the rock. Soon afterwards the wind fell, and they were enabled to row safely to shore.

Some years passed, until Bishop Guðmundur visited that part of his diocese, in order to bind the malignant monsters in rocks and waters and mountains, by his prayers. When he came to Hólmar, he was asked by the priest to consecrate the island Skrúður; but the same night, the bishop had a dream, in which a tall and splendidly dressed man came to him and said, "Do not obey the priest's injunction, nor consecrate Skrúður, for it will be very difficult for me to move away with all my chattels before your arrival. Besides this, I may as well tell you, that if you come out to visit that island, it will be your last journey in this life." So the bishop refused on the morrow to consecrate the island at all, and the troll was left in peace.

Told by Sigríður Pálsdóttir to Jón Árnason, translated by
Eiríkur Magnússon and George E. J. Powell

⟶≫ ≪⟵

Trolls are sometimes said to live in big cliffs close to the shore. Guðmundur, who is mentioned in the story, was born in 1161 and was Bishop of Hólar in Hjaltadalur; he was usually called Guðmundur *góði* (Guðmundur the Good). He was famous for travelling the country and blessing difficult routes, scree slopes and fjords, and consecrating springs and wells. Various folk legends are connected to his blessings, such as the one told here.

Boot-Lout

The following stories about the origin of Boot-Lout are in circulation in Arnarfjörður in the west:

It happened that a shepherd of the priest in Selárdalur was herding sheep out by Verdalir. It was then that he found a beached corpse of a well-dressed young man. Among other things, he wore new leather boots. In those days, only well-to-do men had that type of footwear. The boy found them very desirable and started to pull them off the corpse. This went well with the first boot, but when he was going to take the second, the foot of the corpse was so clenched that he could not get it off. The story says that he then became frustrated and threw both corpse and boot into the sea and returned home once he had done so. After this, it became apparent that there was haunting, and those with second sight believed themselves to see a man walking around after dusk in only one boot. He targeted the shepherd the most, who told the whole story when questioned by the priest. The priest then got a magician to take care of the ghost. The magician clearly stated that no human or animal may be outdoors on the evening that he was to attempt this. That evening at bedtime a great din was heard in Selárdalur, as if something were dragged down the roof or chased across the farmyard. The women were very scared, but the young men said that there was little danger. The shepherd said that he would show them whether he dared to go out, and before one could look around, he had already ripped open the entrance to the farmstead. In that second the ghost attacked him and turned his head in such a way that his face pointed straight up from his shoulder. The workers who had come out after him helped him back inside. He was laid on a bed in the living room, but died shortly afterwards. It is said of the sorcerer that, following this, he said people should not look to him anymore for help dealing with the ghost, since his advice had not been followed. But the man claimed that the ghost had been stunned in a way that meant he should not be of harm to people anymore, but would still be able to cause trouble.

After the death of the shepherd, the ghost followed the people of Selárdalur. He was generally seen with a boot on one foot and for that reason was called Boot-Lout.

Once, when I was little, I saw Boot-Lout. I would likely have been nine or ten years old. My parents lived in Uppsalir, in Selárdalur. There it was the custom then, and is surely still, that people would row out to sea in the autumn. It was not so far from the sea that people were not able to sleep at home [rather than at specific fishing stations] and they would get up between three and four in the morning to check the weather. The living room was up in the loft; my parents slept there, and I was in a bed across from them. I woke up as my father left the room, and I heard him go down the stairs and across the hallway to open the entrance to the farmstead. I then immediately heard someone come across the hallway and up the stairs, more forcefully than usual. I saw right then something pale and in the likeness of a human come in through the door and move itself towards my bed. It supported itself with its left hand upon a table that was between the beds, and it was as if it was going to reach towards my mother. I then became scared and called out to her what this was. She saw nothing, and when she started speaking the ghost disappeared. I told my mother what I had seen. She said that it was just nonsense, that I should make the sign of the cross and read my prayers. When I went back to sleep, I dreamed that a man with a shoe on only one foot came to my mother and asked her for help. I described my dream when I woke up. People said: "You have dreamed of Boot-Lout."

The next day, conditions were not suitable for seafaring and therefore people did not row out. A man then came to find my father, and he sat by the foot of my bed and my mother sat in her bed. When he stood up to say thank you for the coffee, he supported himself by his left hand on exactly the same spot as the being had done during that night. Everybody believed that I had seen Boot-Lout there that night because he was known to haunt the man who came.

*Told by Jarþrúður Nikulásdóttir to Jón Thorarensen,
translated by Alice Bower*

Many legends tell of foreign bodies that have washed ashore. In these stories, the importance of respecting the body is often highlighted, as is the duty of those who find it to tend to the corpse. Ignoring it showed great disrespect, and even worse was if someone went as far as stealing something from the body, taking clothes or money, for example. As Terry Gunnell points out, this posed a difficult moral choice for Icelanders, who were already wary of those foreigners who did not belong within the community and out of necessity were used to making use of everything they found washed up on the shore. Nevertheless, in Icelandic legends, the general belief seems to have been be that if any part of the deceased (or any of their possessions) was removed from the body, this was likely to disturb their eternal peace; they would return as a vengeful ghost, both to reclaim their property and to seek revenge. These types of legends are also well known in other parts of Europe.[15]

The Sealskin

There was once a man who lived in Mýrdalur, in the east, who was walking past cliffs down by the sea one morning, earlier than when people would usually leave the house. He came to the entrance of a cave and heard the sound of dancing and merriment from inside, while outside he saw very many sealskins. He took one of the sealskins with him, carried it home and locked it in a chest. Later that day, he came back to the cave entrance. There sat a young and pretty woman. She was completely naked and cried a lot. It was the seal whose skin the man had taken. The man gave the young woman clothes, comforted her and took her home with him. She was loyal to him, but appeared to enjoy the company of others less. She often sat and looked out towards the sea. After some time, the man married her. Things went well between them and they were blessed with children. The man always kept the skin locked in the chest and took the key with him wherever he went. Many years later, he rowed out to sea and accidentally left the key under the edge of his pillow at home. Others say that he had gone with the other inhabitants of his farm to a church service on Christmas Eve, but that his wife had been ill and unable to go with him, and that he had forgotten to take the key out of the pocket of his everyday clothes when he changed. When he returned home, the chest was open and both his wife and the skin had disappeared. She had taken the key and looked in the chest out of curiosity, and there she had found the skin. Unable to withstand the temptation, she had said goodbye to her children, donned the skin and plunged into the sea. It is said that before she plunged into the sea, she had let this out of her mouth:

> Woe is me,
> I have seven children in the sea
> And seven children on land.

It is said that this caused the man much hurt.

When the man next rowed out to sea, a seal often swam around his boat, and it was as if tears ran from its eyes. He had very good luck in fishing after this, and many good fortunes washed up on his shores. People often saw that when the couple's children walked by the sea, a seal swam close to the shore, both when they walked on the beach and on land, and threw fish of many colours and beautiful shells up to them. But their mother never returned to land.

Told by Hólmfríður Þorvaldsdóttir to Magnús Grímsson,
Jón Árnason and Skúli Gíslason, translated by Alice Bower

Two kinds of seal are commonly found around Iceland: the harbour seal and the grey seal. Other types of seals nonetheless visit Iceland regularly, and in the nineteenth century some of them could be found by Icelandic shores all year round, including the harp seal, the ringed seal, the hooded seal, the bearded seal and walrus. All of these animals were hunted for their meat, skin and blubber whenever possible.[16]

In Iceland a great deal of folk belief surrounded seals. One of the best-known beliefs is the idea that seals are humans. In his collection, Jón Árnason notes that the origin of the seal was said to be traced back to the biblical story of Pharaoh, who, following Moses over the Red Sea, disappeared into the ocean with all his men. According to folk belief, these men did not drown but were turned into seals: "Since then, the seals live as a distinct generation beneath the sea, but have human form, nature and characteristics within their seal costumes."[17] This was said to be proved by similarities between the bones of seals and those of humans, as well as the human-like eyes of the seal. According to the legends, the seals can come onto land as humans once a year, and dance and sing on the shore. The story above tells of how a female seal that comes to shore is trapped by a farmer whom she encounters.

Seals Take Revenge

In Suðursveit, a farmer had a habit of taking his pregnant wife out to sea with him, proudly displaying her to the seals before mercilessly hunting them down. However, as the saying goes, "even the clever get what is coming," and the seals contemplated revenge. Once, when the woman was pregnant and went to the beach with the farmer, they noticed an unusual number of seals, of all sizes and varieties, encircling them. Initially unsuspecting, they soon found themselves under attack. Despite the farmer's efforts to defend them, the seals overwhelmed them, viciously tearing the woman apart. Devastated, the farmer then returned home.

*Told by Guðrún Runólfsdóttir to Sigfús Sigfússon,
translated by Sigurður Líndal*

⸻⸻

While in some stories, seals were said to be people, more gruesome legends of seals are also known in Iceland, telling of seals that hunt and eat pregnant women. A few legends, mostly found in the collection of Sigfús Sigfússon, also tell of farmers who took their pregnant wives out to sea in order to attract seals, which they then hunted. This usually ends badly for them, as the seal manages to kill the woman and eat the fetus. In his collection, Sigfús notes that this belief, that seals could be attracted to pregnant women, was well known in other Nordic countries and that in Iceland, farmers in the north were extremely fond of this method to lure in seals.[18]

It is interesting to note that in all other legends included in this chapter, it is men who venture to the shore by themselves; this belief that seals eat pregnant women seems to have given the storytellers a reason to have a woman go to the shore, a place that is otherwise often out of their reach in the Icelandic legend corpus.

Epilogue

Good stories possess the ability to transport us to another place and time, allowing us to forget our surroundings and become fully immersed in the narrative. When I first heard the story of my family ghost, Ennis-Móri, I was transported from my parents' car to the farming society of the nineteenth century. Furthermore, legends have the power to affect us: we might experience joy or sadness on hearing them, and they can spark fear or curiosity within us. Their influence can also inspire, inform and even transform us. Today, whenever I drive the same road we drove all these years ago, passing the farm where the ghost in the form of a fly found the girl and killed her, I think of the ghost and its origin. The legend has also changed the way I feel in the dark: I now see it as imbued with ghosts, which I can easily imagine lurking in the shadows around me. Once, I was a passenger in a car with one of my cousins. As we were driving along the road where Ennis-Móri is often found, she suddenly took her cap off and used it to cover the rear-view mirror. I was surprised and asked her why she had done this, and she replied that she was so afraid that the ghost would suddenly appear in the back seat that she always covered her mirror when driving through the area. She too had been affected by the story (as well as, perhaps, by ghost stories of vanishing hitchhikers), and it changed her thinking and even behaviour.

In the past, legends could change the way people acted, for example in relation to seafaring and their interactions with the landscape, and many recall being extremely afraid of the dark as a result of such tales. Legends have the ability to bring the landscape to life, imbuing it with meaning and thereby altering how people viewed it, whether it was specific places, such as hills in which the hidden people were said to live, or more general settings like the wilderness or the dark. While the stories were indeed shaped by the landscape and people's surroundings, the ruling ideology of the time and the world views of those who told them, they could also affect people's idea of their own place in the world and what was considered appropriate behaviour.

Although it is possible to draw out specific themes from the Icelandic legend material, it is clear that the ideas people had about the supernatural varied. The legend collections often reveal contradictions, as the tales were gathered from many different storytellers, who were affected by their own perspectives and the legends that they themselves had heard before. There was thus not one legend tradition in Iceland, but many.

One of the many messages conveyed by the legends is related to communication with others. The legends show how to avoid conflict and highlight the importance of showing other people respect and kindness, especially those in need, as seen for example in the legends "The Raven at Skíðastaðir", "The Grateful Elf Woman" and "Pjakkur", where those who help are greatly rewarded, and those who do not are punished. This common theme may have arisen because people in the past never knew when trouble might come their way. The qualities of being brave, hardworking, strong and a quick thinker are highlighted as desirable, as can be seen in the legends "The Worker and the Water Elves", "The Shepherd of Silfrúnarstaðir", "The Sorcerers in the Westman Islands" and "The Skeleton in Hólar Church". However in many of the stories, greed and being stingy are shown as negative qualities that may be punished, as for example in "The Hidden Woman in Múli", "The Raven at Skíðastaðir", "Pjakkur" and "Boot-Lout".

The themes of Christianity and the Church are also present in every chapter of this book, as they formed a prominent part of people's lives in Iceland during the nineteenth century. Priests held a powerful position within Icelandic society, and it is worth noting how the different classes are portrayed in the legends. In many cases, the stories affirm restrictive gender and class roles upholding the current social order. While we might see objections to or rebellion against these ideas, they are usually diminished in the end.[1] It is important that, while we read the legends and travel back in our minds to nineteenth-century Icelandic farming society, we remember that we bring with us in our baggage our own world views, shaped by the present. Nevertheless, we must also keep revisiting the legends and researching them from new points of view; to understand what has shaped our present, it is necessary to know where our ideas and world views come from.

These legends are frequently migratory, and similar stories and beliefs can be found in many other parts of the world. Similar motifs or legend types to those found in the Icelandic legend material are usually found elsewhere in Europe. However, when the tales are adapted to new surroundings, elements are lost and new aspects are added.

In the Icelandic legend corpus, we can clearly see the effect that both the landscape and the weather have had on the stories. Both appear as fateful powers that determine the course of events. This is especially true for stories that take place in the wilderness or out at sea, for example in the legends "Jón from the Farm Parthús", "Pjakkur", "Anna at Bessastaðir", "Ketilríður" and "The Grímsey Man and the Bear". The legends also highlight the importance of respecting nature, as can be seen in the belief that the homes of the hidden people, concealed in the landscape, must not be ruined, a belief that still resides in Icelandic society. One must also be careful around big rocks or cliffs, for they might once have been powerful trolls. There are in fact laws in Iceland that are meant to protect places connected to stories of the supernatural if the story was recorded over a hundred years ago. These sites are safeguarded against destruction owing to the cultural value of the legends attached to them.[2] In 2013 I interviewed people who lived on farms that included places that were said to be inhabited or owned by hidden people, such as in the legend "The Hidden Woman in Múli". The people I spoke to had a variety of feelings towards these places: while some did not care, most were quite proud of the connections and took care of these sites, looking after them and not removing rocks or grass where it was forbidden. While few would say outright that they believed in the stories, many noted that they wanted to respect the place, the story itself or the feelings of those who believed in it.[3]

As a folklorist, it is also important not to dismiss the fact that in some legends, people are simply describing their experiences of the supernatural or something that they could not quite explain. In Iceland almost everyone knows someone who has seen something that can be categorized as out of the ordinary. My great-grandmother would tell me the story of when she was herding sheep many years ago and sat down to rest next to a giant rock and heard beautiful singing coming from inside it – a well-known feature of Icelandic stories of the hidden people. Since it is not nice to accuse one's grandmother of lying, I can hardly deny the possibility that there were indeed hidden people living in the rock. And as noted, it does not matter: for her it was an experience that she held dear, and, as I have endeavoured to underline, the legends always contain a certain kind of truth.

As has been pointed out by Terry Gunnell, stories that are connected to specific places in the landscape can also work as a map: they taught people how to interact with the landscape and how to navigate it.[4] For example, stories would often be connected to places where it could be dangerous for children to play, or places where the ocean could pose a threat to fishermen. Caves and canyons where trolls were said to live are often located far from the main path: if you reach one, you have gone too far. However, legends not only served the function of being warnings. They were also told for their entertainment value; some of them were meant to send shivers down the listener's spine, while others were filled with humour. It is also important to remember that supernatural beings in legends are commonly used as vehicles to act out everyday human conflicts, making it easier for people to process them themselves.[5]

When categorizing the legends for this book based on their setting, it became clear to me that it is difficult to escape the divisions created by the original collectors of the legends, who categorized the stories based on the supernatural beings that appear in them. This was partly due to the importance of introducing these supernatural beings to those who might be less familiar with them. It is also clear that some of the legends included here could easily have fitted into other chapters, as they take place in more than one setting. In those instances, I chose the most prominent setting. However, the setting of a story certainly affects what the story conveys, and certain supernatural beings are of course more closely associated with one specific setting than another, such as the trolls and outlaws that inhabit the wilderness, or the sea monsters that are usually connected to either the ocean or the shore. Many similarities can be identified between the wilderness, the darkness, the ocean and the shore. All these places are affected by the mystery that surrounds them. Darkness turns the known into the unknown, and when the stories were originally told, both the wilderness and the ocean were to a degree uncharted territory. There, the lines between the natural and supernatural become blurred as outlaws appear as troll-like figures and animals gain human-like abilities. Additionally, the wilderness and the ocean, along with the shore, were places mainly visited by men at the time, something that is reflected in the legend material. On the other hand, legends that take place on the farm often tell of women. It is worth noting that in the supernatural realm, however, the gender roles often appear reversed, with women seeming to be in charge, such as among the hidden people and trolls.

The seasons in which the legends are noted to take place are also important here, as different seasons call for different tasks. People went into the wilderness when collecting herbs over the summertime, and, most commonly, autumn is when they went to search for lost sheep, something that underlines the importance of livestock in the past.

Some of the legends, especially those that take place in a farm setting, speak of the haymaking season. Many others take place during winter, which is perhaps not so strange considering that it is the longest season of the year in Iceland. And many of those winter legends take place around Christmas, which was considered to be a magical or liminal time when anything could happen.

Many of the legends included in this book are still told in Iceland, though many have been forgotten, too. Some are told among specific groups of people: fishermen are more likely to tell stories of sea monsters, while teenagers often enjoy ghost stories. Tour guides keep many of the folk legends alive, as they often tell these stories to those who visit Iceland, and can situate them in the landscape, within their proper setting.

The supernatural world has also long been an inspiration to artists, authors, playwrights and film-makers, who draw inspiration and ideas from the folk legends. This is evidenced by the illustrations that can be found in this book, which date from the sixteenth century to the present day. Another example is *The Lord of the Rings* by J.R.R. Tolkien, which among other things drew on Icelandic folk stories. A recent example is the Icelandic television drama *KATLA*, which was produced by Netflix and premiered on the streaming service in 2021. References to folklore and folk music can also often be seen in Icelandic music, and numerous novels and children's books in Iceland include supernatural elements or beings.

Today, new stories continue to emerge, stories that fit our present world views while also drawing from the old legend tradition. These deal with subjects and conflicts that are pressing in our times, warning, for example, of the ruin of the homes of the hidden people in the context of environmental issues and preservation of the natural world. It is important to allow the tradition to evolve and to continue to collect the stories. For those legends that are both found in the legend collections and still told in oral tradition, it would be interesting to see if, and how, they have changed, for, as mentioned earlier, they are always shaped by the time and space in which they are told, as well as the individual storyteller. Indeed, stories must maintain their relevance to society to still be told; it does not matter whether it is the messages contained in them or their entertainment value that ensures their continuity.

Just as the story of Ennis-Móri sparked my curiosity about the Icelandic legends all those years ago, I hope that you have enjoyed this glimpse into the world of folk tales and the farming society of nineteenth-century Iceland. I also hope that these stories have changed you in some way, as good stories often do, and that they imbue your surroundings with enchantment and magic.

REFERENCES

Note on References

While a great deal has been written about the Icelandic folk legends in English, it is also a fact that even more has been written by scholars in Icelandic. This is partly because of how inaccessible the material is, owing to the language barrier. It was therefore impossible to write this book without referencing important Icelandic scholarly work where appropriate. I have nevertheless tried to keep the number of references to a reasonable number, although, as evident, with mixed success.

Editor's Note

1 For further information on their translation, see Terry Gunnell, "Jón Árnason and the Collection of Icelandic Folk Legends: Ripples, Flotsam, Nets and Reflections", in *Grimm Ripples: The Legacy of the Grimms' "Deutsche Sagen" in Northern Europe* (Leiden and Boston, MA, 2022), pp. 415–17.

2 Júlíana Gottskálksdóttir and Ólafur Kvaran, *Íslensk listasaga: Frá síðari hluta 19. aldar til upphafs 21. aldar*, 5 vols (Reykjavík, 2011), vol. I, pp. 31–2.

Introduction

1 There he is called Sólheima-Móri; see Jón Árnason, *Íslenzkar þjóðsögur og ævintýri*, 6 vols (Reykjavík, 1954–61), vol. I, pp. 376–7.

2 Guðbjörg Jónsdóttir, *Gamlar glæður: Þættir úr daglegu lífi á Ströndum á síðari hluta 19. aldar* (Reykjavík, 1943), p. 85.

3 Gunnar Karlsson, *Iceland's 1100 Years: History of a Marginal Society* (London, 2000), p. 37.

4 Sigurður Gylfi Magnússon, *Wasteland with Words: A Social History of Iceland* (London, 2010), p. 21.

5 Gísli Ágúst Gunnlaugsson, *Family and Household in Iceland, 1801–1930: Demographic Socio-Economic Development, Social Legislation and Family and Household Structures* (Uppsala, 1988); Guðmundur Hálfdanarson, "Íslensk þjóðfélagsþróun á 19. öld", in *Íslensk þjóðfélagsþróun 1880–1990: Ritgerðir*, ed. Guðmundur Hálfdanarson and Svanur Kristjánsson (Reykjavík, 1993); Erla

Hulda Halldórsdóttir, "Að vera sjálfstæð: Ímyndir, veruleiki og frelsishugmyndir kvenna á 19. öld", *Saga*, xxxv/1 (1997), pp. 57–94.

6 Anna Sigurðardóttir, *Vinna kvenna á Íslandi í 1100 ár* (Reykjavík, 1985); Gunnar Sveinsson, *Alþingisbækur Íslands 10: 1711–1720* (Reykjavík, 1967); Vilhelm Vilhelmsson, *Sjálfstætt fólk: Vistarband og íslenskt samfélag á 19. öld* (Reykjavík, 2017).

7 Erla Hulda Halldórsdóttir and Guðrún Dís Jónatansdóttir, *Ártöl og áfangar í sögu íslenskra kvenna* (Reykjavík, 1998).

8 Erla Hulda Halldórsdóttir, "Að vera sjálfstæð", pp. 57–94; Sigurður Gylfi Magnússon, *Menntun, ást og sorg: Einsögu rannsókn á íslensku sveitasamfélagi 19. og 20. aldar* (Reykjavík, 1997), p. 76.

9 Magnús Gíslason, *Kvällsvaka: En Isländsk kulturtradition belyst genom studier i bondefolkningens vardagsliv och miljö under senere hälften av 1800-talet och början av 1900-talet* (Uppsala, 1977); Júlíana Þóra Magnúsdóttir, "Women of the Twilight: The Narrative Spaces of Women in the Icelandic Rural Community of the Past", *Folklore: Electronic Journal of Folklore*, lxxxiv (2022), pp. 107–10.

10 Árni Björnsson, ed., *Úr torfbæjum inn í tækniöld 1* (Reykjavík, 2003).

11 Erla Hulda Halldórsdóttir, *Nútímans konur: Menntun kvenna og mótun kyngervis á Íslandi 1850–1903* (Reykjavík, 2011), p. 107; Loftur Guttormsson, *Almenningsfræðsla á Íslandi 1880–2007* (Reykjavík, 2008), pp. 32–4.

12 Símon Jón Jóhannsson and Ragnhildur Vigfúsdóttir, *Íslandsdætur: Svipmyndir úr lífi íslenskra kvenna 1850–1950* (Reykjavík, 1991), p. 107.

13 Gísli Ágúst Gunnlaugsson, *Family and Household in Iceland*, pp. 138–41; Gunnar Karlsson, *Iceland's 1100 Years*, pp. 231–3.

14 Guðmundur Jónsson and Magnús S. Magnússon, *Hagskinna: Sögulegar hagtölur um Ísland* (Reykjavík, 1997), pp. 86, 90; Gísli Ágúst Gunnlaugsson, "Fólksfjölda- og byggðaþróun 1880–1990", in *Íslensk þjóðfélagsþróun 1880–1990*, ed. Guðmundur Hálfdanarson and Svanur Kristjánsson, pp. 107–8.

15 Anna Lísa Rúnarsdóttir, *Á tímum torfbæja: Híbýlahættir og efnismenning í íslenska torfbænum frá 1850* (Reykjavík, 2007), p. 9.

16 Gunnar Karlsson, *Iceland's 1100 Years*, pp. 280–84, 319–23.

17 Diarmuid Ó Giolláin, *Locating Irish Folklore: Tradition, Modernity, Identity* (Cork, 2000), pp. 4–24; Terry Gunnell, "Daisies Rise to Become Oaks: The Politics of Early Folktale Collection in Northern Europe", *Folklore*, cxxi/1 (2010), pp. 12–37.

18 Jacob and Wilhelm Grimm, *Deutsche Sagen*, 2 vols, 2nd edn (Berlin, 1865), vol. 1, pp. v–xxi; Terry Gunnell, ed., *Grimm Ripples: The Legacy of the Grimms' "Deutsche Sagen" in Northern Europe* (Leiden and Boston, ma, 2022), pp. 2–3.

19 Terry Gunnell, "Jón Árnason and the Collection of Icelandic Folk Legends: Ripples, Flotsam, Nets and Reflections", in *Grimm Ripples*, ed. Terry Gunnell, pp. 385–419.

20 Rósa Þorsteinsdóttir, "Konrad Maurer: Cultural Conduit and Collector", in *Grimm Ripples*, ed. Terry Gunnell, pp. 359–84.

21 Terry Gunnell, "Clerics as Collectors of Folklore in Nineteenth-Century Iceland", *ARV: Nordic Yearbook of Culture*, LXVIII (2012), pp. 45–66.

22 Jón Árnason, *Íslenzkar þjóðsögur og ævintýri*, 6 vols (Reykjavík, 1954–61), vol. I, p. xvii.

23 Rósa Þorsteinsdóttir, *Sagan upp á hvern mann: Átta íslenskir sagnamenn og ævintýrin þeirra* (Reykjavík, 2011).

24 Ibid., pp. 64–5, 123–59.

25 Linda Dégh, *Folktales and Society: Story-Telling in a Hungarian Peasant Community* (Bloomington, IN, 1989), p. 93; Rosan A. Jordan and Susan J. Kalcik, eds, *Women's Folklore, Women's Culture* (Philadelphia, PA, 1985), p. ix; Michel Foucault, "Skipan orðræðunnar", in *Spor í bókmenntafræði 20. aldar*, ed. Garðar Baldvinsson, Kristín Birgisdóttir and Kristín Viðarsdóttir, trans. Gunnar Harðarson (Reykjavík, 1991), p. 193; Terry Gunnell, "Clerics as Collectors".

26 See www.sagnagrunnur.com; Trausti Dagsson and Olga Holownia, "Legends, Letters and Linking: Lessons Learned from Amassing and Mapping Folklore and Viewing It as Part of Nineteenth-Century Culture Creation", *ARV: Nordic Yearbook of Folklore*, LXXVI (2020), pp. 55–74.

27 Jacob and Wilhelm Grimm, *Deutsche Sagen*, vol. I, pp. v–vi.

28 Max Lüthi, *Once Upon a Time: On the Nature of Fairy Tales*, trans. Lee Chadeayne and Paul Gottwald (Bloomington, IN, 1986), pp. 6–7, 12, 24.

29 Elliott Oring, "Legendry and the Rhetoric of Truth", *Journal of American Folklore*, CXXI/480 (2008), pp. 127–66.

30 Linda Dégh, *Legend and Belief: Dialectics of a Folklore Genre* (Bloomington, IN, 2001), p. 97.

31 Bengt Holbek, *Interpretation of Fairy Tales: Danish Folklore in a European Perspective* (Helsinki, 1987), p. 435; Guðrún Bjartmarsdóttir, *Bergmál: Sýnisbók íslenskra þjóðfræða* (Reykjavík, 1988), p. 22; Anna-Leena Siikala, *Interpreting Oral Narrative* (Helsinki, 1990), p. 39; Timothy Tangherlini, *Interpreting Legends: Danish Storytellers and Their Repertoires* (New York, 1994), pp. 15–17; Ülo Valk, "Folk and the Others: Constructing Social Reality in Estonian Legends", in *Legends and Landscape: Articles Based on Plenary Papers Presented at the 5th Celtic–Nordic–Baltic Folklore Symposium*, ed. Terry Gunnell (Reykjavík, 2008), p. 153.

32 Ulf Palmenfelt, "On the Understanding of Folk Legends", in *Telling Reality: Folklore Studies in Memory of Bengt Holbek*, ed. Michael Chesnutt (Copenhagen, 1993), p. 149.

33 Linda Dégh, *Folktales and Society*, p. 181.

34 Anna-Leena Siikala, "Reproducing Social Worlds: The Practice and Ideology of Oral Legends", in *Legends and Landscape*, ed. Terry Gunnell, p. 39.

35 Terry Gunnell, ed., *Legends and Landscape*, p. 15.

36 Patrick B. Mullen, "The Relationship of Legend and Folk Belief", *Journal of American Folklore*, LXXXIV/334 (1971), pp. 406–13.

37 John Miles Foley, *How to Read an Oral Poem* (Urbana, IL, 2002), p. 60.

38 Carl Wilhelm von Sydow, "Geography and Folk-Tale Oicotypes", in *Selected Papers on Folklore*, ed. Laurits Bødker (Copenhagen, 1948), pp. 50–52.
39 Antti Aarne and Stith Thompson, *The Types of the Folktale: A Classification and Bibliography*, trans. and enlarged by Stith Thompson (Helsinki, 1961); later developed in Hans-Jörg Uther, Antti Aarne and Stith Thompson, *The Types of International Folktales: A Classification and Bibliography*, 2 vols, Folklore Fellows Communications 284 (Helsinki, 2004).
40 See, for example, Reidar Th. Christiansen, *The Migratory Legends: A Proposed List of Types with a Systematic Catalogue of the Norwegian Variants*, Folklore Fellows Communications 175 (Helsinki, 1958); Bengt af Klintberg, *The Types of the Swedish Folk Legend*, Folklore Fellows Communications 330 (Helsinki, 2010).
41 Aðalheiður Guðmundsdóttir, *Handan Hindarfjalls* (Reykjavík, 2021).

1 The Farm

1 Anna Lísa Rúnarsdóttir, *Á tímum torfbæja: Hýbílahættir og efnismenning í íslenska torfbænum frá 1850* (Reykjavík, 2007).
2 Sigfús Sigfússon, *Íslenzkar þjóðsögur og sagnir*, 11 vols (Reykjavík, 1982–93), vol. II, pp. 90–91.
3 Anna Lísa Rúnarsdóttir, *Á tímum torfbæja*, pp. 12–18; Sigurður Gylfi Magnússon, *Wasteland with Words: A Social History of Iceland* (London, 2012), pp. 48–53; Jónas Jónasson, *Íslenzkir þjóðhættir* (Reykjavík, 1945), pp. 438–65.
4 Ólöf Sigurðardóttir, "Bernskuheimilið mitt", *Eimreiðin*, XII/2 (1906), pp. 96–111.
5 Þorkell Bjarnason, "Fyrir 40 árum", *Tímarit hins íslenzka bókmentafélags*, XIII (1892), pp. 177–8.
6 J. Ross Browne, *Íslandsferð J. Ross Browne 1862* (Reykjavík, 1976), p. 59.
7 Henry Holland, *Dagbók í Íslandsferð 1810* (Reykjavík, 1960), p. 60.
8 Greta Karen Friðriksdóttir, *"Ósjálfrátt býður flestum við mjög óhreinlátum mönnum": Mismunandi sjónarhorn á hreinlæti í torfbæjarsamfélaginu* (Reykjavík, 2017).
9 See, for example, Ólafur Sigurðsson, "Fyrir 40 árum", *Tímarit hins íslenzka bókmentafélags*, XV (1894), pp. 198–206.
10 Gísli Ágúst Gunnlaugsson, *Saga og samfélag: Þættir úr félagssögu 19. og 20. aldar* (Reykjavík, 1997), pp. 20–27; Gunnar Karlsson, *Iceland's 1100 Years: History of a Marginal Society* (London, 2000), p. 250; Anna Lísa Rúnarsdóttir, *Á tímum torfbæja*, pp. 9, 34–5.
11 Loftur Guttormsson, "Barnaeldi Barnaeldi, ungbarnadauði og viðkoma á Íslandi 1750–1860", in *Athöfn og orð: Afmælisrit helgað Matthíasi Jónassyni áttræðum*, ed. Sigurjón Björnsson (Reykjavík, 1983), pp. 137–68.
12 Gunnar Karlsson, *Iceland's 1100 Years*, p. 37.
13 Jón Jónsson, *Á mörkum mennskunar* (Reykjavík, 2018), pp. 164–5.

14 Guðmundur Hálfdanarson, "Íslensk þjóðfélagsþróun á 19. öld", in *Íslensk þjóðfélagsþróun 1880–1990: Ritgerðir*, ed. Guðmundur Hálfdanarson and Svanur Kristjánsson (Reykjavík, 1993), p. 18.

15 Símon Jón Jóhannsson and Ragnhildur Vigfúsdóttir, *Íslandsdætur: Svipmyndir úr lífi íslenskra kvenna 1850–1950* (Reykjavík, 1991), pp. 79–98.

16 For further information on elves, see, for example, Terry Gunnell, "How Elvish Were the Álfar?" in *Constructing Nations, Reconstructing Myth: Essays in Honour of T. A. Shippey*, ed. Andrew Wawn, Graham Johnson and John Walter (Turnhout, 2007), pp. 111–30; and Alan Bruford, "Trolls, Hillfolk, Finns and Picts: The Identity of the Good Neighbors in Orkney and Shetland", in *The Good People: New Fairylore Essays*, ed. Peter Narváez (New York, 1997), pp. 116–41.

17 Jón Jónasson, *Íslenzkir þjóðhættir*, p. 407.

18 Jón Árnason, *Íslenzkar þjóðsögur og ævintýri*, 6 vols (Reykjavík, 1954–61), vol. 1, p. 3.

19 Please note that in 1974 the question combines belief in both dreams and precognition; see Erlendur Haraldsson, *Þessa heims og annars: Könnun á dulrænni reynslu Íslendinga, trúarviðhorfum og þjóðtrú* (Reykjavík, 1978), p. 16; and Ásdís Aðalbjörg Arnaldsdóttir, Ragna Benedikta Garðarsdóttir and Unnur Diljá Teitsdóttir, *Könnun á íslenskri þjóðtrú og trúarviðhorfum* (Reykjavík, 2008). The newest figures were sent to me by Terry Gunnell.

20 See further Bo Almqvist, "Midwife to the Fairies", in *Legends and Landscape: Articles Based on Plenary Papers Presented at the 5th Celtic–Nordic–Baltic Folklore Symposium*, ed. Terry Gunnell (Reykjavík, 2008), pp. 273–325.

21 For similar legends in Sweden, see Bengt af Klintberg, *The Types of the Swedish Folk Legend* (Helsinki, 2010), p. 208.

22 Ulf Palmenfelt, "Understanding of Folk Legends", in *Telling Reality: Folklore Studies in Memory of Bengt Holbek*, ed. Michael Chesnutt (Copenhagen, 1993), pp. 143–67.

23 Jón Árnason, *Íslenzkar þjóðsögur og ævintýri*, vol. 1, p. 41.

24 Eva Þórdís Ebenezersdóttir, *Umskiptingur eða ei: Umskiptingasagnir í nýju ljósi* (Reykjavík, 2010).

25 Valdimar Hafstein, "The Elves' Point of View: Cultural Identity in Contemporary Icelandic Elf-Tradition", *Fabula: Zeitschrift für Erzählforschung*, XLI (2000), pp. 87–104.

26 Terry Gunnell, "The Coming of Christmas Visitors: Folk Legends Concerning the Attacks on Icelandic Farmhouses Made by Spirits at Christmas", *Northern Studies*, XXXVIII (2004), pp. 51–75; for similar legends in Norway, see Reidar Th. Christiansen, *The Migratory Legends: A Proposed List of Types with a Systematic Catalogue of the Norwegian Variants*, Folklore Fellows Communications 175 (Helsinki, 1958), pp. 144–55.

27 Dagrún Ósk Jónsdóttir, "'She Did Not Want a Husband, and Least of All This One': Marriage and Gendered Power Relations in Icelandic Folk Legends", *ARV: Nordic Yearbook of Folklore*, LXXIX (2023), pp. 99–101.

2 The Wilderness

1   Guðmundur Páll Ólafsson, *Hálendið í náttúru Íslands* (Reykjavík, 2013), p. 204.
2   ÞMS [Þjóðminjasafn Íslands/National Museum of Iceland], *Questionnaire 63: Ferðalög og flutningar* (1986), no. 7779, available at www.sarpur.is, accessed 20 July 2024.
3   Guðmundur Páll Ólafsson, *Hálendið*, pp. 219–27, 279.
4   Einar E. Sæmundsen, Gísli Gíslason and Yngvi Þór Loftsson, *Miðhálendi Íslands: Svæðisskipulag 2015* (Reykjavík, 1999), p. 214.
5   Gils Guðmundsson, *Öldin okkar: Minnisverð tíðindi 1901–1903* (Reykjavík, 1950), p. 33.
6   Ibid.
7   Jón Árnason, *Íslenzkar þjóðsögur og ævintýri*, 6 vols (Reykjavík, 1954–61), vol. I, pp. 136–7.
8   See, for example, Reimund Kvideland and Henning K. Sehmsdorf, *Scandinavian Folk Belief and Legend* (Minneapolis, MN, 1999), p. 299; Bengt af Klintberg, *The Types of the Swedish Folk Legend*, Folklore Fellows Communications 330 (Helsinki, 2010), pp. 151, 196; Jacqueline Simpson, *Icelandic Folktales and Legends* (Stroud, 2004), pp. 16–17; Einar Ólafur Sveinsson, *The Folk-Stories of Iceland*, trans. Anthony Faulkes (London, 2003), pp. 167–9.
9   Terry Gunnell, "Sagnagrunnur: En kartlagt database over de islandske folkesagn", in *Saga och Sed: Kungl. Gustav Adolfs Akademiens Årsbok*, ed. Gunnar Ternhag (Uppsala, 2015), pp. 15–40.
10 Jónas Jónasson, *Íslenzkir þjóðhættir* (Reykjavík, 1945), p. 407; Ólína Þorvarðardóttir, *Álfar og tröll* (Reykjavík, 1995), p. 19.
11 Helga Kress, *Máttugar meyjar* (Reykjavík, 1993), p. 119.
12 Ólína Þorvarðardóttir, *Álfar og tröll*, p. 33; see also Dagrún Ósk Jónsdóttir, "'[She] Was Very Eager for Men and Hated Living Alone': Supernatural Women That Pose a Threat to Men in Icelandic Legends", *Ethnologia Europaea*, LIII/1 (2023), pp. 8–15.
13 Kirsten Hastrup, *Culture and History in Medieval Iceland: An Anthropological Analysis of Structure and Change* (Oxford, 1985), p. 137.
14 Jón Árnason, *Íslenzkar þjóðsögur og ævintýri*, vol. IV, p. 257.
15 Kirsten Hastrup, *Culture and History in Medieval Iceland*, p. 143; Einar Ólafur Sveinsson, *The Folk-Stories of Iceland*, pp. 217–24; see also Stuart Hall, "The Spectacle of the 'Other'", in *Representation: Cultural Representations and Signifying Practices*, ed. Jessica Evans, Sean Nixon and Stuart Hall (London, 1997), pp. 223–90.
16 Kirsten Hastrup, *Nature and Policy in Iceland, 1400–1800: An Anthropological Analysis of History and Mentality* (Oxford, 1990), p. 258.
17 Kristinn Schram and Jón Jónsson, "Visitations: The Social and Cultural History of Polar Bear Narratives in Iceland and the North Atlantic", in *The Bear: Culture, Nature, Heritage*, ed. Owen Nevin, Ian Convery and Peter Davis (New York, 2019), p. 148; Alice Bower and Kristinn Schram, "Polar

Bear Narratives from Gendered and Post-Human Perspectives",
Arctic and Antarctic, xv (2021), pp. 63–80; Jón M. Halldórsson,
"Hvað hafa margir ísbirnir komið til Íslands?", *Vísindavefurinn* (2005),
available at www.visindavefur.is, accessed 20 July 2024.

18 Kristinn Schram and Jón Jónsson, "Visitations", p. 151.

19 Ibid., p. 154.

20 Anon., "Örn rændi barni", *Morgunblaðið*, x/2 (1944), pp. 46–7;
Daníel Bergmann, "Konungur fuglanna", *Morgunblaðið*, xxiv (2004),
pp. 28–9; Guðlaug Guðmunda Ingibjörg Bergsveinsdóttir, "Örninn
gegnum aldirnar: Kynskipting, náernir og opinn þarfagangur", *Kreddur*
(2022), available at www.thjodfraedi.is, accessed 20 July 2024.

21 Alice Bower and Kristinn Schram, "Polar Bear Narratives from Gendered
and Post-Human Perspectives", pp. 63–80.

22 Ari Trausti Guðmundsson, *Íslandseldar: Eldvirkni á Íslandi í 10.000 ár*
(Reykjavík, 1986).

3 The Dark

1 Þms, *Questionnaire 7: Kvöldvakan og hlutdeild heimilisins í íslensku
þjóðaruppeldi* (1962), no. 434, available at www.sarpur.is, accessed
20 July 2024.

2 Sigfús Sigfússon, *Íslenskar þjóðsögur og sagnir*, ii vols (Reykjavík, 1982–93),
vol. iv, pp. 273–4.

3 Ibid., p. 273.

4 Ibid., p. 274.

5 Guðmundur Hálfdanarson, "Private Spaces and Private Lives: Privacy,
Intimacy, and Culture in Icelandic Nineteenth-Century Rural Homes",
in *Power and Culture: New Perspectives on Spatiality in European History*,
ed. Pieter François, Taina Syrjämaa and Henri Terho (Pisa, 2008),
pp. 109–24.

6 Gísli Ágúst Gunnlaugsson, "Ljós, lestur og félagslegt taumhald", *Ný saga*, v/1
(1991), pp. 62–6.

7 Þms, *Questionnaire 96: Rafvæðingin 1 – Þegar rafmagnið kom* (1999), no. 13299,
available at www.sarpur.is, accessed 20 July 2024.

8 Jónas Jónasson, *Íslenzkir þjóðhættir* (Reykjavík, 1945), p. 333.

9 Þms, *Questionnaire 96*, no. 13220.

10 Jónas Jónasson, *Íslenzkir þjóðhættir*, p. 302.

11 Þms, *Questionnaire 4: Andlát og útfarasiðir* (1961), nos 219, 532, 1904, available
at www.sarpur.is, accessed 20 July 2024.

12 Árni Björnsson, *Merkisdagar á mannsævinni* (Reykjavík, 1996), p. 393.

13 Ibid., p. 403; Jónas Jónasson, *Íslenskir þjóðhættir*, p. 302.

14 Jónas Jónasson, *Íslenzkir þjóðhættir*, p. 428.

15 Ibid., pp. 429–30.

16 Ólafur Halldórsson, Hilmar Stephensen, Jón Sigurðsson and Oddgeir
Stephensen, *Lovsamling for Island* (Copenhagen, 1853), pp. 171–2.

17 Matthias Egeler, *Landscape, Religion and the Supernatural: Nordic Perspectives on Landscape Theory* (Oxford, 2024).

18 Terry Gunnell, "Waking the Dead: Folk Legends Concerning Magicians and Walking Corpses in Iceland", in *News from Other Worlds: Studies in Nordic Folklore, Mythology and Culture*, ed. Merrill Kaplan and Timothy Tangherlini (Berkeley and Los Angeles, CA, 2012), pp. 235–66.

19 Jón Árnason, *Íslenzkar þjóðsögur og ævintýri*, 6 vols (Reykjavík, 1954–61), vol. I, pp. 304–6.

20 Similar legends are also known in Germany; see Jón Hnefill Aðalsteinsson, "Þjóðsögur og sagnir", in *Íslensk þjóðmenning*, 4 vols (I, V, VI, VII), ed. Frosti F. Jóhansson, Haraldur Ólafsson, Jón Hnefill Aðalsteinsson and Þór Magnússon (Reykjavík, 1987–90), vol. VI, pp. 280–83.

21 Haraldur Bessason and Robert J. Glendinning, eds, *Laws of Early Iceland: Grágás: The Codex Regius of Grágás with Material from Other Manuscripts* (Winnipeg, MB, 1980), pp. 30–31.

22 Jónas Jónasson, *Íslenzkir þjóðhættir*, p. 308.

23 "Arfur Miklabæjar-Solveigar", *Byggðasafn Skagfirðinga*, available at www.glaumbaer.is, accessed 20 July 2024.

24 *Kristni saga*, in *Íslenzk fornrit XV* (2): *Biskupa sögur I*, ed. Jónas Kristjánsson (Reykjavík, 2003), p. 36.

25 Már Jónsson, *Dulsmál 1600–1900: Fjórtán dómar og skrá* (Reykjavík, 2000), p. 13.

26 Juha Pentikäinen, *The Nordic Dead-Child Tradition*, trans. Antony Landon (Helsinki, 1968); Bo Almqvist, "Norwegian Dead-Child Legends Westward Bound", in *Viking Ale: Studies on Folklore Contacts between the Northern and the Western Worlds*, ed. Éilís Ní Dhuibhne-Almqvist and Séamas Ó Catháin (Aberystwyth, 1991), pp. 155–67; and Reimund Kvideland and Henning K. Sehmsdorf, *Scandinavian Folk Belief and Legend* (Minneapolis, MN, 1999), pp. 113–15.

27 Dagrún Ósk Jónsdóttir, "'It Was Ill Done, My Mother, to Deny Me Life': Rejecting the Role of Motherhood in Icelandic Folk Legends", *Western Folklore*, LXXXI/4 (2022), pp. 321–55.

28 Már Jónsson, *Dulsmál 1600–1900*, pp. 50–51.

29 Dagrún Ósk Jónsdóttir, "'It Was Ill Done, My Mother, to Deny Me Life'", pp. 321–55.

30 Már Jónsson, *Galdur og guðlast á 17. öld: Dómar og bréf* (Reykjavík, 2021), pp. 88–90.

31 Terry Gunnell, "Mists, Magicians and Murderous Children: International Migratory Legends Concerning the 'Black Death' in Iceland", in *Northern Lights: Following Folklore in North-Western Europe*, ed. Séamas Ó Catháin (Dublin, 2021), pp. 47–59.

32 Similar methods of getting rid of ghosts are also known, for example, in England, where ghosts are conjured into a bottle, a snuffbox or occasionally into a boot. See Jacqueline Simpson, *Icelandic Folktales and Legends* (Stroud, 2004), pp. 172–3.

4 The Church

1   Terry Gunnell, "Pantheon? What Pantheon? Concepts of a Family of Gods in Pre-Christian Scandinavian Religions", in *Scripta Islandica: Isländska Sällskapets Årsbok 66*, ed. Lasse Mårtensson and Veturliði Óskarsson (Uppsala, 2015), p. 57.

2   Terry Gunnell, "Ansgar's Conversion of Iceland", in *Scripta Islandica: Isländska Sällskapets Årsbok 60*, ed. Daniel Sävborg (Uppsala, 2009), pp. 105–18; Gunnar Karlsson, *Iceland's 1100 Years: History of a Marginal Society* (London, 2000), pp. 33–7.

3   Gunnar Karlsson, *Iceland's 1100 Years*, pp. 128–33.

4   Jón Árnason, *Íslenzkar þjóðsögur og ævintýri*, 6 vols (Reykjavík, 1954–61), vol. II, pp. 73–4.

5   Ibid., vol. I, p. 7.

6   Hjalti Hugason, "Kristnir trúarhættir", in *Íslensk þjóðmenning*, 4 vols (I, V, VI, VII), ed. Frosti F. Jóhansson, Haraldur Ólafsson, Jón Hnefill Aðalsteinsson and Þór Magnússon (Reykjavík, 1987–90), vol. V, pp. 78–9.

7   Jónas Jónasson, *Íslenzkir þjóðhættir* (Reykjavík, 1945), pp. 345–6.

8   Ibid., p. 345.

9   ÞMS, *Questionnaire 63: Ferðalög og flutningar* (1986), no. 7927, available at www.sarpur.is, accessed 20 July 2024.

10   Hjalti Hugason, "Kristnir trúarhættir", p. 258.

11   Þórunn Valdimarsdóttir, "Öld frelsis, lýðvalds og jafnaðar", in *Kristni á Íslandi: Til móts við nútímann*, ed. Gunnar F. Guðmundsdóttir et al. (Reykjavík, 2000), pp. 9–195.

12   Terry Gunnell, "Clerics as Collectors of Folklore in Nineteenth-Century Iceland", *ARV: Nordic Yearbook of Culture*, LXVIII (2012), pp. 45–66.

13   Jón Jónsson, *Á mörkum mennskunar* (Reykjavík, 2018), pp. 112–16.

14   Terry Gunnell, "Clerics as Collectors".

15   Michel Foucault, *Discipline and Punish: The Birth of the Prison*, trans. Alan Sheridan (London, 1991), pp. 218–28; and Gísli Sigurðsson, "Þjóðsögur", in *Íslensk bókmenntasaga*, ed. Halldór Guðmundsson (Reykjavík, 1996), vol. III, pp. 409–94.

16   Dagrún Ósk Jónsdóttir, "'[She] Was Very Eager for Men and Hated Living Alone': Supernatural Women That Pose a Threat to Men in Icelandic Legends", *Ethnologia Europaea*, LIII/1 (2023), pp. 8–15.

17   Jónas Jónasson, *Íslenzkir þjóðhættir*, pp. 245–8; Hjalti Hugason, "Kristnir trúarhættir", pp. 294–8.

18   Guðbjörg Jónsdóttir, *Gamlar glæður: Þættir úr daglegu lífi á Ströndum á síðari hluta 19. aldar* (Reykjavík, 1943), p. 144.

19   Þórunn Valdimarsdóttir, "Öld frelsis, lýðvalds og jafnaðar", p. 132.

20   Hjalti Hugason, "Kristnir trúarhættir", pp. 323–30.

21   Ásdís Aðalbjörg Arnaldsdóttir, Ragna Benedikta Garðarsdóttir and Unnur Diljá Teitsdóttir, *Könnun á íslenskri þjóðtrú og trúarviðhorfum* (Reykjavík, 2008). The newest figures were sent to me by Terry Gunnell.

22 Similar versions are known in Scandinavia, in which people dance themselves to death on a mountain to music played by the Devil; see Júlíana Þóra Magnúsdóttir, "Hvað getið þið sagt mér um dansinn í Hruna?", *Vísindavefur* (2014), availalble at www.visindavefurinn.is, accessed 20 July 2024.

23 Dagrún Ósk Jónsdóttir, "'Obey My Will or Suffer': Violence Against Women in Icelandic Folk Legends", *Journal of Ethnology and Folkloristics*, XIV/2 (2020), pp. 17–43. For similar legends in Europe, see Jacqueline Ní Fhearghusa, "The Devil's Son as Priest: Distribution, Form and Function of a Story on the Borderline between Folktale and Folk Legend", *Béaloideas: Sounds from the Supernatural: Papers Presented at the Nordic–Celtic Legend Symposium*, 62–3 (1994–5), pp. 89–108; ATU 764.

24 For similar legends in Europe, see Bengt af Klintberg, *The Types of the Swedish Folk Legend*, Folklore Fellows Communications 330 (Helsinki, 2010), p. 156; and for Norway, see Reidar Th. Christiansen, *The Migratory Legends*, Folklore Fellows Communications 175 (Helsinki, 1958), p. 156.

25 Jacqueline Simpson, *Icelandic Folktales and Legends* (Stroud, 2004).

26 These stories bear similarities to ATU 362B, "The Youth and the Corpse"; see further Hans-Jörg Uther, Antti Aarne and Stith Thompson, *The Types of International Folktales: A Classification and Bibliography*, 2 vols (Helsinki, 2004), vol. I, p. 211.

27 The story bears a resemblance to those of the tale type ATU 470, "Friends in Life and Death", ibid., pp. 275–6.

28 For similar legends in Sweden, see, for example, Bengt af Klintberg, *The Types of the Swedish Folk Legend*, p. 152.

29 Terry Gunnell, "The Return of Sæmundur: Origins and Analogues", in *Þjóðlíf og þjóðtrú: Ritgerðir helgaðar Jóni Hnefli Aðalsteinssyni*, ed. Jón Jónsson, Terry Gunnell, Valdimar Tr. Hafstein and Ögmundur Helgason (Reykjavík, 1988), pp. 87–100.

30 Ólína Kjerúlf Þorvarðardóttir, *Brennuöldin* (Reykjavík, 2000), pp. 282–3; and Matthías Viðar Sæmundsson, *Galdrar á Íslandi* (Reykjavík, 1992), p. 40.

31 These legend types are also known for example in Norway and Scotland; see further Terry Gunnell, "The Return of Sæmundur", pp. 87–111.

5 The Ocean

1 Viðar Hreinsson, *Jón lærði og náttúrur náttúrunnar* (Reykjavík, 2016), pp. 147–8.

2 Peder Hansen Resen, *Íslandslýsing* (Reykjavík, 1991), pp. 152–62.

3 Handritadeild Landsbókasafns Íslands – Lbs 5134 4to [Unpublished manuscript at the National and University Library of Iceland]. *Dagbók Jóns Jónssonar 1846–1879*.

4 See Davíð Ólafsson, *Frá degi til dags: Dagbækur, almanök og veðurbækur 1720–1920* (Reykjavík, 2021), pp. 105–18, 127–36.

5 Sigfús Sigfússon, *Íslenzkar þjóðsögur og sagnir*, 11 vols (Reykjavík, 1982–93), vol. IV, p. 181.

6 Lúðvík Kristjánsson, *Íslenskir sjávarhættir*, 5 vols (Reykjavík, 1980–86), vol. II, pp. 32–3.
7 Ibid., pp. 485–6.
8 Ibid., pp. 480–81.
9 Páll Einarsson, "Synt og svamlað", *Sagnir*, 5 (1984), pp. 88–92.
10 Lúðvík Kristjánsson, *Íslenskir sjávarhættir*, vol. III, p. 127.
11 Jón Árnason, *Íslenzkar sagnir og ævintýri*, 6 vols (Reykjavík, 1954–61), vol. I, p. 657.
12 Lúðvík Kristjánsson, *Íslenzkir sjávarhættir*, vol. V, p. 327.
13 Símon Jón Jóhansson, *Stóra hjátrúarbókin* (Reykjavík, 1999), pp. 332–5.
14 Ibid., p. 5.
15 Lúðvík Kristjánsson, *Íslenzkir sjávarhættir*, vol. V, p. 329.
16 Ibid., vol. III, pp. 211–21.
17 Cristina Bacchilega and Marie Alohalani Brown, *The Penguin Book of Mermaids* (London, 2019).
18 Sigfús Sigfússon, *Íslenskar þjóðsögur og sagnir*, vol. IV, p. 5.
19 Ibid., p. 104.
20 Ibid., vol. IV, pp. 167–8.
21 Jón Árnason, *Íslenzkar þjóðsögur og ævintýri*, vol. I, pp. 625–7.
22 See further Sigurður Ægisson, *Meeting with Monsters: An Illustrated Guide to the Beasts of Iceland* (Reykjavík, 2023).
23 Lúðvík Kristjánsson, *Íslenzkir sjávarhættir*, vol. III, pp. 207–10.
24 Ulf Palmenfelt, "Seductive, Generous and Dangerous like the Sea Itself: Gotlandic Mermaid Legends as Moral Examples", in *Islanders and Water-Dwellers*, ed. Patricia Lysaght, Séamas Ó Catháin and Dáithí Ó hÓgáin (Dublin, 1999), pp. 261–7.
25 This tale type is also known in Scandinavia, and similar legends are told about leprechauns in Ireland; see further Michael Chesnutt, "The Three Laughs: A Celtic–Norse Tale in Oral Tradition and Medieval Literature", in *Islanders and Water-Dwellers*, ed. Patricia Lysaght, Séamas Ó Catháin and Dáithí Ó hÓgáin, pp. 37–49.
26 Jón Árnason, *Íslenzkar þjóðsögur og ævintýri*, vol. I, pp. 4–5; Ólafur Davíðsson, *Íslenzkar þjóðsögur*, 4 vols (Reykjavík, 1978–80), vol. I, pp. 3–4.
27 Ásdís Aðalbjörg Arnaldsdóttir, Ragna Benedikta Garðarsdóttir and Unnur Diljá Teitsdóttir, *Könnun á íslenskri þjóðtrú og trúarviðhorfum* (Reykjavík, 2008). The newest figures were sent to me by Terry Gunnell.
28 Similar tales are known all around Europe, for example in Ireland, Scotland and Scandinavia (F103B, "Child unintentionally uses the word *näck*"); for Sweden see Bengt af Klintberg, *The Types of the Swedish Folk Legend*, Folklore Fellows Communications 330 (Helsinki, 2010), p. 123.

6 The Shore

1 Lúðvík Kristjánsson, *Íslenzkir sjávarhættir*, 5 vols (Reykjavík, 1980–86), vol. I, pp. 37–9.

2 Torfhildur Hólm, *Þjóðsögur og sagnir* (Reykjavík, 1962), pp. 192–4.
3 Lúðvík Kristjánsson, *Íslenzkir sjávarhættir*, vol. I, pp. 278–80.
4 See, for example, Arnold van Gennep, *The Rites of Passage* (Chicago, IL, 1960); and Victor Turner, *The Ritual Process: Structure and Anti-Structure* (Chicago, IL, 1969).
5 Terry Gunnell, "On the Border: The Liminality of the Seashore in Icelandic Folk Legends of the Past", in *Northern Atlantic Islands and the Sea: Seascapes and Dreamscapes*, ed. Andrew Jennings, Silke Reeploeg and Angela Watt (London, 2017), pp. 1–23.
6 Árnastofnun, *Kirkjuból Grímur Benediksston: Viðbætur, svör við spurningum og uppdráttur* (1999), available at www.nafnid.is, accessed 20 July 2024.
7 *Norges gamle love indtil 1387*, 5 vols (Christiania, 1846–95).
8 Guðmundur Páll Ólafsson, *Ströndin í náttúru Íslands* (Reykjavík, 1995), p. 170.
9 For further information on this execution in Árneshreppur, see Már Jónsson, *Galdur og guðlast á 17. öld: Dómar og bréf* (Reykjavík, 2021), pp. 222–35.
10 ÞMS, *Questionnaire 56: Lifnaðarhættir í þéttbýli V – Dagamunur og félagslíf* (1983), no. 6921, available at www.sarpur.is, accessed 20 July 2024.
11 Jónas Jónasson, *Íslenzkir þjóðhættir* (Reykjavík, 1945), p. 423.
12 Terry Gunnell, "An Invasion of Foreign Bodies: Legends of Washed Up Corpses in Iceland", in *Eyðvinur: Heiðursrit til Eyðun Andreassen*, ed. Malan Marnersdóttir, Jens Cramer and Anfinnur Johansen (Tórshavn, 2005), pp. 72–3.
13 Sigfús Sigfússon, *Íslenzkar þjóðsögur og sagnir*, 11 vols (Reykjavík, 1982–93), vol. IV, p. 264.
14 Sigurður Ægisson, *Meeting with Monsters: An Illustrated Guide to the Beasts of Iceland* (Reykjavík, 2023).
15 Ibid., p. 77.
16 Sigurður Ægisson, *Íslenskar kynjaskepnur* (Reykjavík, 2011), p. 95.
17 Similar ideas and stories (in the shape of stories about selkies) can be found in other northerly places of the world, such as in the Faroe Islands, the British Isles and Norway; see further David Thomson, *People of the Sea: A Journey in Search of the Seal Legend* (New York, 2001).
18 Sigfús Sigfússon, *Íslenzkar þjóðsögur og sagnir*, vol. IV, p. 198.

Epilogue

1 Dagrún Ósk Jónsdóttir, *Trapped within Tradition: Women, Femininity and Gendered Power Relations in Icelandic Folk Legends* (Reykjavík, 2022).
2 Alþingi, *Lög um menningarminjar*, article 3 (2012), available at www.althingi.is, accessed 20 July 2024.
3 Dagrún Ósk Jónsdóttir and Jón Jónsson, *Álagablettir á Ströndum* (Strandir, 2021).
4 Terry Gunnell, "The Power in the Place: Icelandic Álagablettir Legends in a Comparative Context", in *Stories and Supernatural Places: Studies in Spatial*

and Social Dimensions of Folklore and Sagas, ed. Ülo Valk and Daniel Sävborg (Helsinki, 2018), pp. 27–41.

5 Ulf Palmenfelt, "On the Understanding of Folk Legends", in *Telling Reality: Folklore Studies in Memory of Bengt Holbek*, ed. Michael Chesnutt (Copenhagen, 1993), p. 149.

BIBLIOGRAPHY

List of Legends

The list below provides details of where the original legends in Icelandic can be found, as well as the translations made by George E. J. Powell and Eiríkur Magnússon. References have been abbreviated in this section as follows:

J. Árnason   Jón Árnason, *Íslenzkar þjóðsögur og ævintýri*, 6 vols (Reykjavík, 1954–61)

G.E.J. Powell & E. Magnússon   George E. J. Powell and Eiríkur Magnússon, *Icelandic Legends*, 2 vols (London, 1864–6)

S. Sigfússon   Sigfús Sigfússon, *Íslenskar þjóðsögur og sagnir*, 11 vols (Reykjavík, 1982–93)

Ó. Davíðsson   Ólafur Davíðsson, *Íslenzkar þjóðsögur*, 4 vols (Reykjavík, 1978–80)

1 *The Farm*

"Young Woman Helps a Hidden Woman to Give Birth" ("Stúlka hjálpar álfkonu í barnsnauð"), in J. Árnason, vol. III, p. 33

"The Grateful Elf Woman" ("Álfkonan þakkláta"), in J. Árnason, vol. I, pp. 10–11; translation in G.E.J. Powell & E. Magnússon, vol. I, pp. 23–4

"The Magic Scythe" ("Kaupamaðurinn"), in J. Árnason, vol. I, pp. 12–14; translation in G.E.J. Powell & E. Magnússon, vol. I, pp. 27–34

"The Elfin-Lover" ("Huldupilturinn"), in J. Árnason, vol. I, pp. 68–70; translation in G.E.J. Powell & E. Magnússon, vol. I, pp. 58–65

"The Father of Eighteen Elves" ("Átján barna faðir í álfheimum"), in J. Árnason, vol. I, pp. 43–4; translation in G.E.J. Powell & E. Magnússon, vol. I, pp. 41–4

"The Hidden Woman in Múli" ("Álfkonan í Múla"), in J. Árnason, vol. I, pp. 36–7

"Una the Elf Woman" ("Una álfkona"), in J. Árnason, vol. I, pp. 101–2; translation in G.E.J. Powell & E. Magnússon, vol. I, pp. 80–84

"The Worker and the Water Elves" ("Vinnumaðurinn og sæfólkið"), in J. Árnason, vol. I, pp. 112–14; translation in G.E.J. Powell & E. Magnússon (there called "The Man-Servant and the Water Elves"), vol. I, pp. 95–9

"Nineteen Outlaws" ("Nítján útilegumenn"), in J. Árnason, vol. II, pp. 233–4

"The Raven at Skíðastaðir" ("Hrafninn á Skíðastöðum"), in J. Árnason, vol II, pp. 45–7; translation in G.E.J. Powell & E. Magnússon, vol. II, pp. 53–6

2 The Wilderness

"Troll's Stone" ("Skessusteinn"), in J. Árnason, vol. I, pp. 147–8; translation in G.E.J. Powell & E. Magnússon, vol. I, pp. 122–4

"Ólafur and the Trolls" ("Um Trölla-Láfa"), in J. Árnason, vol. I, pp. 184–5; translation in G.E.J. Powell & E. Magnússon, vol. I, pp. 135–8

"The Shepherd of Silfrúnarstaðir" ("Smalinn á Silfrúnarstöðum"), in J. Árnason, vol. I, pp. 190–92; translation in G.E.J. Powell & E. Magnússon, vol. I, pp. 140–47

"Up! My Six, in Jesu's Name!" ("Upp mínir sex í Jesú nafni"), in J. Árnason, vol. II, pp. 170–71; translation in G.E.J. Powell & E. Magnússon, vol. II, pp. 109–12

"Ketilríður" ("Sagan af Ketilríði bóndadóttur"), in J. Árnason, vol. II, pp. 234–7; translation in G.E.J. Powell & E. Magnússon, vol. II, pp. 178–85

"The Eagle" ("Örninn"), in S. Sigfússon, vol. IV, p. 239

"The Bear on Breiðdalsheiði" ("Bangsi á Breiðdalsheiði"), in S. Sigfússon, vol. IV, pp. 203–4

"Jón from the Farm Parthús" ("Parthúsa-Jón"), in Ó. Davíðsson, vol. I, pp. 329–31

"Katla" ("Katla eða Kötlugjá"), in J. Árnason, vol. I, pp. 175–6; translation in G.E.J. Powell & E. Magnússon, vol. I, pp. 134–5

3 The Dark

"The Darkness Is Delightful" ("Skemmtilegt er myrkrið"), in J. Árnason, vol. I, pp. 219–20

"The Deacon of Myrká" ("Djákninn á Myrká"), in J. Árnason, vol. I, pp. 270–72; translation in G.E.J. Powell & E. Magnússon, vol. I, pp. 173–7

"Miklabæjar-Solveig", in J. Árnason, vol. I, pp. 284–6

"Pjakkur", in J. Árnason, vol. III, p. 416

"Mother Mine in the Pen, Pen" ("Móðir mín í kví kví"), in J. Árnason, vol. I, pp. 217–18

"Did Not See the Sun" ("Sá ekki sólina"), in Torfhildur Hólm, *Þjóðsögur og sagnir* (Reykjavík, 1962), pp. 76–7

"The Story of Ábæjar or Nýjabæjarskotta" ("Árbæjar- eða nýjabæjarskotta"), in J. Árnason, vol. I, pp. 360–61

"The Sorcerers in the Westman Islands" ("Galdramennirnir í Vestmanneyjum"), in J. Árnason, vol. I, pp. 308–10; translation in G.E.J. Powell & E. Magnússon (there called "The Wizards in the Westmann Islands"), vol. I, pp. 237–44

"The White Cap" ("Draugshúfan"), in J. Árnason, vol. I, p. 231; translation in G.E.J. Powell & E. Magnússon, vol. I, pp. 157–8

"A Naked Woman Deals with a Ghost" ("Nakin kona fæst við draug"), in
Torfhildur Hólm, *Þjóðsögur og sagnir*, pp. 3–4

4 The Church

"The Dance at Hruni" ("Dansinn í Hruna"), in J. Árnason, vol. II, pp. 11–12
"The Son of the Ghost" ("Bakkadraugurinn"), in J. Árnason, vol. I, pp. 274–6;
    translation in G.E.J. Powell & E. Magnússon (there called "The Son of the
    Goblin"), vol. I, pp. 177–81
"Who Built Reynir Church?" ("Kirkjusmiðurinn á Reyni"), in J. Árnason, vol. III,
    pp. 74–5; translation in G.E.J. Powell & E. Magnússon, vol. I, pp. 49–51
"Murder Will Out" ("Upp koma svik um síðir"), in J. Árnason, vol. I, pp. 225–6;
    translation in G.E.J. Powell & E. Magnússon, vol. I, pp. 155–6
"The Skeleton in Hólar Church" ("Beinagrindin í Hólakirkju"), in J. Árnason, vol. I,
    pp. 292–3; translation in G.E.J. Powell & E. Magnússon, vol. I, pp. 235–7
"More Dirt, More Dirt" ("Meiri mold, meiri mold"), in J. Árnason, vol. III, pp. 310–11
"The Troll of Mjóifjörður" ("Mjóafjarðar skessan"), in J. Árnason, vol. I, pp. 146–7;
    translation in G.E.J. Powell & E. Magnússon, vol. I, pp. 120–22
"Tungustapi", in J. Árnason, vol. I, pp. 32–5; translation in G.E.J. Powell &
    E. Magnússon, vol. I, pp. 35–41
"The Black School" ("Svartiskóli"), in J. Árnason, vol. I, pp. 475–6; translation in
    G.E.J. Powell & E. Magnússon, vol. I, pp. 226–8
"Sæmundur Gets the Living of Oddi" ("Sæmundur Fróði fær Oddann"), in
    J. Árnason, vol. I, p. 478; translation in G.E.J. Powell & E. Magnússon, vol. I,
    pp. 230–31

5 The Ocean

"Rauðkembingur [Red-Comb]", in S. Sigfússon, vol. IV, pp. 176–7
"The Mermaid in Grindavík" ("Hafmeyin í Grindavík"), in S. Sigfússon, vol. IV,
    pp. 14–15
"The Merman's Laughter" ("Þá hló marbendill"), in J. Árnason, vol. III, pp. 202–3;
    translation in G.E.J. Powell & E. Magnússon, vol. I, pp. 103–6
"The Fisherman of Götur" ("Sjómaðurinn á Götum"), in J. Árnason, vol. I, p. 8;
    translation in G.E.J. Powell & E. Magnússon, vol. I, pp. 21–3
"Anna in Bessastaðir" ("Anna á Bessastöðum"), in J. Árnason, vol. I, p. 346
"The Man-Whale" ("Rauðhöfði"), in J. Árnason, vol. III, pp. 150–51; translation in
    G.E.J. Powell & E. Magnússon, vol. I, pp. 65–72
"The Girl in Álftamýri Parish" ("Stúlkan í Álftamýrarsókn"), in J. Árnason, vol. I,
    p. 286
"Priest Hálfdán and Ólöf of Lónkot" ("Hálfdán Prestur og Ólöf í Lónkoti"), in
    J. Árnason, vol. I, pp. 500–501; translation in G.E.J. Powell & E. Magnússon,
    vol. I, pp. 244–5
"The Grímsey Man and the Bear" ("Grímseyingurinn og bjarndýrið"), in J. Árnason,
    vol. I, pp. 606–7; translation in G.E.J. Powell & E. Magnússon, vol. II,
    pp. 657–9

"The Nixie" ("Nykur"), in J. Árnason, vol. I, pp. 131–2; translation in G.E.J. Powell
& E. Magnússon (there called "Nennir, or the One Who Feels Inclined"),
vol. I, pp. 106–8

6 The Shore

"A Ghost Doffs His Cap" ("Draugur tekur ofan"), in J. Árnason, vol. I, p. 333
"The Story of the Man with the Lantern and the Sea Monster" ("Sagan um karlinn
með luktina og sjóskrímslið"), in S. Sigfússon, vol. IV, pp. 135–6
"Jón at Stokkseyri and the Monster" ("Jón á Stokkseyri og skrímslið"), in
Ó. Davíðsson, vol. I, pp. 140–41
"A Man from Sea and a Man from Land" ("Maður úr sjó og maður úr landi"),
in Ó. Davíðsson, vol. I, pp. 119–20
"Naddi", in J. Árnason, vol. I, pp. 134–5; translation in G.E.J. Powell &
E. Magnússon, vol. I, pp. 109–10
"Stories of the Beach Creep" ("Fjörulabbi"), in S. Sigfússon, vol. IV, pp. 106–7
"The Troll in the Skrúður" ("Tröllið í Skrúðnum"), in J. Árnason, vol. I, pp. 186–7;
translation in G.E.J. Powell & E. Magnússon, vol. I, pp. 138–40
"Boot-Lout" ("Stígvélabrokkur"), in Jón Thorarensen, Rauðskinna hin nýrri, 3 vols
(Reykjavík, 1971), vol. I, pp. 117–18
"The Sealskin" ("Selshamurinn"), in J. Árnason, vol. I, pp. 629–30
"Seals Take Revenge" ("Selir hefna sín"), in S. Sigfússon, vol. IV, p. 191

Other Selected Works

This select bibliography is largely limited to works in English on the Icelandic legend
tradition (along with some additional sources on folk legends) and Icelandic farming
society in the nineteenth century. Please note that this list does not include all the sources
referenced in the book. According to Icelandic convention, Icelandic authors are ordered
by their personal names rather than their patronymic names.

Almqvist, Bo, "Midwife to the Fairies (ML 5070) in Icelandic Tradition", in Legends
and Landscape: Plenary Papers from the 5th Celtic–Nordic–Baltic Folklore
Symposium, ed. Terry Gunnell (Reykjavík, 2008), pp. 273–325
Alver, Brynjulf, "Historical Legends and Historical Truth", in Nordic Folklore:
Recent Studies, ed. Reimund Kvideland and Henning K. Sehmsdorf
(Bloomington, IN, 1989), pp. 137–49
Anderson, Benedict, Imagined Communities: Reflections on the Origin and Spread
of Nationalism (London, 1983)
Anna Lísa Rúnarsdóttir, Á tímum torfbæja: Híbýlahættir og efnismenning í íslenska
torfbænum frá 1850 (Reykjavík, 2007)
Ármann Jakobsson, The Troll Inside You: Paranormal Activity in the Medieval
North (New York, 2017)
Arngrímur Sigurðsson, Museum of Hidden Beings: Mythological Beings of Icelandic
Folk Tales (Reykjavík, 2016)

Árni Björnsson, *Merkisdagar á mannsævinni* (Reykjavík, 1996)

Bower, Alice, and Kristinn Schram, "Polar Bear Narratives from Gendered and Post-Human Perspectives", *Arctic and Antarctic*, XV (2021), pp. 63–80

Dagrún Ósk Jónsdóttir, "'You Have a Man's Spirit in a Woman's Heart': Women That Break Hegemonic Ideas about Femininity in Icelandic Legends", *Folklore*, CXXXIII/3 (2021), pp. 290–312

——, "'[She] Was Very Eager for Men and Hated Living Alone': Supernatural Women That Pose a Threat to Men in Icelandic Legends", *Ethnologia Europaea*, LIII/1 (2023), pp. 8–15

Davíð Erlingsson, "Ormur, Marmennill, Nykur: Three Creatures of the Watery World", in *Islanders and Water-Dwellers*, ed. Patricia Lysaght, Séamas Ó Catháin and Dáithí Ó hÓgáin (Dublin, 1999), pp. 61–80

Dégh, Linda, *Legend and Belief: Dialectics of a Folklore Genre* (Bloomington, IN, 2001)

Egeler, Matthias, *Landscape, Religion and the Supernatural: Nordic Perspectives on Landscape Theory* (Oxford, 2024)

Einar Ólafur Sveinsson, *The Folk-Stories of Iceland*, trans. Anthony Faulkes (London, 2003)

Foley, John Miles, *How to Read an Oral Poem* (Urbana, IL, 2002)

Frosti F. Jóhannsson, Haraldur Ólafsson, Jón Hnefill Aðalsteinsson and Þór Magnússon, eds, *Íslensk þjóðmenning*, 4 vols (I, V, VI, VII) (Reykjavík, 1987–90)

Gísli Ágúst Gunnlaugsson, *Family and Household in Iceland, 1801–1930: Demographic Socio-Economic Development, Social Legislation and Family and Household Structures* (Uppsala, 1988)

Guðrún Bjartmarsdóttir, *Bergmál: Sýnisbók íslenskra þjóðfræða* (Reykjavík, 1988)

Gunnar Karlsson, *Iceland's 1100 Years: History of a Marginal Society* (London, 2000)

Gunnell, Terry, "An Invasion of Foreign Bodies: Legends of Washed Up Corpses in Iceland", in *Eyðvinur: Heiðursrit til Eyðun Andreassen*, ed. Malan Marnersdóttir, Jens Cramer and Arnfinnur Johansen (Tórshavn, 2005), pp. 70–79

——, "Daisies Rise to Become Oaks: The Politics of Early Folktale Collection in Northern Europe", *Folklore*, CXXI/1 (2010), pp. 12–37

——, "The Álfar, the Clerics and the Enlightenment: Conceptions of the Supernatural in the Age of Reason in Iceland", in *Fairies, Demons and Nature Spirits*, ed. Michael Ostling (London, 2017), pp. 191–212

——, ed., *Legends and Landscape: Articles Based on Plenary Papers Presented at the 5th Celtic–Nordic–Baltic Folklore Symposium* (Reykjavík, 2008)

——, ed., *Grimm Ripples: The Legacy of The Grimms' "Deutsche Sagen" in Northern Europe* (Leiden and Boston, MA, 2022)

Hastrup, Kirsten, *Culture and History in Medieval Iceland: An Anthropological Analysis of Structure and Change* (Oxford, 1985)

——, "The Environment", in *Nature and Policy in Iceland, 1400–1800*, ed. Kirsten Hastrup (Oxford, 1990), pp. 244–72

Holbek, Bengt, *Interpretation of Fairy Tales: Danish Folklore in a European Perspective*, Folklore Fellows Communications 239 (Helsinki, 1987)

Honko, Lauri, "Methods in Folk Narrative Research", in *Nordic Folklore*, ed. Reimund Kvideland and Henning K. Sehmsdorf (Bloomington, IN, 1989), pp. 23–39

Jónas Jónasson, *Íslenzkir þjóðhættir* (Reykjavík, 1945)

Júlíana Þóra Magnúsdóttir, "Gender, Legend, and the Icelandic Countryside in the Long Nineteenth Century: Re-Engaging the Archives as a Means of Giving Voice to the Women of the Past", *Folklore*, CXXIX/2 (2018), pp. 129–47

——, "Women of the Twilight: The Narrative Spaces of Women in the Icelandic Rural Community of the Past", *Folklore: Electronic Journal of Folklore*, LXXXIV (2022), pp. 97–126

af Klintberg, Bengt, *The Types of the Swedish Folk Legend*, Folklore Fellows Communications 330 (Helsinki, 2010)

Kristinn Schram and Jón Jónsson, "Visitations: The Social and Cultural History of Polar Bear Narratives in Iceland and the North Atlantic", in *The Bear: Culture, Nature, Heritage*, ed. Owan Nevin, Ian Convery and Peter Davis (New York, 2019), pp. 147–59

Kvideland, Reimund, and Henning K. Sehmsdorf, *Scandinavian Folk Belief and Legend* (Minneapolis, MN, 1999)

Lúðvík Kristjánsson, *Íslenskir sjávarhættir*, 5 vols (Reykjavík, 1980–86)

Lüthi, Max, *Once Upon a Time: On the Nature of Fairy Tales*, trans. Lee Chadeayne and Paul Gottwald (Bloomington, IN, 1986)

Ólína Þorvarðardóttir, *Álfar og tröll: Íslenskar þjóðsögur* (Reykjavík, 1995)

Palmenfelt, Ulf, "On the Understanding of Folk Legends", in *Telling Reality: Folklore Studies in Memory of Bengt Holbek*, ed. Michael Chesnutt (Copenhagen, 1993), pp. 143–67

Pentikäinen, Juha, *The Nordic Dead-Child Tradition*, trans. Antony Landon (Helsinki, 1968)

Röhrich, Lutz, *Folktales and Reality*, trans. Peter Tokofsky (London, 1991)

Rósa Þorsteinsdóttir, "'Ég kann langar sögur um kónga og drottningar': Eight Icelandic Storytellers and Their Fairy Tales", *ARV: Nordic Yearbook of Folklore*, LXXI (2015), pp. 67–98

Sigurður Ægisson and Jón Baldur Hlíðberg, *A Meeting with Monsters: An Illustrated Guide to the Beasts of Iceland* (Reykjavík, 2023)

Sigríður Dúna Kristmundsdóttir, *Doing and Becoming: Women's Movements and Women's Personhood in Iceland, 1870–1990* (Reykjavík, 1997)

Sigurður Gylfi Magnússon, *Wasteland with Words: A Social History of Iceland* (London, 2010)

Siikala, Anna-Leena, *Interpreting Oral Narrative*, Folklore Fellows Communications 245 (Helsinki, 1990)

——, "Reproducing Social Worlds: The Practice and Ideology of Oral Legends", in *Legends and Landscape: Articles Based on Plenary Papers Presented at the 5th Celtic–Nordic–Baltic Folklore Symposium*, ed. Terry Gunnell (Reykjavík, 2008), pp. 39–67

Simpson, Jacqueline, *Icelandic Folktales and Legends* (Berkeley and Los Angeles, CA, 1979)

——, *Scandinavian Folktales* (London, 1988)

Tangherlini, Timothy, *Interpreting Legends: Danish Storytellers and Their Repertoires* (New York, 1994)

Trausti Dagsson and Olga Holownia, "Legends, Letters and Linking: Lessons Learned from Amassing and Mapping Folklore and Viewing It as Part of Nineteenth-Century Culture Creation", *ARV: Nordic Yearbook of Folklore*, LXXVI (2020), pp. 55–74

Uther, Hans-Jörg, Antti Aarne and Stith Thompson, *The Types of International Folktales: A Classification and Bibliography*, 2 vols, Folklore Fellows Communications 284 (Helsinki, 2004)

Valdimar Tr. Hafstein, "The Elves' Point of View", *Fabula*, XLI (2000), pp. 87–104

Valk, Ülo, "Folk and the Others: Constructing Social Reality in Estonian Legends", in *Legends and Landscape: Articles Based on Plenary Papers Presented at the 5th Celtic–Nordic–Baltic Folklore Symposium*, ed. Terry Gunnell (Reykjavík, 2008), pp. 153–70

ACKNOWLEDGEMENTS

There is little question about the truth of the old saying "Enginn er eyland" (No person is an island). First, I would like to express my gratitude to professor Sigurður Gylfi Magnússon, who suggested that I write a book on Icelandic folk legends and put me in contact with Reaktion Books, thereby making this book possible. I am also deeply appreciative of the assistance, valuable suggestions, conversations, readings and feedback from my fellow folklorists, friends and colleagues at the University of Iceland, including Áki Guðni Karlsson, Rósa Þorsteinsdóttir and Sigurlaug Dagsdóttir. My thanks also extend to friends and folklorists elsewhere. Matthias Egeler and Kristín Linnet for their readings of the text, suggestions and feedback. Particular gratitude is also expressed to Alice Bower and Sigurður Líndal for their exceptional translations of a portion of the legends featured here. And many thanks are also due to Guðný Ósk Laxdal for her complete reading of the work and important suggestions.

I would also like to thank my PhD supervisor, professor Terry Gunnell. Parts of this book are built on my PhD thesis on the portrayal of women in Icelandic folk legends, which I could not have done without Terry's professional guidance and valuable support. Terry also reviewed large sections of the book and provided valuable feedback. A very special thanks also goes to my father, the folklorist Jón Jónsson, who initially sparked my interest in folklore by telling me the story of Ennis-Móri and has continued to stoke this interest over the years, and who offered his advice during the writing of this book.

I would like to take the opportunity to express my gratitude to all those who helped me in collecting or by giving permission to reproduce the photographs and other illustrative material used in this book. There are a variety of images showing how Icelandic artists imagined the supernatural. The illustrations mostly come from the National Gallery of Iceland, and I am very grateful for their help. Ragnheiður Vignisdóttir brought to my attention many of the beautiful illustrations done by Ásgrímur Jónsson, found in the gallery. Dagný Heiðdal provided me with important information regarding artwork related to folk legends and beliefs, also found in the gallery, and Elín Guðjónsdóttir located the appropriate images. I would also like to thank the National Museum of Iceland for the illustration found in their collection, and especially Kristín Halla Baldvinsdóttir and Ágústa Kristófersdóttir for their help. The photographs come from both private and public collections. I am immensely grateful to the artists who provided me with their own works: Arngrímur Sigurðsson, Brian Pilkington, Jón Jónsson and Sunneva Guðrún Þórðardóttir, as well as Andrés Úlfur Helguson, who gave me permission to use the illustration done by his grandmother Þórdís Tryggvadóttir.

Last but not least, I would like to thank the great people at Reaktion Books, and especially Michael Leaman, for entrusting me with writing this book, and Alex Ciobanu and Emma Devlin for all their patience and assistance.

PHOTO ACKNOWLEDGEMENTS

The author and publishers wish to express their thanks to the sources listed below for illustrative material and/or permission to reproduce it:

From Jón Árnason, and George E. J. Powell and Eiríkur Magnússon, trans., *Icelandic Legends* (London, 1864), photos UNC Chapel Hill University Library: pp. 116, 240; David Rumsey Map Collection, David Rumsey Map Center, Stanford Libraries, CA: p. 191; from Paul Gaimard, *Voyage en Islande et au Groenland . . . Atlas historique* (Paris, 1838), vol. II, photo ETH-Bibliothek Zurich: p. 115; from *Illustreret Tidende*, XXIV/1211 (10 December 1882): p. 33; photo Dagrún Ósk Jónsdóttir: p. 37; photos Jón Jónsson: pp. 28, 78; © National Gallery of Iceland (Listasafn Íslands), Reykjavík: pp. 74 (LÍÁJ-768/238), 123 (LÍÁJ-898/156), 150 (LÍÁJ-435/308), 153 (LÍÁJ-711-A/10), 156 (LÍÁJ-709/15), 193 (LÍÁJ-761/18), 196 (LÍ-4475), 227 (LÍÁJ-772-A/345); National Library of Norway (Nasjonalbiblioteket), Oslo: pp. 186–7; National Museum of Iceland (Þjóðminjasafn Íslands), Reykjavík (Sch-5): p. 19; © Brian Pilkington, photo courtesy the artist: p. 77; © Sunneva Guðrún Þórðardóttir, photos courtesy the artist: pp. 118, 134; © Arngrímur Sigurðsson, photo courtesy the artist: p. 229; © Þórdís Tryggvadóttir, photo National Gallery of Iceland (Listasafn Íslands), Reykjavík (LÍ-8912): p. 55.

INDEX

This index is designed to enhance the usability of the book by including a range of terms that may be of interest to readers. It features place names, names of people, types of supernatural beings and other words that are integral to the Icelandic folk legends presented here. As throughout the book, Icelandic names are ordered here by their personal names rather than their patronymic names.

For place and people's names, the index specifies only the pages where these terms are mentioned, even though entire stories were narrated, collected or translated by certain individuals or set in particular locations. For types of supernatural beings (such as ghosts, trolls and the hidden people), the index provides descriptions of them and the stories where they appear in different entries. For the stories' entries, the index references the complete stories, providing a broader context for understanding their role in the legends.

Page numbers in *italics* refer to illustrations